Stand Out
Lesson Planner

Y0-BSM-938

Rob Jenkins

Staci Lyn Sabbagh

THOMSON
HEINLE

Australia • Canada • Mexico • Singapore • Spain • United Kingdom • United States

THOMSON
HEINLE

Stand Out 1
Lesson Planner
Rob Jenkins and Staci Lyn Sabbagh

Acquisitions Editor
Sherrise Roehr

Managing Editor
James W. Brown

Developmental Editor
Ingrid Wisniewska

Associate Developmental Editor
Sarah Barnicle

Contributing Editor
Alfred Meyer

Marketing Manager
Eric Bredenberg

Director, Global ESL Training & Development
Evelyn Nelson

Production Editor
Jeff Freeland

Senior Manufacturing Coordinator
Mary Beth Hennebury

Compositor
TSI Graphics

Text Printer/Binder
Banta

Cover Printer
Phoenix Color Corporation

Designers
Elise Kaiser
Julia Gecha

Cover Designer
Gina Petti

Illustrators
James Edwards represented by Sheryl Beranbaum
Vilma Ortiz-Dillon
Michael DiGiorgio

Cover Art
Diana Ong/SuperStock

PHOTO CREDITS

Front Matter:
Page V: Courtney Sabbagh

Pre-Unit:
Page P2: Top: Gary Connor/PhotoEdit; Michael Newman/PhotoEdit; Bottom: Mark Richards/PhotoEdit; Jonathan Nourok/PhotoEdit
Page P3: Mark Richards/PhotoEdit; Johnathan Nourok/PhotoEdit
Page P5: Top:©Steve Cole/PhotoDisk/PictureQuest; ©Corbis Images/PictureQuest Bottom: Bonnie Kamin/PhotoEdit/PictureQuest; Bob Daemmrich/The Image Works

Unit 1:
Page 2: Top: Michael Newman/PhotoEdit; Jonathan Nourok/PhotoEdit Bottom: Michael Newman/PhotoEdit; Mark Richards/PhotoEdit
Page 5: Top: Michael Newman/PhotoEdit; Jonathan Nourok/PhotoEdit; Michael Newman/PhotoEdit Bottom: Gary Connor/PhotoEdit; Digital Vision/PictureQuest; Michael Freeman/PhotoEdit
Page 6: Gary Connor/PhotoEdit; Jonathan Nourok/PhotoEdit; Michael Newman/PhotoEdit
Page 13: Top: Bettman/CORBIS; Right: Jean Coughlin; Middle: Jean Coughlin; Bottom: Corbis Images/PictureQuest; Jose Carrillo/PhotoEdit; Corbis Images/PictureQuest
Page 15: Jean Coughlin all except Center: Spencer Grant/PhotoEdit
Page 18: Jean Coughlin

Unit 2:
Page 23: Jean Coughlin
Page 24: Top: Heinle & Heinle; Middle: Heinle & Heinle and Jean Coughlin; Bottom: Jean Coughlin
Page 30: Top: Jean Coughlin; Far Right: Erv Schowengerdt; Middle and Bottom: Jean Coughlin

Unit 3:
Page 42: Jean Coughlin
Page 49: Top: Jean Coughlin; Bottom Jean Coughlin; Right: Erv Schowengerdt
Page 54: Left Jean Coughlin; Center and Right: Erv Schowengerdt

Unit 4:
Page 64: Jean Coughlin
Page 68: Michael Newman/PhotoEdit; Billl Aron/PhotoEdit; Michael Newman/PhotoEdit; Erv Schowengerdt

Unit 6:
Page 108: Top: Dennis Brack/Black Star Publishing/PictureQuest; David Young-Wolff/PhotoEdit Bottom: Donna Day/Stone/Getty Images; Felicia Martinez/PhotoEdit
Page 110: Julian Calder/Stone Images; Tom Carter/PhotoEdit; Dana White/PhotoEdit
Page 115: Michael Freeman/PhotoEdit; Mark Richards/PhotoEdit; Rhoda Sidney, PhotoEdit; David Young-Wolf/PhotoEdit

Unit 7:
Page 121: Richard Hutchins/PhotoEdit; Michael Newman/PhotoEdit; Stephen Frisch/Stock, Boston/PictureQuest; Bill Aron/PhotoEdit; Michael Newman/PhotoEdit
Page 125: David Young-Wolff/PhotoEdit/PictureQuest
Page 128: Top: Jean Coughlin; Jean Coughlin; David Young-Wolff/PhotoEdit; Jean Coughlin; Heinle & Heinle
Page 130: Jean Coughlin
Page 137: Michael Newman/PhotoEdit; Michael Newman/PhotoEdit; Stephen Frisch/Stock, Boston/PictureQuest

Unit 8:
Page 143: Corbis Images/PictureQuest; Bob Daemmrich/The Image Works; Jean Coughlin; Bonnie Kamin/PhotoEdit/PictureQuest; Anton Vengo/SuperStock; Frank Siteman/Stock, Boston, Inc./PictureQuest
Page 151: Pictor International/Pictor International Ltd./PictureQuest; Walter Hodges/CORBIS; Michael Newman/PhotoEdit/PictureQuest; David Young-Wolf/PhotoEdit; Jonathan Nourok/PhotoEdit; Michael Newman/PhotoEdit
Page 152: David Kelly Crow/PhotoEdit; David Young-Wolff/PhotoEdit; Rachel Epstein/The Image Works

TEXT CREDIT

Lesson Planner page 178, **Suggestions for Computer Use** adapted with permission from Susan Gaer and "The Web Rangers."

ACKNOWLEDGMENTS

The authors and publisher would like to thank the following reviewers, consultants, and participants in focus groups:

Elizabeth Aderman
(New York City Board of Education, New York, NY)

Shannon Bailey
(Austin Community College, Austin, TX)

Sharon Baker
(Roseville Adult School, Roseville, CA)

Lillian Barredo
(Stockton School for Adults, Stockton, CA)

Linda Boice
(Elk Grove Adult Education, Elk Grove, CA)

Chan Bostwick
(Los Angeles Unified School District, Los Angeles, CA)

Rose Cantu
(John Jay High School, San Antonio, TX)

Toni Chapralis
(Fremont School for Adults, Sacramento, CA)

Melanie Chitwood
(Miami-Dade Community College, Miami, FL)

Geri Creamer
(Stockton School for Adults, Stockton, CA)

Irene Dennis
(San Antonio College, San Antonio, TX)

Eileen Duffell
(P.S. 64, New York, NY)

Nancy Dunlap
(Northside Independent School District, San Antonio, TX)

Gloria Eriksson
(Old Marshall Adult Education Center, Sacramento, CA)

Judy Finkelstein
(Reseda Community Adult School, Reseda, CA)

Lawrence Fish
(Shorefront YM-YWHA English Language Program, Brooklyn, NY)

Victoria Florit
(Miami-Dade Community College, Miami, FL)

Kathleen Flynn
(Glendale Community College, Glendale, CA)

Rhoda Gilbert
(New York City Board of Education, New York, NY)

Kathleen Jimenez
(Miami-Dade Community College, Miami, FL)

Nancy Jordan
(John Jay High School Adult Education, San Antonio, TX)

Renee Klosz
(Lindsey Hopkins Technical Education Center, Miami, FL)

David Lauter
(Stockton School for Adults, Stockton, CA)

Patricia Long
(Old Marshall Adult Education Center, Sacramento, CA)

Maria Miranda
(Lindsey Hopkins Technical Education Center, Miami, FL)

Karen Moore
(Stockton School for Adults, Stockton, CA)

Erin Nyhan
(Triton College, Chicago, IL)

Marta Pitt
(Lindsey Hopkins Technical Education Center, Miami, FL)

Sylvia Rambach
(Stockton School for Adults, Stockton, CA)

Myra Redman
(Miami Dade Community College, Miami, FL)

Charleen Richardson
(San Antonio College, San Antonio, TX)

Eric Rosenbaum
(Bronx Community College, New York, NY)

Laura Rowley
(Old Marshall Adult Education Center, Sacramento, CA)

Sr. M. B. Theresa Spittle
(Stockton School for Adults, Stockton, CA)

Andre Sutton
(Belmont Adult School, Los Angeles, CA)

Jennifer Swoyer
(Northside Independent School District, San Antonio, TX)

Claire Valier
(Palm Beach County School District, West Palm Beach, FL)

The authors would like to thank Joel and Rosanne for believing in us, Eric for seeing our vision, Nancy and Sherrise for going to bat for us, and Jim, Ingrid, and Sarah for making the book a reality.

Rob Jenkins

Staci Lyn Sabbagh

I love teaching. I love to see the expressions on my students' faces when the light goes on and their eyes show such sincere joy of learning. I knew the first time I stepped into an ESL classroom that this was where I needed to be and I have never questioned that resolution. I have worked in business, sales, and publishing, and I've found challenge in all, but nothing can compare to the satisfaction of reaching people in such a personal way.

Thanks to my family who have put up with late hours and early mornings, my friends at church who support me, and everyone at Santa Ana College, School of Continuing Education who believe in me and are a source of tremendous inspiration.

Ever since I can remember, I've been fascinated with other cultures and languages. I love to travel and every place I go, the first thing I want to do is meet the people, learn their language, and understand their culture. Becoming an ESL teacher was a perfect way to turn what I love to do into my profession. There's nothing more incredible than the exchange of teaching and learning from one another that goes on in an ESL classroom. And there's nothing more rewarding than helping a student succeed.

I would especially like to thank Mom, Dad, CJ, Tete, Eric, my close friends and my Santa Ana College, School of Continuing Education family. Your love and support inspired me to do something I never imagined I could. And Rob, thank you for trusting me to be part of such an amazing project.

We are lesson plan enthusiasts! We have learned that good lesson planning makes for effective teaching and, more importantly, good learning. We also believe that learning is stimulated by task-oriented activities in which students find themselves critically laboring over decisions and negotiating meaning from their own personal perspectives.

The need to write **Stand Out** came to us as we were leading a series of teacher workshops on project-based simulations designed to help students apply what they have learned. We began to teach lesson planning within our workshops in order to help teachers see how they could incorporate the activities more effectively. Even though teachers showed great interest in both the projects and planning, they often complained that lesson planning took too much time that they simply didn't have. Another obstacle was that the books available to the instructors were not conducive to planning lessons.

We decided to write our own materials by first writing lesson plans that met specific student-performance objectives. Then we developed the student pages that were needed to make the lesson plans work in the classroom. The student book only came together after the plans! Writing over 300 lesson plans has been a tremendous challenge and has helped us evaluate our own teaching and approach. It is our hope that others will discover the benefits of always following a plan in the classroom and incorporating the strategies we have included in these materials.

ABOUT THE SERIES

The *STAND OUT* series is designed to facilitate *active* learning while challenging students to build a nurturing and effective learning community.

Stand Out Book 1 is divided into eight distinct units mirroring competency areas most useful to newcomers. These areas are outlined in CASAS assessment programs and different state model standards for adults. Each unit is then divided into eight lessons and a team project activity. Lessons are driven by performance objectives and are filled with challenging activities that progress from teacher-presented to student-centered tasks.

USER QUESTIONS ABOUT *STAND OUT*

- **What are SCANS and EFF and how are they integrated into the book?**

SCANS is the Secretary's Commission on Acquiring Necessary Skills. SCANS was developed to encourage students to prepare for the workplace. The standards developed through SCANS have been incorporated throughout the *STAND OUT* student books and their components.

STAND OUT addresses SCANS a little differently than other books. SCANS standards elicit effective teaching strategies by incorporating essential skills such as critical thinking and group work. We have incorporated SCANS standards in every lesson, not isolating these standards to the work unit as is typically found.

EFF, or Equipped for the Future, is another set of standards established to address students' roles as parents, workers, and citizens with a vision of student literacy and lifelong learning. *STAND OUT* addresses these standards and integrates them into the materials similarly to SCANS.

- **What about CASAS?**

The federal government has mandated that states show student outcomes as a prerequisite to funding. Some states have incorporated the Comprehensive Adult Student Assessment System (CASAS) testing to standardize agency reporting. Unfortunately, many of our students are unfamiliar with standardized testing and struggle with it, so adult schools need to develop lesson plans to address specific concerns. *STAND OUT* was developed with careful attention to CASAS skill areas in most lessons and performance objectives.

- **Are the tasks too challenging for my students?**

Students learn by doing and learn more when challenged. *STAND OUT* provides tasks that encourage critical thinking in a variety of ways. The tasks in each lesson move from teacher-directed to student-centered so the learner clearly understands what's expected and is willing to "take a risk." The lessons are expected to be challenging; when students work together as a learning community, anything becomes possible. The satisfaction of accomplishing something as both an individual and as a member of a team results in greater confidence and effective learning.

- **Do I need to understand lesson planning to teach from the student book?**

If you don't understand lesson planning when you start, you will when you finish! Teaching from *STAND OUT* is like a course on lesson planning, especially if you use the *STAND OUT Lesson Planner* on a daily basis.

STAND OUT does *stand out* from other series because, in the writing of this text, performance objectives were first established for each lesson. Then lesson plans were designed, followed by the book pages. The introduction to each lesson varies because different objectives demand different approaches. The greater variety of tasks makes learning more interesting for the students.

- **What are project activities?**

The final lesson of each unit is a **project.** The project is often a team simulation that incorporates the objectives of the unit and provides one further opportunity for students to apply in active circumstances what they have learned. It allows students to produce something that represents their progress in learning. These end-of-unit projects were created with a variety of learning styles and individual skills in mind. While the projects can be skipped or simplified, we encourage instructors to implement them as presented, enriching the overall student experience.

- **Is this a grammar-based or a competency-based series?**

This is a competency-based series with grammar identified more clearly and more boldly than in other similar series. We believe that grammar instruction in context is extremely important. In *Stand Out Book 1,* different structures are identified as principle objectives in 16 lessons. Students are first given a context incorporating the grammar, followed by an explanation and practice. In level one, we expect students to acquire the language structure after hearing and reading grammar in useful contexts. For teachers who want to enhance grammar instruction, the *Activity Bank 1 CD-ROM* and/or the *Stand Out Grammar Challenge 1* workbook will provide ample opportunities.

The six competencies that drive **STAND OUT** are basic communication, consumer economics, community resources, health, occupational knowledge, and lifelong learning (The unit on government and law replaces lifelong learning in Books 3 and 4).

- **Are there enough activities so I don't have to supplement?**

STAND OUT stands alone in providing 231 hours of instruction and activities, even without the additional suggestions of the *Lesson Planner.* The *Lesson Planner* also shows you how to streamline lessons to provide 115 hours of class work and still have thorough lessons if you meet less often. When supplementing with the *Activity Bank 1 CD-ROM,* the **STAND OUT** ExamView® Pro *Test Bank,* and the *Stand Out Grammar Challenge 1,* your opportunities to extend class hours and continue to provide activities related directly to each lesson objective are unlimited. Calculate how many hours your class meets in a semester and look to **STAND OUT** to address the full class experience.

THE *LESSON PLANNER*

The *Stand Out Lesson Planner* is in full color with 77 complete lesson plans, taking the instructor through each stage of a lesson, from warm-up and review through application. The *Lesson Planner* is a new and innovative approach. As many seasoned teachers know, good lesson planning can make a substantial difference in the classroom. Students continue coming to class, understanding, applying, and remembering more of what they learn. They are more confident in their learning when good lesson planning techniques are incorporated.

Each lesson is written in the following lesson plan format. All of the lessons have three practices that help extend the lesson for longer class periods and for students who may need more practice with the same objective(s).

1. Warm-up and/or review
Use previously learned content and materials that are familiar to students from previous lessons to begin a lesson.

2. Introduction
Begin focusing the students' attention on the lesson by asking questions, showing visuals, telling a story, etc. State the objective of the lesson and tell students what they will be doing. The objective should address what you expect students to be able to do by the end of the lesson.

3. Presentation

Introduce new information to the students through visuals, realia, description, explanation, or written text. Check on students' comprehension.

4. Practice

Have students practice what they have just learned through different activities. These activities can be done as a class, in small groups, pairs, or individually. The practice is guided through materials. Model each activity, monitor progress, and provide feedback.

5. Evaluation

Evaluate students on attainment of the objective. This can be oral, written, or by demonstrated performance.

6. Application

Students apply new knowledge to their own lives or new situations.

HOW TO USE THE *LESSON PLANNER*

Each lesson plan page is placed next to the *Stand Out 1 Student Book* page for easy reference. In your *Lesson Planner 1*, the answers to the *Student Book* exercises are filled in on the student pages.

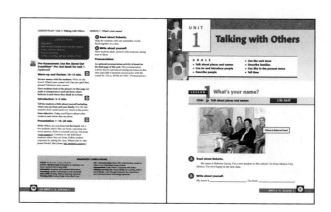

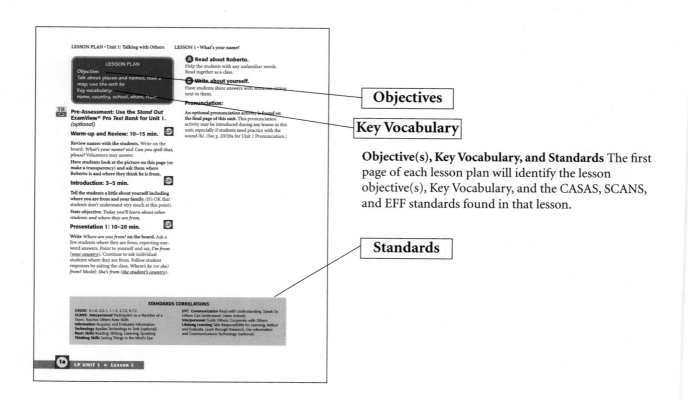

Objectives

Key Vocabulary

Objective(s), Key Vocabulary, and Standards The first page of each lesson plan will identify the lesson objective(s), Key Vocabulary, and the CASAS, SCANS, and EFF standards found in that lesson.

Standards

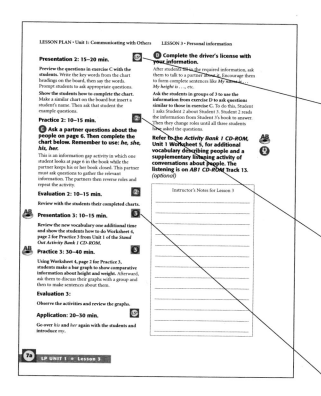

Class Length

The lesson planner includes lessons for classes that are from 1½ hours in length up to 3 hours in length.

1.5+ Instructors who teach 1½ hour classes should follow the steps of the lesson plan next to these icons. There may be additional exercises in the *Stand Out Student Book* or activities on the *Activity Bank CD-ROM* that you don't have time for in class, but those exercises can be assigned for homework.

1.5+ **2+** Instructors who teach two-hour classes should follow the steps of the lesson plan next to these icons. Again, there may be some additional exercises in the *Student Book* or activities on the *Activity Bank* that you don't have time for in class, but those exercises can be assigned for homework.

1.5+ **2+** **3** Instructors who teach three-hour classes should follow the steps of the lesson plan next to these icons. Sufficient activities are available for homework.

SUPPLEMENTAL MATERIALS

- **The *Stand Out Activity Bank CD-ROM*** contains supplemental listening, grammar, reading, and writing activities, as well as project sheets. These activities are all presented in Word format and can be downloaded and modified to meet the needs of your class. If you see this icon in a lesson plan, it indicates that there is an activity worksheet or template that you can print out to use with your students.

- **How do I use the *Activity Bank CD-ROM*?**
  To use the *Stand Out Activity Bank,* put the CD-ROM into your computer and open it. Find the folder for the unit you are working on and open it. Inside you will see all of the extra worksheets for that unit. (There is a Table of Contents that gives you a brief description of each activity.) Open the file you want and customize it for your class. Save the file on your computer's hard drive or on a disk or CD and print it out. All the worksheets are reproducible and modifiable, so make as many copies as you want!

- **Listening Components:** The main listening scripts are found in the back of the *Stand Out Student Book.* Teachers will find all listening scripts in the *Lesson Planner.* Cassette tapes and audio CD-ROMs are available for all listening activities described in the *Stand Out Student Book.* The recordings for the supplemental listenings can only be found on the *Activity Bank CD-ROM.*

- *Stand Out Grammar Challenge 1* is a workbook that offers further grammar explanation and challenging practice. While incorporating the same contexts and vocabulary studied in the *Stand Out 1 Student Book,* the *Grammar Challenge 1* workbook complements all the grammar objectives taught. Additional grammar challenges reinforce structures passively introduced throughout the *Student Book.*

- *Stand Out* ExamView® Pro *Test Bank CD-ROM* allows teachers to customize pre- and post-tests for each unit as well as a pre- and post-test for the book. *ExamView®Pro* is an easy-to-use, innovative test bank system. Each unit has a set of test questions from which unit quizzes can be generated.

- **How can teachers create tests using the *Stand Out* ExamView® Pro *Test Bank CD-ROM?***
In order to compose a test, teachers indicate the number of questions that they want. They either can have questions randomly selected or they can select the questions themselves. Teachers can further customize quizzes by combining questions from the *Test Bank* with original, teacher-generated questions. They can then simply print out the pre-formatted quiz for the students to take a traditional paper and pencil test. The *Stand Out* ExamView® Pro *Test Bank CD-ROM* also allows the test to be administered by computer. It can even be administered on-line with automatic scoring. When the test is given on-line, the test results can be automatically e-mailed to the instructor!

- **What types of questions appear in the ExamView® Pro *Test Bank?***
The tests and quizzes give students practice with a number of different question types including multiple choice, true/false, completion, yes/no, numeric response, and matching. For students who need more practice with CASAS testing, the first ten questions in each test bank are CASAS-style questions, and there is a CASAS-style answer sheet on the *Stand Out Activity Bank CD-ROM.*

STAND OUT **is a comprehensive approach to adult language learning, meeting needs of students and instructors completely and effectively.**

LESSON PLANNER CONTENTS

STUDENT BOOK CONTENTS

Theme	Unit and page number	Life Skills	Language Functions	Grammar	Vocabulary
Basic communication	**Pre-unit Welcome to our Class** *Page P2*	• Say alphabet and numbers • Write names and numbers • Understand classroom instructions	• Greet your friends • Spell aloud • Say and understand numbers	❖ Simple present of *be* ❖ Contracted forms with *be* ❖ Personal pronouns ❖ Imperative verb forms for classroom instructions	• Names, numbers • Classroom vocabulary • Verbs: *listen, read, write, speak*
	1 Talking with Others *Page1*	• Talk about places and names • Read a world map • Interpret information on a driver's license • Plan weekly schedules • Tell time	• Introduce people • Exchange personal information • Describe people • Describe families • Talk about likes • Talk about ways to practice English • Tell time	◆ Simple present of *be* ◆ Simple present of *have* ◆ Personal subject pronouns ◆ Simple present of *like* ❖ *Wh* questions with *be* ❖ Possessive *s* ❖ Possessive adjectives	• Physical descriptions: Eye color, hair color, hairstyle • Age, height, weight • Marital status: *married, single, divorced* • Family members • Times of the day
Consumer economics	**2 Let's Go Shopping** *Page 21*	• Count money • Read receipts • Understand numbers and prices • Make purchases in a store • Write a check	• Talk about where to buy goods • Ask about prices • Identify clothing • Ask about color and size of objects	◆ Singular and plural nouns ◆ *This, that, these, those* ◆ Possessive adjectives ❖ Adjectives ❖ Questions with *or*	• Types of stores • Pricing, unit price • Tax and total cost • Clothing • Adjectives for color, size, pattern, age • *Cash, check, and credit*
	3 Food *Page 41*	• Read and follow instructions • Read a menu and order food • Write a shopping list • Compare prices • Read recipes • Understand food label instructions	• Talk about eating habits and meals • Order food from a menu • Talk about prices of food • Understand instructions for machines • Read and write a recipe	◆ Count and non-count nouns ◆ Simple present tense of regular verbs ◆ *How much is / How much are* ◆ Negative simple present of regular verbs ◆ Imperative forms - affirmative and negative ❖ *Wh* questions with *do*	• Food items • Meals: *breakfast, lunch, dinner* • Containers for food: *jar, box, bottle, package, bag, carton* • Verbs: *eat, bring, go, get* • Cooking verbs: *chop, boil, peel, cook, mix, whip*
	4 Housing *Page 61*	• Identify types of housing • Identify rooms in a home • Read and interpret classified ads • Interpret and make a family budget	• Describe housing • Make an appointment • Describe location of objects • Ask about cost of rent	◆ Present continuous ◆ Prepositions of location ❖ *There is / There are* ❖ *Wh* questions in present continuous ❖ Questions with *What type of ____?*	• Types of housing: *apartment, house, mobile home, condo* • Rooms in a home • Furniture • Verbs: *call, work, talk, look* • *Rent, utilities, budget, income, expenses, savings*

◆ Grammar points that are explicitly taught.   ❖ Grammar points that are presented in context.

EFF	SCANS (Workplace)	Math	CASAS
• Speaking so others can understand • Listening actively	• Listening • Speaking • Sociability	• Understand and write numerals 0–20	**1:** 0.1.1, 0.1.4, 0.2.1 **2:** 0.2.1, 0.1.6 **3:** 0.1.5, 0.2.1 **4:** 0.1.2, 0.1.5, 0.1.6
Most EFF skills are incorporated into this unit, with an emphasis on: • Conveying ideas in writing • Taking responsibility for learning • Reflecting and evaluating (Technology is optional.)	Most SCANS are incorporated into this unit, with an emphasis on: • Acquiring information • Interpreting and evaluating information • Writing (Technology is optional.)	• Use units of measurement: feet, inches, pounds • State dates: day, month, and year • Tell time: hour, half hour, and quarter hour • Write times of the day in numerals	**1:** 0.1.6, 0.2.1, 1.1.3, 2.7.2, 6.7.2 **2:** 0.1.4, 0.2.1 **3:** 0.1.2, 0.2.1, 0.2.2 **4:** 0.1.2 **5:** 0.1.2 **6:** 0.1.2, 0.2.1, 0.2.4 **7:** 0.1.2, 0.1.5, 0.2.1 **R:** 7.1.1, 7.1.4, 7.4.1, 7.4.9, 7.4.10, 7.5.1 **TP:** 4.8.1, 4.8.5
Most EFF skills are incorporated into this unit, with an emphasis on: • Using mathematics in problem solving and communication • Solving problems and making decisions • Reflecting and evaluating (Technology is optional.)	Most SCANS are incorporated into this unit, with an emphasis on: • Allocating money • Serving customers • Organizing and maintaining information • Decision making (Technology is optional.)	• Interpret data on a bar graph • Create a bar graph • Use addition and multiplication to calculate totals • Count U.S. currency • Understand and write prices • Write a check	**1:** 1.3.8, 1.3.9, 4.8.1 **2:** 1.1.6, 1.3.9, 1.6.4 **3:** 1.2.1, 1.3.1, 1.3.9 **4:** 0.1.2, 1.3.9 **5:** 1.3.9, 7.2.3 **6:** 1.3.1, 1.8.2 **7:** 0.1.2, 1.2.2, 1.2.4 **R:** 7.1.1, 7.1.4, 7.4.1, 7.4.9 **TP:** 4.6.1, 4.8.1, 4.8.5
Most EFF skills are incorporated into this unit, with an emphasis on: • Using mathematics in problem solving and communication • Learning through research (Technology is optional.)	Most SCANS are incorporated into this unit, with an emphasis on: • Allocating money • Understanding systems • Creative thinking • Seeing things in the mind's eye (Technology is optional.)	• Interpret and create a bar graph • Use addition to calculate totals • Understand U.S. units of measurement: *pounds, ounces, gallons, pints* • Interpret measurements in recipes • Compare prices per pound and per unit • Compare prices and calculate savings	**1:** 1.1.3, 1.3.8, 6.7.2 **2:** 1.3.6, 1.3.8, 2.2.1, 6.1.1 **3:** 1.3.8, 2.6.4 **4:** 1.1.7, 1.2.1, 1.3.8 **5:** 1.2.1 **6:** 1.1.7, 1.2.1, 1.2.2, 1.2.4 **7:** 1.1.1, 1.1.4 **R:** 7.1.1, 7.1.4, 7.4.1, 7.4.9 **TP:** 4.6.1, 4.8.1, 4.8.5, 6.1.1
Most EFF skills are incorporated into this unit, with an emphasis on: • Solving problems and making decisions • Planning • Reflecting and evaluating (Technology is optional.)	Most SCANS are incorporated into this unit, with an emphasis on: • Acquiring and evaluating information • Creative thinking • Seeing things in the mind's eye (Technology is optional.)	• Interpret and create a pie chart • Compare rents of apartments and houses • Interpret categories in a family budget • Make a budget plan • Use addition and subtraction to calculate expenses and savings	**1:** 1.4.1, 6.7.4 **2:** 1.4.1 **3:** 1.4.1, 1.4.2 **4:** 1.4.2 **5:** 4.6.1 **6:** 1.5.1, 6.1.1 **7:** 1.5.1, 1.5.2 **R:** 7.1.1, 7.1.4, 7.4.1, 7.4.9, 7.4.10, 7.5.1 **TP:** 4.8.1, 4.8.5

CASAS standards: Numbers in bold indicate lesson numbers; **R** indicates review lesson; **TP** indicates team project.

STUDENT BOOK CONTENTS

◆ Grammar points that are explicitly taught.   ❖ Grammar points that are presented in context.

EFF	SCANS (Workplace)	Math	CASAS
Most EFF skills are incorporated into this unit, with an emphasis on: • Reading with understanding • Solving problems and making decisions • Learning through research (Technology is optional.)	Most SCANS are incorporated into this unit, with an emphasis on: • Acquiring and evaluating information • Reading • Seeing things in the mind's eye • Sociability (Technology is optional.)	• Interpret spatial relationships: *in, on, between, next to, across from, in the corner* • Understand phone numbers • Create a bar graph	**1:** 2.5.1 **2:** 1.1.3, 1.9.4, 2.2.1, 2.2.5 **3:** 1.1.3, 1.9.4, 2.2.1, 2.2.5, 2.5.4 **4:** 1.1.3, 1.3.7, 2.5.4 **5:** 2.1.1, 2.5.1, 2.5.2, 2.5.3 **6:** 2.1.7, 2.1.8 **7:** 0.2.3 **R:** 7.1.1, 7.1.4, 7.4.1, 7.4.9, 7.4.10, 7.5.1 **TP:** 4.8.1, 4.8.5
Most EFF skills are incorporated into this unit, with an emphasis on: • Solving problems and making decisions • Reflecting and evaluating • Learning through research (Technology is optional.)	Most SCANS are incorporated into this unit, with an emphasis on: • Interpreting and communicating information • Understanding systems • Decision making (Technology is optional.)	• Interpret data in a Venn diagram • Complete a Venn diagram • Determine temperatures on a thermometer using Celsius and Fahrenheit	**1:** 3.1.1 **2:** 1.1.5, 3.1.1 **3:** 3.1.1, 3.3.1 **4:** 3.3.1, 3.3.2, 3.4.1 **5:** 0.1.6, 2.1.2 **6:** 2.2.1, 2.5.1, 2.5.4 **7:** 3.5.9 **R:** 7.1.1, 7.1.4, 7.4.1, 7.4.9, 7.4.10, 7.5.1 **TP:** 4.8.1, 4.8.5
Most EFF skills are incorporated into this unit, with an emphasis on: • Solving problems and making decisions • Learning through research (Technology is optional.)	Most SCANS are incorporated into this unit, with an emphasis on: • Organizing and maintaining information • Understanding systems • Creative thinking • Decision making (Technology is optional.)	• Interpret and compare information about wages • Interpret data including dates in an employment application	**1:** 4.1.8, 4.8.1 **2:** 4.1.3, 4.1.6, 4.1.8 **3:** 4.1.8, 4.1.2 **4:** 4.1.5, 4.1.7 **5:** 4.1.2, 4.1.8, 4.5.1 **6:** 4.3.1 **7:** 4.4.1, 4.4.4 **R:** 7.1.1, 7.1.4, 7.4.1, 7.4.9, 7.4.10, 7.5.1 **TP:** 4.8.1, 4.8.2, 4.8.5
Most EFF skills are incorporated into this unit, with an emphasis on: • Planning • Taking responsibility for learning • Reflecting and evaluating (Technology is optional.)	Most SCANS are incorporated into this unit, with an emphasis on: • Understanding systems • Monitoring and correcting performance • Knowing how to learn • Self-management (Technology is optional.)	• Tell time • Use multiplication and addition to calculate totals • Estimate time spent on different activities • Use ordinal numbers	**1:** 6.7.2, 7.1.1, 7.3.1, 7.3.2, 7.4.1 **2:** 7.1.4, 7.4.1, 7.4.3 **3:** 2.3.1, 6.6.6, 7.1.1, 7.1.4, 7.4.1 **4:** 7.1.1, 7.1.4, 7.2.3 **5:** 7.11, 7.2.6 **6:** 7.1.1, 7.5.1 **7:** 7.1.4, 7.4.1 **R:** 7.1.1, 7.1.3, 7.1.4, 7.4.1, 7.4.9, 7.5.10, 7.5.1 **TP:** 7.1.1, 7.1.2, 7.1.3, 7.1.4, 7.4.1

CASAS standards: Numbers in bold indicate lesson numbers; **R** indicates review lesson; **TP** indicates team project.

Welcome to Our Class

GOALS
- Greet your friends
- Spell aloud
- Say and understand numbers
- Understand classroom instructions

LESSON 1 Hello!

GOAL ▶ Greet your friends

Life Skill

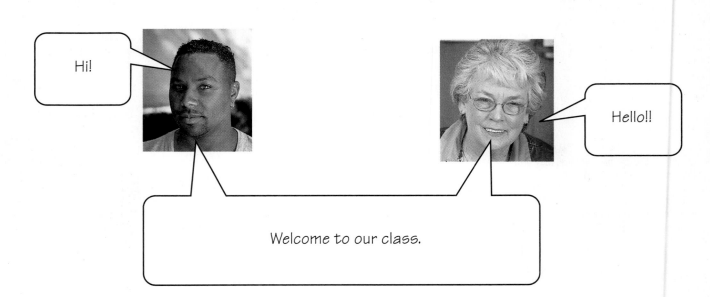

Hi!

Hello!!

Welcome to our class.

How are you?

Fine! How are you?

> **LESSON PLAN**
>
> *Objective:*
> Greet friends and classmates
> *Key vocabulary:*
> hello, hi, fine, welcome, How are you?

Warm-up and Review: 5–10 min.

Write on the board *Hi!, Hello!, How are you? Fine! How are you?* Shake hands with several students while saying the phrases above. Ask students to repeat.

Introduction: 1 min.

State objective: *Today we will learn how to say hello in three different ways.*

Presentation 1: 5–10 min.

Look at the pictures on this page with the students and review the new vocabulary introduced in the Warm-up. Demonstrate the American way to shake hands: curl your fingers around the other person's hand and clasp it firmly. Write the greeting exchanges from the page on the board in dialog form. See Teaching Hints for help with presenting dialogs.

Practice 1: 5–10 min.

A Greet your class.

Ask each student to greet five others. Write the number *5* on the board.

Evaluation 1:

Observe students greeting others.

Presentation 2: 15–20 min.

Ask the class, *Who did you talk to?* Most will not remember. Then write on the board, *My name's*

_____. *What's yours?* Now do the greeting dialog with one student, ending it with the phrases you just wrote. Practice this new, lengthier exchange with the students a few times.

Practice 2: 10–15 min.

Ask students to learn the names of ten students they don't know. Ask them to say *hello* before introducing themselves. Demonstrate how to do this. Write this expression on the board at the end of the conversation: *Welcome to the class.*

Evaluation 2: 5–10 min.

Ask for volunteers to state the names of a few students they have just met.

Presentation 3: 15–20 min.

Using a wad of paper or a soft ball, learn student names by passing or tossing the ball to a student, greeting him or her, and asking for that student's name. Offer yours in return. The student then hands the object to another and repeats the dialog.

Practice 3: 20–30 min.

Toss the ball out of order. Provide less help.

Evaluation 3:

Make sure the object is passed to everyone. Listen to responses.

Application: 15–20 min.

Ask students to form groups of four or five. Each group sends a representative to the other groups to greet, introduce, and exchange first names with all their members. Then the representatives return and share the names with their groups.

STANDARDS CORRELATIONS

CASAS: 0.1.1, 0.1.4, 0.2.1
SCANS: **Resources** Allocates Human Resources
Interpersonal Participates as a Member of a Team, Teaches Others New Skills
Information Acquires and Evaluates Information, Organizes and Maintains Information

Basic Skills Listening, Speaking
Personal Qualities Sociability
EFF: **Communication** Speak So Others Can Understand, Listen Actively
Interpersonal Cooperate with Others

LESSON PLAN

Objective:
Spell aloud
Key vocabulary:
spell, aloud, partner, first name, last name

Warm-up and Review: 5–10 min.

Challenge individuals to name every student in the class.

Introduction: 1 min.

State objective: *Today we will learn to spell our names in English.*

Presentation 1: 15–20 min.

A Listen and repeat. *(Audio CD Track 1)*

Play the recording several times. Have students repeat and then speak along with the recording.

Write the alphabet on the board. Next, in random order, point to all the letters for the students to say. Don't spend much time on pronunciation; just make sure students can be understood by others.

B Practice spelling aloud. Listen and repeat. *(Audio CD Track 2)*

Ask the students to listen and then practice spelling their names.

Practice 1: 10–15 min.

C Listen and write. *(Audio CD Track 3)*

Play the recording a few times, allowing students to write what they hear in the spaces provided. If the students don't have their books yet, write exercise C on the board and have students spell the names they hear.

Evaluation 1: 10–15 min.

Ask volunteers to write the names on the board.

Presentation 2: 20–30 min.

Review exercise A. Turn it into a dialog by adding *What's your name?* on the board, followed by *Can you spell that, please?*

Practice 2: 10–15 min.

D Spell your name to your partner. Listen and write your partner's name.

Have the students greet each another and exchange names with five students. Have them make a chart, spell, and write the names.

| 1 | Gabriela |
| 2 | Duong |

Evaluation 2: 5–10 min.

Ask for volunteers to write the names of a few other students on the board.

Presentation 3: 15–20 min.

Write *first name* and *last name* on the board. Read a few last names from your roll sheet and ask students to write them down. If they have trouble spelling some, point to *Can you spell that, please?* on the board. Make clear that they will get the correct spelling if they ask the question.

Practice 3: 15–20 min.

Give the students a dictation in which they listen to and write student last names. Spell the names for students who ask.

Evaluation 3: 5–10 min.

Ask volunteers to write the last names on the board.

Application: 10–15 min.

Write several last names on the board. Ask the students to find who belongs to each last name.

STANDARDS CORRELATIONS

CASAS: 0.2.1, 0.1.6
SCANS: **Information** Acquires and Evaluates Information
Basic Skills Listening, Speaking
Thinking Skills Visualizing, Knowing How to Learn

Personal Qualities Sociability
EFF: **Communication** Speak So Others Can Understand, Listen Actively

LESSON 2 Spell your name

GOAL ▶ **Spell aloud**

Life Skill

A Listen and repeat.

Hi! I'm Gabriela.
G–A–B–R–I–E–L–A

Hello! I'm Duong.
D–U–O–N–G

B Practice spelling aloud. Listen and repeat.

Aa   Bb   Cc   Dd   Ee   Ff   Gg
Hh   Ii   Jj   Kk   Ll   Mm   Nn
Oo   Pp   Qq   Rr   Ss   Tt   Uu
Vv   Ww   Xx   Yy   Zz

C Listen and write.

1. Hi! I'm   *Susan*   .

2. Hello! My name's   *Bill*   .

3. How are you? I'm   *Annette*   .

4. Hi! My name's   *Tony*   .

D Spell your name to your partner. Listen and write your partner's name.

(Answers will vary.)

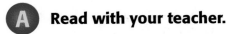

LESSON 3 Numbers

GOAL ▶ Say and understand numbers   **Life Skill**

A **Read with your teacher.**

There are 12 students in our class. We study English for 6 hours every week. Our school address is 19 Lincoln Street, Los Angeles. The zip code is 78014.

B **Listen and practice saying the numbers 0 to 20.**

0	1	2	3	4	5	6	7	8	9	10
11	12	13	14	15	16	17	18	19	20	

C **Listen and write the numbers you hear.**

a. _____5_____   c. _____9_____   e. _____0_____

b. _____8_____   d. _____3_____   f. _____10_____

D **Write these numbers. Say the numbers to your partner. Listen and write your partner's numbers.**

	You	Your partner
1. The number of people in your family.	*(Answers will vary.)*	
2. Your phone number.		
3. Your house number.		
4. Your zip code.		

E **Listen and write the missing numbers.**

My name is Gabriela. My address is _____14_____ Main Street. The zip code is _____06119_____. The phone number is _____401-555-7248_____. There are _____16_____ students in my class.

LESSON PLAN

Objective:
Say and understand numbers
Key vocabulary:
numbers, house number, zip code,
family, favorite, day of birth (birthday)

Warm-up and Review: 20–30 min.

Ask students to identify other students in the class by last name. Ask students in groups to make a list correctly spelled first and last names of classmates.

Introduction: 1 min.

State objective: *Today we will learn to say and understand numbers.*

Presentation 1: 15–20 min.

A Read with your teacher.

Read the passage with the class, giving special emphasis to the numbers. Read it again and ask students to circle the numbers. Write the first sentence on the board and circle *12* so they understand what to do.

B Listen and practice saying the numbers 0 to 20. *(Audio CD Track 4)*

Play the recording. Ask the students to repeat the first few times you play it and then to say the numbers with the recording. As a class, change the reading in exercise A by inserting information from your school.

Practice 1: 10–15 min.

C Listen and write the numbers you hear. *(Audio CD Track 5)*

Play the recording. Ask students to compare answers with a partner.

Evaluation 1: 5–10 min.

Review the numbers.

Presentation 2: 15–20 min.

Write the following words on the board and help the students understand the meanings: *house number, zip code, family, favorite.* Demonstrate how to do exercise D. For the second column, one student reads the sentence while the other gives the information.

Practice 2: 10–15 min.

D Write these numbers. Say the numbers to your partner. Listen and write your partner's numbers.

Allow the students to write their own numbers first. Be sure they don't look at each other's books.

Evaluation 2:

Observe the partner exchanges.

Presentation 3: 10–15 min.

Write *What is the number of your house (or apartment)?* on the board and practice with the students.

Practice 3: 10–15 min.

Ask the students to form a line in the order of the day of the month they were born, left to right. To help them understand, ask four students the birthday question and put them in the right place in the line.

Evaluation 3:

Observe the activity.

Application: 15–20 min.

E Listen and write the missing numbers. *(Audio CD Track 6)*

Play the recording. Then ask the students to copy the paragraph and write their own information.

STANDARDS CORRELATIONS

CASAS: 0.1.5, 0.2.1, 4.8.2
SCANS: Information Acquires and Evaluates Information
Basic Skills Reading, Writing, Listening, Speaking
Thinking Skills Decision Making

Personal Qualities Sociability
EFF: Communication Read with Understanding, Speak so Others Can Understand, Listen Actively
Interpersonal Guide Others, Cooperate with Others

> ### LESSON PLAN
>
> Objective:
> Understand classroom instructions
> Key vocabulary:
> write, read, listen, speak, stand up, sit down, take out, pen, pencil, paper, book, similar, (audio or cassette) tape, please, excuse me, pardon me

Warm-up and Review: 10–15 min.

Ask volunteers to read the paragraphs they wrote about themselves for Lesson 3, exercise E.

Introduction: 1 min.

State objective: *Today we are going to learn and follow classroom instructions.*

Presentation 1: 10–15 min.

With books closed, ask students to identify some **actions.** Pantomime a few and write the corresponding words on the board. Pay special attention to which words the students know. Show them *write, read, listen, speak, stand up, sit down,* and *take out (your book, a pencil/ pen, some paper).* Challenge students to name your action.

Practice 1: 10–15 min.

A Write the correct word below each picture.

B Use the words from the box to complete these classroom instructions.

Students can read and do these exercises in pairs.

Evaluation 1:

Observe the pair activity.

Presentation 2: 15–20 min.

Teach the students simple actions to demonstrate *listen, speak, read, write, stand up, sit down,* and *take out (your book, a pencil/ pen, some paper).*

Quiz the students on the new vocabulary by having them pantomime and name the actions in small groups.

Practice 2: 10–15 min.

C Listen and follow the instructions.
(Audio CD Track 7)

Play the recording several times to give students ample practice .

(Lesson 4, Practice 2 is continued on the next page.)

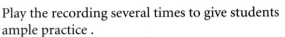

STANDARDS CORRELATIONS

CASAS: 0.1.2, 0.1.5, 0.1.6
SCANS: Basic Skills Listening, Speaking, Reasoning
Personal Qualities Responsibility, Self-Esteem, Sociability, Self-Management, Integrity/Honesty

EFF: Communication Speak So Others Can Understand, Listen Actively

GOAL ▶ **Understand classroom instructions**   **Life Skill**

 A **Write the correct word below each picture.**

| write | read | listen | speak |

write
_____

listen
_____

read
_____

speak
_____

B **Use the words from the box to complete these classroom instructions.**

EXAMPLE: **_Write_** your answers on the board.

1. _____*Listen*_____ to the tape and repeat.

2. _____*Write*_____ your answers on a piece of paper.

3. _____*Read*_____ the story and answer the questions.

4. _____*Speak*_____ with your partner and make a new conversation.

 C **Listen and follow the instructions.**

Tell your partner.

Please stand up.
Please take out your book and open to page fifteen.
Please sit down.
Please write my name on a piece of paper.
Please read my name.

 Practice the conversation with your teacher.

Teacher: Please open your books to page fifteen.
You: What page?
Teacher: Page fifteen. That's one, five.
You: Thank you.

 Practice with a partner.

Student B's book is closed.
Student A says:

1. Please open your book to page six.
2. Please open your book to page fourteen.
3. Please open your book to page sixteen.
4. Please open your book to page eight.
5. Please open your book to page nine.
6. Please open your book to page twenty.

Student A's book is closed.
Student B says:

7. Please open your book to page three.
8. Please open your book to page twelve.
9. Please open your book to page eleven.
10. Please open your book to page four.
11. Please open your book to page seventeen.
12. Please open your book to page nineteen.

Practice 2 (continued):

 Tell your partner.

Students should do exercise D in pairs. One partner closes the book and responds to the instructions read by the other. Then they reverse roles.

Evaluation 2:

Observe student responses to partner instructions.

Presentation 3: 10–15 min.

Prepare students for exercises E and F. Have students practice opening their books (or any book) to specific pages.

Write the following clarification phrases on the board: *Excuse me? Pardon me? What page? What did you say?* To prompt, say something muddled so the students can't understand. Explain that they can ask for clarification by using one of the phrases.

Practice the conversation with your teacher.

Review the dialog in exercise E with the students. Practice a few times with them by changing the page number. Ask for a volunteer pair to demonstrate. Shorter classes may practice with friends or family for homework.

Practice 3: 15–20 min.

Practice with a partner.

Evaluation 3: 10–15 min.

Listen for clarification exchanges. Remind students by pointing to the phrases on the board.

Application: 10–15 min.

Ask individual students to write four instructions to give other students. Review the clarification statements with the students and ask them to give the instructions to three or four other students. Ask the students receiving the directions to follow or pantomime the different instructions.

Refer to the *Activity Bank 1 CD-ROM*, Pre-unit Worksheet 1, for practice filling out a Personal Information form. *(optional)*

LESSON PLAN

Objective:
Talk about places and names; read a map; use the verb *be*
Key vocabulary:
name, country, school, where, from

Pre-Assessment: Use the *Stand Out* ExamView® Pro *Test Bank* for Unit 1. *(optional)*

Warm-up and Review: 10–15 min. 〔1.5⁺〕

Review names with the students. Write on the board: *What's your name?* and *Can you spell that, please?* Volunteers may answer.

Have students look at the picture on this page (or make a transparency) and ask them where Roberto is and where they think he is from.

Introduction: 3–5 min. 〔1.5⁺〕

Tell the students a little about yourself including where you are from and your family. (It's OK that students don't understand very much at this point).

State objective: *Today you'll learn about other students and where they are from.*

Presentation 1: 10–20 min. 〔1.5⁺〕

Write *Where are you from?* on the board. Ask a few students where they are from, expecting one-word answers. Point to yourself and say, *I'm from (your country).* Continue to ask individual students where they are from. Follow student responses by asking the class, *Where's he (or she) from?* Model: *She's from (the student's country).*

A) Read about Roberto.

Help the students with any unfamiliar words. Read together as a class.

B) Write about yourself.

Have students share answers with someone sitting next to them.

Pronunciation:

An optional pronunciation activity is found on the final page of this unit. This pronunciation activity may be introduced during any lesson in this unit, especially if students need practice with the sound /h/. (See p. 20/20a for Unit 1 Pronunciation.)

STANDARDS CORRELATIONS

CASAS: 0.1.6, 0.2.1, 1.1.3, 2.7.2, 6.7.2
SCANS: Interpersonal Participates as a Member of a Team, Teaches Others New Skills
Information Acquires and Evaluates Information
Technology Applies Technology to Task (optional)
Basic Skills Reading, Writing, Listening, Speaking
Thinking Skills Seeing Things in the Mind's Eye

EFF: Communication Read with Understanding, Speak So Others Can Understand, Listen Actively
Interpersonal Guide Others, Cooperate with Others
Lifelong Learning Take Responsibility for Learning, Reflect and Evaluate, Learn through Research, Use Information and Communications Technology (optional)

UNIT 1

Talking with Others

GOALS

- Talk about places and names
- Use *be* and introduce people
- Describe people
- Use the verb *have*
- Describe families
- Use *like* in the present tense
- Tell time

LESSON 1 ## What's your name?

GOAL ▶ **Talk about places and names**   **Life Skill**

Where is Roberto from?

A Read about Roberto.

My name is Roberto Garcia. I'm a new student in this school. I'm from Mexico City, Mexico. I'm very happy in my new class.

B Write about yourself.

My name is _____*(Answers will vary.)*_____ . I'm from _____.

C **Listen and fill in the missing information.**

Names: *Roberto, Eva, Gabriela, Duong*
Countries: *Argentina, Vietnam, Poland, Mexico*

Name: _____*Roberto*_____ Garcia
Age: 43
City: Mexico City
Country:_____*Mexico*_____

Name: _____*Duong*_____ Bui
Age: 30
City: Hanoi
Country:_____*Vietnam*_____

Name: _____*Eva*_____ Malinska
Age: 60
City: Warsaw
Country:_____*Poland*_____

Name: _____*Gabriela*_____ Ramirez
Age: 26
City: Buenos Aires
Country:_____*Argentina*_____

D **Make sentences about each person.**

EXAMPLE: *__Roberto is 43 years old. He is from Mexico City, Mexico.__*

1. *Duong is 30 years old. He is from Hanoi, Vietnam.*

2. *Eva is 60 years old. She is from Warsaw, Poland.*

3. *Gabriela is 26 years old. She is from Buenos Aires, Argentina.*

Practice 1: 10–15 min.

Teach the students the principles of focused listening. See Teaching Hints for how to use focused listening in the class. Show students that it is not necessary for them to understand every word of a conversation to be able to understand the main idea or to gather information. Tell them to listen only for names and countries in exercise C.

 ## ⓒ Listen and fill in the missing information. *(Audio CD Track 8)*

Play the recording several times until the students hear the information.

Evaluation 1: 10–15 min.

Review the answers with the class. Ask the students where each person comes from.

Presentation 2: 5–10 min.

Review the phrase *How do you spell that?* Ask the students if they spelled the names in exercise C correctly. Ask them if they need clarification from you.

Practice 2: 10–15 min.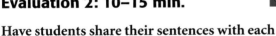

ⓓ Make sentences about each person.

Model the example sentence for students. Ask students to work alone at first and to write the three sentences.

Evaluation 2: 10–15 min.

Have students share their sentences with each other and attempt to peer edit. Encourage students to read for understanding.

Presentation 3: 10–15 min.

E Find Roberto's, Duong's, Eva's, and Gabriela's countries. Mark them with an "X."

A large map of the world in the classroom would be helpful for this exercise.

While doing exercise E, begin to incorporate the sentences in F, but in the third person. Then present the dialog in exercise F with the students. Practice it with them, using Roberto, Duong, Eva, and Gabriela until they can recite the short dialogue without relying on their books.

Practice 3: 10–15 min.

F Practice the conversation with five students. Ask where they are from and mark the places on the map.

Perform a practice conversation with a student using *I* and *you* instead of *he* and *she*.

Evaluation 3: 10–15 min.

Ask volunteers to demonstrate in front of the class.

Application: 15–30 min.

Take a class poll and write down where all the students in the class come from. Draw a bar graph on the board. The vertical axis represents the number of students. The horizontal axis represents countries. You may also use the bar graph template on the *Activity Bank 1 CD-ROM,* Unit 1 Worksheet 1 *(optional)*. If the class is basically homogeneous, use regions or cities instead of countries. Show the students how to create the graph. Ask students, in groups of three or four, to talk to other students and groups in the class and to create their own bar graphs. Then compare bar graphs between groups. The graph can be designed on the computer (optional). See Teaching Hints for computer suggestions.

G Active Task: Go to the library or use the Internet to find out more about your classmates' hometowns or countries.

Ask students to discover one new fact about a county they are not familiar with and share it with the class.

Refer to the *Activity Bank 1 CD-ROM* Unit 1 for a bar graph template (Worksheet 1) and additional practice with names and countries (Worksheet 2). *(optional)*

Instructor's Notes for Lesson 1

_____

_____

_____

_____

_____

_____

_____

_____

_____

_____

_____

_____

_____

_____

_____

_____

_____

_____

_____

E Find Roberto's, Duong's, Eva's, and Gabriela's countries. Mark them with an "X".

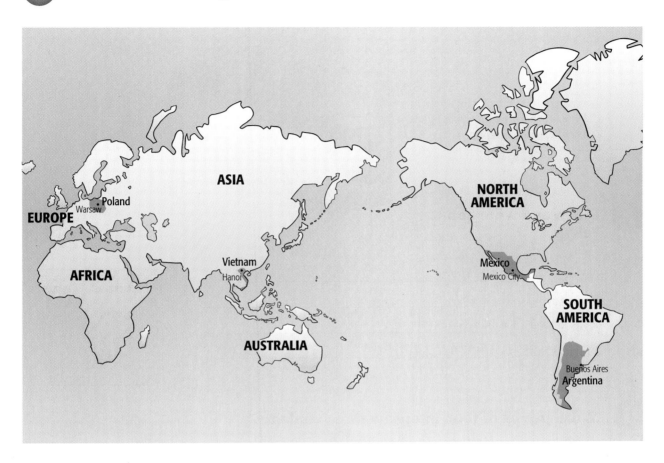

F Practice the conversation with five students. Ask where they are from and mark the places on the map.

EXAMPLE:
Student A: Where are you from?
Student B: I'm from Mexico City, Mexico. It's right here on the map.

 G **Active Task:** Go to the library or use the Internet to find out more about your classmates' hometowns or countries.

LESSON 2 Introductions

GOAL ▶ Use *be* and introduce people

Grammar

Where are the people in the picture?
What are they saying?

A Listen and write about Felipe.

Name: ___*Felipe*___

Country: ___*Cuba*___

Age: ___*23 years old*___

Marital Status: ___*Single*___

Marital Status:

single

married

divorced

B Make groups of four. Interview three students.

(Answers will vary.)

What's your name?	Where are you from?	How old are you?	Are you married or single?
Ex. *Roberto*	*Mexico*	*43 years old*	*married*
1.			
2.			
3.			

C Listen and write.

My name is Tatsuya. This is my new friend, Felipe. Felipe ___*is*___ ___*from*___ Cuba. ___*He*___ ___*is*___ 23 years old. He ___*is*___ ___*single*___. We ___*are*___ students in this class.

D Introduce one new friend in your group to another group. Follow the example in exercise C.

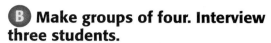

LESSON PLAN

Objective:
Use *be* and introduce people
Key vocabulary:
age, marital status, single, married, divorced, interview

Warm-up and Review: 10–15 min.

Ask students to open their books to the world map on page 3. Ask one student: *Where are you from?* Point to the map in your book or, preferably, to a wall map. Have the students ask four students they don't know, *Where are you from?* and find the locations on their maps.

Introduction: 10–15 min.

Ask the students to open their books and look at the picture at the top of page 4. Ask them the questions about the picture from the box and any other appropriate questions.

State objective: *Today, you will learn to introduce people by using the "be" verb. First you will interview them for information.*

Presentation 1: 20–30 min.

Review the box on marital status with the students and make sure they have a clear understanding of what the words mean.

A Listen and write about Felipe.
(Audio CD Track 9)
Remind the students about focused listening. They are only to listen for specific information. Help them understand what *age* means (how old one is). Play the recording.

Practice 1: 10–15 min.

B Make groups of four. Interview three students.

Review the questions in exercise B to prepare students for the activity. Emphasize that an interview is a process by which one person learns information from another.

Evaluation 1: 5–10 min.

Ask volunteer pairs to demonstrate the interview in front of the class.

Presentation 2: 10–15 min.

C Listen and write. *(Audio CD Track 10)*
Play the recording.

Practice 2: 10–15 min.

D Introduce one new friend in your group to another group. Follow the example in exercise C.

Demonstrate how they will do exercise D, by inserting names and information about students in the class. Practice with a few students. Have students form groups of four or five. Ask one student and a partner from each group to visit another group. Give them one or two minutes to conduct an introduction before returning to their group. Repeat this until all students have been introduced at least once.

Evaluation 2:

Observe how the introductions proceed.

STANDARDS CORRELATIONS

CASAS: 0.1.4, 0.2.1
SCANS: **Interpersonal** Participates as a Member of a Team, Teaches Others New Skills
Information Acquires and Evaluates Information, Organizes and Maintains Information, Interprets and Communicates Information

Basic Skills Listening, Speaking
Personal Qualities Sociability
EFF: **Communication** Convey Ideas in Writing, Speak so Others Can Understand, Listen Actively
Interpersonal Guide Others, Cooperate with Others

Presentation 3: 15–25 min.

 Study the chart with your teacher.

Help the students understand the verb *be.* Make special note that to express age we use *be.* Quiz the students about the pictures and the information below the chart.

 Refer to *Stand Out Grammar Challenge 1,* Unit 1, pages 1–3 for more practice. *(optional)*

Practice 3: 10–15 min.

 Write sentences about the pictures.

After the students finish this exercise, ask them to interview several different students in the class and write additional sentences.

Evaluation 3: 5–10 min.

Invite volunteers to write their sentences on the board.

Application: 15–30 min.

Ask the students to design an identification card from which would include the information they learned in this lesson and a place for a photo ID. Then have them interview another student to complete the ID form they created.

 Refer to the *Activity Bank 1 CD-ROM,* Unit 1 Worksheet 3 (two pages), for additional practice with the verb *be.* *(optional)*

Instructor's Notes for Lesson 2

_____

_____

_____

_____

_____

_____

_____

_____

_____

_____

_____

_____

_____

_____

_____

_____

_____

_____

_____

_____

_____

_____

_____

_____

Study the chart with your teacher.

be		
Subject	**Verb**	**Example sentence**
I	am	I am from Mexico.
you	are	You are married.
he, she, it	is	She is 30 years old.
we	are	We are friends.
they	are	They are students.

Roberto Garcia
Age: 43 years old
Marital status: Married
Country: Mexico

Duong Bui
Age: 30 years old
Marital status: Married
Country: Vietnam

Eva Malinska
Age: 60 years old
Marital status: Divorced
Country: Poland

Felipe Rodriguez
Age: 23 years old
Marital status: Single
Country: Cuba

Nam Nguyen
Age: 58 years old
Marital status: Married
Country: Vietnam

Gabriela Ramirez
Age: 26 years old
Marital status: Single
Country: Argentina

 Write sentences about the pictures.

EXAMPLE: (Marital Status) Roberto ***is married***.

1. (Country) Duong and Nam _____ *are from Vietnam* _____.

2. (Marital Status) Gabriela and Felipe _____ *are single* _____.

3. (Age) Nam _____ *is 58 years old* _____ and Felipe _____ *is 23 years old* _____.

4. (Country) Eva _____ *is from Poland* _____ and Roberto _____ *is from Mexico* _____.

LESSON 3 **Personal information**

GOAL ▶ **Describe people**   *Vocabulary*

A **Look at Felipe's driver's license. Complete the sentences about Felipe.**

DMV **CALIFORNIA** DMV
DRIVER LICENSE

Felipe Rodriguez
Address: 8220 State St.
San Francisco   CA   94160

Sex: M   Hair: black   Eyes: brown
Height: 5-11   Weight: 155 lbs

Date of birth: 06-04-78

We write: 5'11"   **We say:** Five feet, eleven inches **or:** Five-eleven

---

1. Felipe is ____*5' 11"*____ tall. (Height)
2. His weight is ___*155*___ pounds.
3. His hair is ____*black*____ and his eyes are ____*brown*____.

4. He is ___*23*___ years old.
5. His address is ____*8220*____ State Street, San Francisco, CA ____*94160*____.

B **Make sentences about Duong and Eva.**

Duong	Eva
His hair is black.	**Her** hair is white.

NEW YORK STATE
DRIVER LICENSE

Duong Bui
ADDRESS: 23 Smith Street, Apt. 305
New York,   NY 10038

DOB: July 2, 1971
SEX: M   EYES: BR   HT: 5'6"
HAIR: BLK   WT: 165 lbs   Age: 30

— *Driver's License* —

Florida Driver's License

EVA MALINSKA
ADDRESS: **175 GARDEN ST.**
TAMPA, FLORIDA 33605

BIRTH DATE   SEX   HGT
02-18-1941   F   5'2"

WT   HAIR   EYES   AGE
110 lbs   WHITE   BLUE   60

EXPIRES
04-10-04

1. Duong is ____*30 years old.*____
2. He ____*is 5' 6" tall.*____
3. His ____*eyes are brown.*____
4. *His hair is black.*

1. Eva is ____*60 years old.*____
2. She____*is 5' 2" tall.*____
3. Her ____*eyes are blue.*____
4. *Her hair is white.*

LESSON PLAN

Objectives:
Describe people, read a driver's license
Key vocabulary:
tall, height, weight, pounds, hair, eyes,
age, address, date of birth, his, her, my

Warm-up and Review: 10–15 min.

Write *tallest* on the board. Show students what you are describing by asking three students to come to the front of the room. Ask the class who of the 3 is tallest. Make sure the students understand. Then determine who is tallest in the entire class. Take a guess at his or her height and say, *I think you're probably (5′11″).* Find out if the tallest student knows his or her height. Now focus on hair color. In turn, ask students with red, then blond, then brown, then white or gray, and finally black hair to stand. Help hesitant students understand that you are broadly categorizing people by elements of their appearance.

Introduction: 1 min.

State objective: *Today we will learn to describe people.*

Presentation 1: 20–30 min.

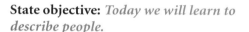 Look at Felipe's driver's license. Complete the sentences about Felipe.

Look at the driver's license with the students and ask questions like: *What is Felipe's height? What color are his eyes?* and so on. Walk through the information on Felipe's driver's license with the students and help them understand inches and feet. Many of them may not know that there are 12 inches in a foot. If possible, bring in a tape

measure, ruler, or yardstick and actually measure some of the students.

Review the lower grammar box on *his* **and** *her* **as you describe students in the classroom.**

Practice 1: 10–15 min.

B Make sentences about Duong and Eva.

This time, the students will have to sift through the abbreviations. Don't help them too much. They need to be willing to guess at meaning at this stage. Make sure the students know that they can use the statements in exercise A to make their new sentences.

Evaluation 1: 10–15 min.

Ask volunteers to write their sentences on the board.

Refer to *Stand Out Grammar Challenge 1,* Unit 1, page 5 for more practice with possessive adjectives. *(optional)*

STANDARDS CORRELATIONS

CASAS: 0.1.2, 0.2.1, 0.2.2
SCANS: **Interpersonal** Teaches Others New Skills
Information Acquires and Evaluates Information,
Organizes and Maintains Information, Interprets and
Communicates Information
Systems Understands Systems

Basic Skills Reading, Writing, Listening, Speaking
Thinking Skills Seeing Things in the Mind's Eye
Personal Qualities Sociability
EFF: **Communication** Read with Understanding, Speak So
Others Can Understand, Listen Actively
Interpersonal Guide Others

Presentation 2: 15–20 min.

Preview the questions in exercise C with the students. Write the key words from the chart headings on the board, then say the words. Prompt students to ask appropriate questions.

Show the students how to complete the chart. Make a similar chart on the board but insert a student's name. Then ask that student the example questions.

Practice 2: 10–15 min.

C Ask a partner questions about the people on page 6. Then complete the chart below. Remember to use: *he, she, his, her.*

This is an information gap activity in which one student looks at page 6 in the book while the partner keeps his or her book closed. This partner must ask questions to gather the relevant information. The partners then reverse roles and repeat the activity.

Evaluation 2: 10–15 min.

Review with the students their completed charts.

Presentation 3: 10–15 min.

Review the new vocabulary one additional time and show the students how to do Worksheet 4, page 2 for Practice 3 from Unit 1 of the *Stand Out Activity Bank 1 CD-ROM*.

Practice 3: 30–40 min.

Using Worksheet 4, page 2 for Practice 3, students make a bar graph to show comparative information about height and weight. Afterward, ask them to discuss their graphs with a group and then to make sentences about them.

Evaluation 3:

Observe the activities and review the graphs.

Application: 20–30 min.

Go over *his* and *her* again with the students and introduce *my*.

D Complete the driver's license with your information.

After students fill in the required information, ask them to talk to a partner about it. Encourage them to form complete sentences like *My name is . . . My height is . . .*, etc.

Ask the students in groups of 3 to use the information from exercise D to ask questions similar to those in exercise C. To do this, Student 1 asks Student 2 about Student 3. Student 2 reads the information from Student 3's book to answer. Then they change roles until all three students have asked the questions.

Refer to the *Activity Bank 1 CD-ROM*, Unit 1 Worksheet 5, for additional vocabulary describing people and a supplementary listening activity of conversations about people. The listening is on *AB1 CD-ROM* Track 13. *(optional)*

Instructor's Notes for Lesson 3

_____

_____

_____

_____

_____

_____

_____

_____

_____

_____

_____

_____

_____

C Ask your partner questions about the people on page 6. Then complete the chart below. Remember to use: *he, she, his, her.*

EXAMPLES:

How tall is Felipe?   What is his weight?
What color are his eyes?   What color is his hair?
How old is he?   What is his address?

Name	Height	Weight	Hair	Eyes	Age	Address
Felipe	5'11"	155 lbs	Black	Brown	23	8220 State Street San Francisco, CA 94160
Duong	5'6"	165 lbs	Black	Brown	30	23 South Street, Apt. 305 New York, NY 10038
Eva	5'2"	110 lbs	White	Blue	60	175 Garden Street Tampa, Florida 33605

D Complete the driver's license with your information.

(Answers will vary.)

Driver's License

Name:_____   Age:_____

Weight:_____   Height:_____

Hair:_____   Eyes:_____   *Your photo here*

Address:_____

City:_____   State:_____

Zip Code:_____

LESSON 4 **What's your hairstyle?**

| GOAL ▶ | Use the verb *have* | *Grammar* |

A **Discuss these new words with your teacher.**

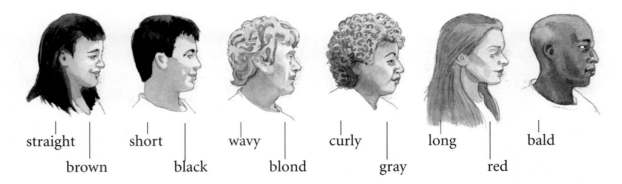

straight | short | wavy | curly | long | bald

brown | black | blond | gray | red

B **In a group, choose and draw the best hair color and hairstyle for each face below.**

Jane | Gustavo | Andres | Maria

C **Write your group's ideas below. Then share your ideas with the class.**

EXAMPLE: Jane **_has_** wavy brown hair. Andres **_is_** bald.

1. _____ *(Answers will vary.)* _____

2. _____

3. _____

4. _____

LESSON PLAN

Objective:
Use the verb have to describe people
Key vocabulary:
straight, brown, short, wavy, blond, curly, gray, black, long, red, bald, same, different, dictation

Warm-up and Review: 10–30 min.

Ask the class to stand and arrange themselves in single file, from the tallest to the shortest. Don't give them too much instruction. Wait to see how they manage. Some leaders will emerge to aid the process. They may use a language other than English, but don't be concerned about it at this time.

After the tall-short arrangement is complete, find where you fit in. Then say, *I'm _____ tall. How tall are you?* Many students may not know. Help them guess by suggesting they judge by your height. You may also want to have on hand a measuring tape or yardstick so students can actually measure themselves.

Introduction: 5–10 min.

Write on the board the words *same* **and** *different.* Make sure that the students understand these words by inviting two students with different hairstyles to the front of the room. Ask the class how the two differ. Lead them to the contrasting hairstyles and write on the board: *Their hair is different.*

State objective: *Today we will learn to use "have" to describe people.* Say, **This student has curly hair and this student has straight hair.**

Presentation 1: 20–30 min.

(A) Discuss these new words with your teacher.

Review the vocabulary on this page with the students, making sure they grasp the new words. Find as many different examples of hairstyles as you can among the class. Use *have* to describe these various hairstyles.

Practice 1: 10–15 min.

(B) In a group, choose and draw the best hair color and hairstyle for each face below.

Give the groups time to reach a consensus. Stress that every group member should add the same colors and hairstyles to the faces in their books. The students will be tempted to do this practice on their own, but that won't allow for sufficient interaction.

(C) Write your group's ideas below. Then share your ideas with the class.

Help students see how the example can aid them in writing their ideas.

Evaluation 1: 5–10 min.

Ask each group to share with the class. Encourage different members of the group to describe the different people in exercise B.

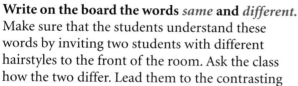

STANDARDS CORRELATIONS

CASAS: 0.1.2, 7.2.3
SCANS: **Interpersonal** Participates as a Member of a Team, Teaches Others New Skills, Exercises Leadership, Works with Cultural Diversity
Information Acquires and Evaluates Information, Organizes and Maintains Information, Interprets and Communicates Information
Basic Skills Listening, Speaking

Thinking Skills Creative Thinking, Decision Making, Problem Solving
EFF: **Communication** Speak So Others Can Understand, Listen Actively, Observe Critically
Decision Making Solve Problems and Make Decisions, Plan
Interpersonal Guide Others, Resolve Conflict and Negotiate, Advocate and Influence, Cooperate with Others

Presentation 2: 10–15 min.

D Study the chart with your teacher.
Again, use examples from the class to help with comprehension. Keep asking questions but also use substitution (substituting words in a model sentence) and transformation (transforming the verb).

Refer to *Stand Out Grammar Challenge 1,* Unit 1, page 7 for more practice. *(optional)*

Practice 2: 10–15 min.

E Write sentences about the students in Roberto's class. Look at the pictures on page 5 to find the information.
By having students work in pairs, you can turn this into an information gap activity. One student looks at the pages and makes statements while the other writes the information. Then they trade places.

Evaluation 2: 10–15 min.

Ask students to write one of their sentences on the board.

Presentation 3: 10–15 min.

Write *dictation* on the board and define it. Explain to students that, at this level, it is very difficult to listen to information and write it down at the same time. Advise them to listen and repeat to themselves what they hear <u>before</u> they begin to write.

Review any spelling problems that you noticed, as with *straight, curly,* and *wavy.*

In listening, students may experience difficulty in distinguishing *have* from *has.* They need to rely on the rule rather than verbal clues, so don't emphasize these words as you give the following dictation.

Practice 3: 10–15 min.

Dictate sentences about the people in Roberto's class and ask the students to write them down as best as they can. See Teaching Hints for help with dictation. Use sentences that the students have already worked with. Also, be sure that their books are closed during the dictation.

Evaluation 3: 10–15 min.

Ask the students in groups to go over each others' sentences and to peer edit. Then read the dictation one additional time, afterward asking volunteers to write their final versions on the board, sentence by sentence.

Application: 10–15 min.

F Describe a student in your class. Your partner can guess who it is.
Practice the example with the students a few times so they understand how to conduct the activity.

G Write sentences about students in your class.
Walk around the class and monitor students' work as they are writing.

Refer to the *Stand Out Activity Bank 1 CD-ROM,* Unit 1 Worksheet 6 (two pages) for additional work on the verb *have.* *(optional)*

Instructor's Notes for Lesson 4

D **Study the chart with your teacher.**

have		
Subject	**Verb**	**Example sentence**
I, you, we, they	have	I have short black hair.
		They have brown eyes.
he, she, it	has	She has long brown hair.

E **Write sentences about the students in Roberto's class. Look at the pictures on page 5 to find the information.**

EXAMPLE:
Roberto has short black hair and brown eyes.

1. Duong _____ *has short black hair and brown eyes* _____.

2. Eva _____ *has short white hair and blue eyes* _____.

3. Gabriela _____ *has long, wavy brown hair and brown eyes* _____.

4. Duong and Nam _____ *have short straight hair* _____.

5. Gabriela and Felipe _____ *have wavy hair and brown eyes* _____.

F **Describe a student in your class. Your partner can guess who it is.**

EXAMPLE:
Student A: She has short white hair. *(Answers will vary.)*
Student B: It's Eva!

G **Write sentences about students in your class.**

EXAMPLE:
Sarina has long brown hair and green eyes.

1. _____ *(Answers will vary.)* _____

2. _____

3. _____

4. _____

GOAL ▶ **Describe families**

Vocabulary

Who is in the picture?
What are they saying?

  A **Listen to the conversation.**

Roberto: Mom and Dad, this is Duong. He is in my English class.
Antonio: Nice to meet you, Duong. Where are you from?
Duong: I'm from Vietnam.
Rebecca: I'm happy to meet you.
Duong: It's nice to meet you, too.
Roberto: Is Julio home?
Antonio: Your brother is at work, but your sister is with Silvia in the other room.

B **Make groups of three students and practice the conversation.**

LESSON PLAN

Objective:
Describe families
Key vocabulary:
father, mother, brother, sister, wife,
husband, son, daughter, children,
parent, family tree

Warm-up and Review: 10–15 min.

Write *brothers* and *sisters* on the board. Ask individual students how many brothers and sisters each has. Encourage them early on by stating how many brothers and sisters you have, even naming them. Take a count in the class of the total number of brothers and sisters, including yours. Write numbers from each student on the board and then ask the students to add them up. Find a volunteer to give you a total and see if the class agrees.

Introduction: 3 min.

State objective: *Today we are going to learn about families.* Write the word *families* on the board.

Presentation 1: 30–40 min.

Instruct the class to study the picture, then ask the two questions in the box. Ask any other questions you consider appropriate.

 ### A Listen to the conversation.
(Audio CD Track 11)

Play the recording. Ask the students to listen first with their books closed and to write down every family word (brother, sister, etc.) they hear. Remind them of focused listening techniques. (See

Teaching Hints.) Keep in mind that the only family vocabulary students may know at this stage was just acquired in the Warm-up and Review.

Play the recording again. This time have students open their books. Ask them to underline the family words they hear and read in the conversation.

Review the words the students have underlined. Make sure they know the enlarging, family-related vocabulary. Help them with any other words they find troublesome.

B Make groups of three students and practice the conversation.

Write the target vocabulary on the board: *father, mother, brother, sister, wife, husband, son, daughter, children, parents.* Introduce the concept of a family tree by drawing your own *family tree* on the board and labeling its branches with both target vocabulary and first names.

Practice 1: 15–20 min.

C **Look at the picture and write the names on the family tree below. Then listen to Roberto and check your answers.** *(Audio CD Track 12)*

After students have completed the chart, remind them of focused listening techniques. See Teaching Hints for help. Then play the recording.

Evaluation 1: 5 min.

Review the answers with the students.

Presentation 2: 10–15 min.

Bring the attention of the class back to your family tree on the board. Ask the students to identify the people on your family tree, following the example in exercise D.

Practice 2: 20–30 min.

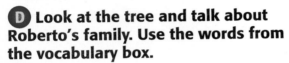

D **Look at the tree and talk about Roberto's family. Use the words from the vocabulary box.**

E **On a separate piece of paper, draw a family tree with the first names of your parents, brothers, and sisters. Show it to a partner. Ask questions about your partner's family tree.**

Ask the students to draw their own family tree. (Keep in mind that some students may have only one parent, none at all, or perhaps a guardian.) You can have them use the template on the *Activity Bank 1 CD-ROM*, Unit 1 Worksheet 7 *(optional)*. When they finish, have them exchange questions and answers with a partner.

Refer to *Stand Out Grammar Challenge 1*, Unit 1, page 6 for more practice. *(optional)*

Evaluation 2:

Observe the activity.

C Look at the picture and write the names on the family tree below. Then listen to Roberto and check your answers.

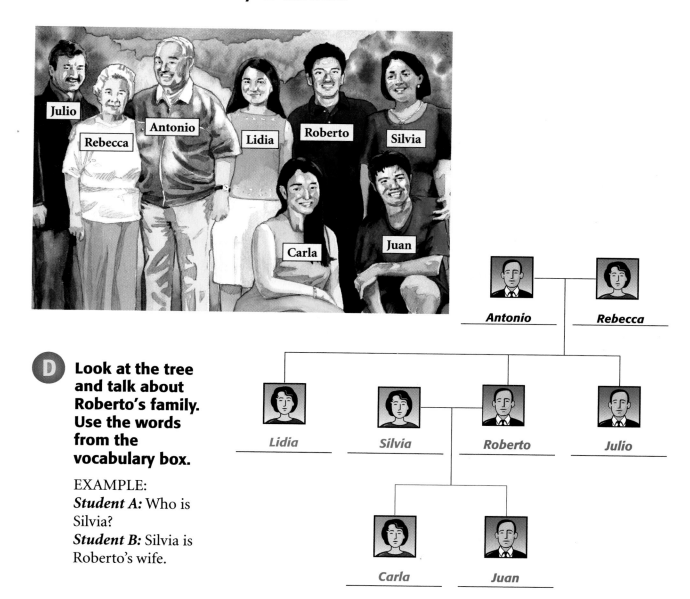

D Look at the tree and talk about Roberto's family. Use the words from the vocabulary box.

EXAMPLE:
Student A: Who is Silvia?
Student B: Silvia is Roberto's wife.

father	mother	brother	sister	wife
husband	son	daughter	children	parents

E On a separate piece of paper, draw a family tree with the first names of your parents, brothers, and sisters. Show it to a partner. Ask questions about your partner's chart.

EXAMPLE:
Student A: Who is Elena?   *Student B:* Elena is my sister.

F **Read Roberto's story and answer the questions.**

My name is Roberto. I am 43 years old. I'm married. My wife's name is Silvia. I have two children, Juan and Carla. Juan is 17 years old. He has straight black hair and brown eyes. Carla is 15. Carla has long, black hair and brown eyes. I love my family.

1. Is Roberto married? _____Yes_____

2. Does Roberto have children? _Yes (He has two children.)_

G **Read Julio's story and answer the questions.**

My name is Julio. I'm single. My parents are wonderful. My father, Antonio, and my mother, Rebecca, have three children, Roberto, Lidia, and me. I am 45 years old. My brother Roberto is 43. He is tall and has short, black hair. My sister, Lidia, is 40 years old. I love my family very much.

1. Is Julio married? _____No_____

2. Does Julio have brothers and sisters? _Yes (He has one brother and one sister.)_

H **Write a paragraph about your family. Use the paragraphs about Roberto and Julio to help you. Bring a photograph of your family to go with your writing and show it to the class.**

(Answers will vary.)

_____

_____

_____

_____

_____

 I **Active Task:** Find examples of family tree charts in the library or on the Internet and show them to your class.

Presentation 3: 10–15 min.

Review the vocabulary one more time in preparation for the reading. Ask the students if they can write a new or similar sentence to the one in exercise G that reads, *My father, Antonio, and my mother, Rebecca, have three children, Roberto, Lidia, and me.* Student sentences should be based on their own personal information.

Practice 3: 15–20 min.

F **Read Roberto's story and answer the questions.**

G **Read Julio's story and answer the questions.**

Allow students to struggle through both stories. Then go back and review the stories with them.

 Refer to *Stand Out Grammar Challenge 1,* Unit 1, page 4 for more practice. *(optional)*

Evaluation 3: 5–10 min.

Ask comprehension questions about the stories.

Application: 15–20 min.

H **Write a paragraph about your family. Use the paragraphs about Roberto and Julio to help you. Bring a photograph of your family to go with your writing and show it to the class.**

This activity probably won't be finished in class, but encourage the students to work on it at home. They can also put their stories on the computer and scan pictures for an extended project. See Teaching Hints for suggestions to enhance the classroom experience with computers.

I **Active Task: Find examples of family tree charts in the library or on the Internet and show them to your class.**

 Refer to the *Activity Bank 1 CD-ROM* Unit 1 for additional activities with family relationship vocabulary (Worksheet 8) and a family tree template (Worksheet 7). *(optional)*

Instructor's Notes for Lesson 5

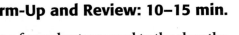

LESSON PLAN

Objective:
Use *like* in the present tense
Key vocabulary:
movies, music, sports, games,
computers, TV, restaurants, parks,
favorite

Warm-Up and Review: 10–15 min.

Have a few volunteers read to the class the
paragraphs they wrote for the previous
application activity.

Introduction: 5 min.

Write the word *like* on the board. Mention
something that you like. You might want to say
that you like your students. Ask students what
they like. Make a list on the board.

State objective: *Today we will learn to use "like"
in the present tense.*

Presentation 1: 10–15 min.

**Look at the pictures with the students and quiz
them on the vocabulary.** Find examples in the
classroom of some of the words (e.g., books or
computers). To further reinforce the vocabulary,
ask individuals if they like these items.

Practice 1: 15–20 min.

Remind the students about focused listening.
(See Teaching Hints for help.)

**A Listen and put an "R" by things
Roberto likes and an "S" by things
Silvia likes.** *(Audio CD Track 13)*

Play the recording as many times as you need to.

B Complete these sentences.

Evaluation 1: 10–15 min.

Ask for volunteers to write the new sentences on
the board.

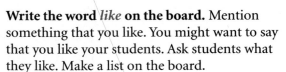

STANDARDS CORRELATIONS

CASAS: 0.1.2, 0.2.1, 0.2.4
SCANS: Information Acquires and Evaluates Information,
Organizes and Maintains Information, Interprets and
Communicates Information

Basic Skills Listening, Speaking
Personal Qualities Sociability
EFF: Communication Speak So Others Can Understand,
Listen Actively, Observe Critically

LESSON 6 I like sports and music.

GOAL ▶ Use *like* in the present tense

Grammar

 A Listen and put an "R" by things Roberto likes and an "S" by things Silvia likes.

movies __R__

music __S__

sports __R and S__

games __R__

computers __R and S__

TV __R and S__

books __R__

restaurants __S__

parks __S__

B **Complete these sentences.** *(Answers may vary.)*

1. Roberto likes **books**.
2. Roberto likes __movies__.
3. Roberto likes __games__.
4. Silvia likes __music__.

5. Silvia likes __restaurants__.
6. Silvia likes __parks__.
7. They both like __computers__.
8. They both like __sports and TV__.

C **Study the chart with your teacher.**

like			
Subject	**Verb**	**Noun**	**Example sentence**
I, you	like	movies	I like computers.
he, she, it	likes	music	She likes sports.
we, they	like	sports	They like music.
		games	
		computers	
		TV	
		books	
		restaurants	
		parks	

D **Talk to a partner and write.**　　*(Answers will vary.)*

1. What do you like?

I like _____.

_____

_____.

2. What does your partner like?

He or she likes _____.

_____.

_____.

3. What do you and your partner like?

We both like _____.

_____.

_____.

E **Introduce your partner to another pair.**

EXAMPLE:

This is my friend Roberto. He is from Mexico. He is married and has two children. Roberto likes movies and books.

Presentation 2: 10–15 min.

C Study the chart with your teacher.

As you go through the chart, show the students that other words can also be used that follow the same rule as *like(s)*. Students are only working with *like* in this lesson, but it serves as an introduction to the simple present.

Refer to *Stand Out Grammar Challenge 1*, Unit 1, page 7 for more practice. *(optional)*

Practice 2: 10–15 min.

D Talk to a partner and write.

Some teachers may want to add *don't* at this stage. That word will be introduced in a future lesson, but if your students are ready, add a fourth box. Head it with *What my partner and I don't like.* This then becomes a Johari Square activity. See the *Activity Bank 1 CD-ROM*, Unit 1 Worksheet 9, for more practice with *don't*.

Evaluation 2: 10–15 min.

Ask students to share what they have written in their boxes.

Presentation 3: 5–10 min.

Review the vocabulary on page 13 again with the students, writing the words on the board. Add any additional new words that have been mentioned during the class. Teach the students how to rank *objects, qualities, events,* etc., by saying *What is your favorite?* Allow each student to name only one favorite. Then ask them to name their second favorite. Write several student responses on the board, assigning the numbers 1 and 2 next to those responses to indicate rank.

Practice 3: 10–15 min.

Ask the students to assign their own ranking to all the items on the board by making a list.

Evaluation 3: 5–10 min.

Ask students to report on their lists.

Application: 15–20 min.

E Introduce your partner to another pair.

Remind students how to introduce each other. Then ask them to gather information about their partner and introduce him or her to three other students, using the example as a guide.

Refer to the *Activity Bank 1 CD-ROM*, Unit 1 Worksheet 10 (two pages), for additional practice with the simple present. *(optional)*

Instructor's Notes for Lesson 6

_____

_____

_____

_____

_____

_____

_____

_____

_____

_____

_____

_____

_____

_____

_____

_____

LESSON PLAN

Objective:
Tell time
Key vocabulary:
go, eat, sleep, wake up, breakfast, lunch, dinner, snack, study, make dinner, go shopping, adverbs of frequency, A.M., P.M., listen, read, practice, watch, write, morning, afternoon, night, break

Warm-Up and Review: 10–15 min.

With books closed, ask the students in groups to compile a list of what makes a good student. Write *comes to school every day* as an example on the board. After the students spend about five or ten minutes thinking and agreeing on a list, ask representatives to write their group's list on the board.

Introduction: 5 min.

Write the words *watch* and *clock* on the board. Help the students understand the difference.

State objective: *Today, we will learn how to read clocks and watches in English.*

Presentation 1: 15–25 min.

(A) When does Roberto practice English? Look at the clocks and read the times.

Review the vocabulary in exercise A with the students. Make sure they understand *morning,*

afternoon, and *night* and see that when we use *night,* we generally say *at night.* Also, explain to them the meanings of A.M. (ante meridian, or before noon) and P.M. (post meridian, or afternoon). Then ask if any students come from countries that use the 24–hour clock. Even if none do, briefly show on the board how this clock works (e.g., 7:30 p.m. equals 19:30 hours).

Walk the students through Roberto's schedule and read the times as a class. Prompt the students by asking such questions as *When does Roberto listen to the radio?* Write *from___* and *to___* on the board, inviting students to fill in the time blanks with oral responses to your questions.

Practice 1: 10–15 min.

(B) Make sentences about Roberto.

Evaluation 1: 10–15 min.

Review by selecting a few students to write their sentences on the board.

STANDARDS CORRELATIONS

CASAS: 0.1.2, 0.1.5, 0.2.1, 7.1.2, 7.1.4
SCANS: **Resources** Allocates Time
Interpersonal Participates as a Member of a Team, Teaches Others New Skills, Exercises Leadership, Works with Cultural Diversity
Information Acquires and Evaluates Information, Organizes and Maintains Information, Interprets and Communicates Information
Systems Understands Systems, Monitors and Corrects Performance, Improves and Designs Systems
Basic Skills Reading, Writing, Listening, Speaking

Thinking Skills Decision Making, Problem Solving, Seeing Things in the Mind's Eye, Knowing How to Learn, Reasoning
Personal Qualities Responsibility, Self-Management
EFF: **Communication** Read with Understanding, Convey Ideas in Writing, Speak So Others Can Understand, Listen Actively, Observe Critically
Decision Making Solve Problems and Make Decisions, Plan
Interpersonal Guide Others, Cooperate with Others
Lifelong Learning Take Responsibility for Learning, Reflect and Evaluate

When do you study?

GOAL ▶ **Tell time**

Life Skill

A **When does Roberto practice English? Look at the clocks and read the times.**

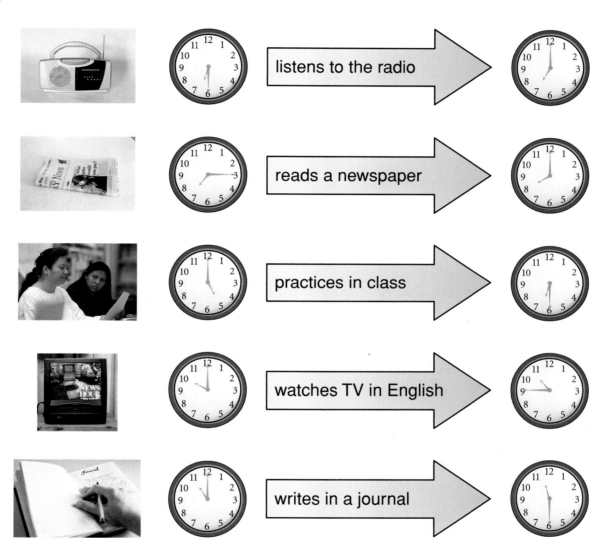

listens to the radio

reads a newspaper

practices in class

watches TV in English

writes in a journal

B **Make sentences about Roberto.**

EXAMPLE: ***Roberto listens to the radio from six thirty to seven o'clock in the morning.*** .

1. He reads a newspaper from _____**seven fifteen /7:15**_____ to _____*eight o' clock /8:00*_____ .

2. He *practices in class from five o' clock /5:00 to six thirty /6:30* _____ .

3. *He watches TV in English from ten o' clock /10:00 to ten forty-five /10:45* _____ .

4. *He writes in a journal from eleven o' clock /11:00 to eleven thirty /11:30.* _____ .

C **When and how do you practice English every day? Fill in the chart with different ways to practice English.**

	From	To	Activity
In the morning			
In the afternoon			
At night			

(Answers will vary.)

D **Make sentences about your daily plan and tell your partner. Listen to your partner's plan and write his or her information here.**

	From	To	Activity
In the morning			
In the afternoon			
At night			

(Answers will vary.)

E **Make sentences about your partner's plan and tell the class.**

Presentation 2: 15–25 min.

With books closed, ask the students if they study in the morning, afternoon, or at night. Review the vocabulary from the previous page again. Ask them what time they start studying and when they finish. Review the simple present with *like* from the previous lesson and show the students once more how this transformation can extend to other verbs. Use examples from page 15.

Practice 2: 10–15 min.

C **When and how do you practice English every day? Fill in the chart with different ways to practice English.**

Ask students to write answers in the simple present, as on page 15.

Evaluation 2: 5–10 min.

Review the work in students' books.

 Presentation 3: 15–25 min.

Ask the students about good study habits. Distribute Worksheet 11 from Unit 1 of the *Activity Bank 1 CD-ROM*.

Define the word *break* for them, denoting *rest* or *stop work for a while*. Then explain that they will study different study schedules and, as a group, decide which is better.

Practice 3: 15–25 min.

Ask student groups to complete Worksheet 11 (page 1).

Evaluation 3: 10–15 min.

Ask the groups to report their conclusions to the class.

 Application: 20–30 min.

D **Make sentences about your daily plan and tell your partner. Listen to your partner's plan and write his or her information here.**

Use Worksheet 11, page 2 from Unit 1 of the *Activity Bank 1 CD-ROM* for expanded work on personal study habits.

E **Make sentences about your partner's plan and tell the class.**

Refer to the *Activity Bank 1 CD-ROM*, Unit 1 Worksheet 12, for additional practice reading about and listening to information on study habits. The listening is on *AB1 CD-ROM* Track 2. *(optional)*

Instructor's Notes for Lesson 7

> ## REVIEW
> Objectives:
> All previous objectives
> Key vocabulary:
> All previous Unit 1 vocabulary

Warm-Up and Review: 10–15 min.

Ask some students to report their partners' plans from the previous lesson.

Introduction: 3–5 min.

State objective: *Today we will review all that we have done in the past unit in preparation for the application project to follow.* Ask students as a class to try to recall all the goals of this unit without looking at their books. Then remind them of the goals they haven't mentioned.

Unit Goals: Talk about places and names, Use be and introduce people, Describe people, Use the verb have, Describe families, Use like in the present tense, Tell the time.

Presentation 1, Practice 1, and Evaluation 1:

Do the Learner Log on page 20. Notes are adjacent to the page.

Presentation 2: 5–15 min.

Review the *be* and *have* verbs with the class. Also review the simple present with *like.*

Practice 2: 10–15 min.

A **Fill in the circle next to the correct answer.**

For students who are not familiar with filling in circles, explain that this method is used on many standardized tests. It is important to fill in the circle completely.

B **What is their relationship? Look back at page 11 and complete the sentences below.**

C **Match the questions and the answers. Write the correct letter next to each number.**

Refer to *Stand Out Grammar Challenge 1,* Unit 1, pages 1–2 for more practice. *(optional)*

Evaluation 2: 5–10 min.

Observe the activities and review student work as a class.

STANDARDS CORRELATIONS

CASAS: 0.1.2, 0.2.1, 7.1.1, 7.1.4, 7.4.1, 7.4.9, 7.4.10, 7.5.1
SCANS: **Information** Acquires and Evaluates Information, Organizes and Maintains Information, Interprets and Communicates Information
Systems Monitors and Corrects Performance
Basic Skills Reading, Writing, Listening, Speaking
Thinking Skills Knowing How to Learn
Personal Qualities Responsibility, Self-Esteem, Self-Management

EFF: **Communication** Read with Understanding, Convey Ideas in Writing, Speak So Others Can Understand, Listen Actively, Observe Critically
Decision Making Make Decisions, Plan
Interpersonal Guide Others, Cooperate with Others
Lifelong Learning Take Responsibility for Learning, Reflect and Evaluate

Review

A Fill in the circle next to the correct answer.

EXAMPLE:
My name _____ Duong.
○ am ● is ○ are

1. I _____ from Vietnam.
   ● am ○ is ○ are

2. Roberto _____ from Mexico.
   ○ am ● is ○ are

3. Roberto and Duong _____ students.
   ○ am ○ is ● are

4. Roberto and Duong both _____ black hair.
   ○ has ● have ○ are

5. Roberto _____ one brother.
   ● has ○ have ○ are

6. Silvia _____ computers.
   ● likes ○ like ○ is like

B What is their relationship? Look back at page 11 and fill in the missing words.

EXAMPLE:
Roberto is Silvia's husband, and Silvia is Roberto's *wife*.

1. Silvia is Juan's mother, and Juan is Silvia's _____ *son* _____.

2. Juan is Carla's brother, and Carla is Juan's _____ *sister* _____.

3. Roberto is Carla's father, and Carla is Roberto's _____ *daughter* _____.

4. Roberto and Silvia are Juan and Carla's _____ *parents (father and mother)* _____.

5. Juan and Carla are Roberto and Silvia's _____ *children (son and daughter)* _____.

C Match the questions and the answers. Write the correct letter next to each number.

1. _d_ What's your name?
2. _f_ Where are you from?
3. _b_ How old are you?
4. _e_ What is your weight?
5. _a_ What is your height?
6. _c_ Are you married?

a. 6 feet 2 inches.
b. 28.
c. Yes, I am.
d. Ernesto Gonzalez.
e. 145 pounds.
f. Colombia.

D How does Roberto practice English? Fill in the missing words.

1. He ___listens___ to the radio.

2. He ___watches___ TV.

3. He ___reads___ the newspaper.

4. He ___writes___ in his journal.

E Write two other ways to practice English. *(Answers will vary.)*

1. ___study my textbook___

2. ___keep a vocabulary notebook___

F What time is it? Write the time under each clock.

1. It's ___11:30___. 2. It's ___8:00___. 3. It's ___10:15___. 4. It's ___7:45___.

G Ask two students about their name, age, and marital status. Write sentences about the two students.

EXAMPLE: Rieko is from Japan. She is 29 years old, and she is married.

1. ___(Answers will vary.)___

2. ___

H Describe two people in your class. What color is his or her hair? What color are his or her eyes? Write one sentence about each person.

1. ___(Answers will vary.)___

2. ___

Presentation 3: 5–15 min.

Write *age* and *marital status* on the board and review these words to make sure students remember them.

Practice 3: 15–25 min.

D **How does Roberto practice English? Fill in the missing words.**

E **Write two other ways to practice English.**

F **What time is it? Write the time under each clock.**

G **Ask two students about their name, age, and marital status. Write sentences about the two students.**

H **Describe two people in your class. What color is his or her hair? What color are his or her eyes? Write one sentence about each person.**

Shorter classes should complete exercises for homework.

 Refer to *Stand Out Grammar Challenge 1,* Unit 1, pages 6–7 for more practice. *(optional)*

Evaluation 3: 10–20 min.

Observe the activities and review student answers and sentences.

Application: 1–2 days

The Team Project Activity on the following page is the application activity to be done on the next day of class.

 Post-Assessment: Use the *Stand Out* ExamView® Pro *Test Bank* for Unit 1. *(optional)*

Note: With the ExamView® Pro *Test Bank* CD-ROM you can design a post-assessment that focuses on what students have learned. It is designed for three purposes:

• To help students practice taking a test similar to current standardized tests.

• To help the teacher evaluate how much the students have learned, retained, and acquired.

• To help students see their progress when they compare their scores to the pre-test they took earlier.

```
Instructor's Notes for Unit 1
_____
_____
_____
_____
_____
_____
_____
_____
_____
_____
_____
_____
_____
_____
_____
_____
_____
_____
_____
```

Unit 1 Application Activity

> ## TEAM PROJECT: CREATING A STUDENT PROFILE
>
> Objective:
> Project designed to apply all the objectives of this unit.
> Product:
> a student profile on Project sheet

Introduction:

Students work together in teams to create a profile about one student on their team. Students will answer questions on student profile Worksheet 13 available in Unit 1 of the *Activity Bank 1 CD-ROM*. The sheet shows students how to describe one another. This project can extend over two days.

Stage 1: 5–10 min.

Form a team with four or five students.

Students decide who will lead which steps as described on the student page. Provide well-defined directions on the board for how students should proceed. Explain to them that every task is to be done by each student. Students don't go to the next stage until the previous one is complete.

Stage 2: 3 min.

Choose one student in your group for a profile.

Stage 3: 10–15 min.

Complete a student profile sheet by asking questions.

Give students the interview project worksheet. Use the *Activity Bank 1 CD-ROM* Unit 1 Worksheet 13. Tell students that each member of the team should ask at least three questions on the sheet. Team members should try to provide additional questions when they complete the questionaire.

Stage 4: 15–20 min.

Write the information on the profile sheet.

Ask the students to complete the profile sheet by writing a paragraph about the selected student. This part of the sheet can be done on the computer. *(optional)*

Encourage students to write sentences using *he* or *she*.

Stage 5: 15–20 min.

Practice introducing the student to the other groups.

Use the profile worksheet.

Stage 6: 20–40 min.

Repeat with other student profiles.

If time, repeat profile process and present the members of your team to the other groups. Encourage students to ask questions if information is unclear.

STANDARDS CORRELATIONS

CASAS: 0.1.2, 0.2.1, 4.8.1, 4.8.5
SCANS: **Resources** Allocates Time, Allocates Material and Facility Resources
Interpersonal Teaches Others New Skills
Information Organizes and Maintains Information, Interprets and Communicates Information, Uses Computers to Process Information (optional)
Systems Understands Systems, Monitors and Corrects Performance, Improves and Designs Systems
Technology Applies Technology to Task (optional)
Basic Skills Reading, Writing, Listening, Speaking

Thinking Skills Creative Thinking, Decision Making
Personal Qualities Responsibility, Self-Esteem, Sociability, Self-Management
EFF: **Communication** Convey Ideas in Writing, Speak So Others Can Understand, Listen Actively, Observe Critically
Decision Making Make Decisions, Plan
Interpersonal Guide Others, Cooperate with Others
Lifelong Learning Take Responsibility for Learning, Reflect and Evaluate, Learn through Research, Use Information and Communications Technology (optional)

T E A M
P R O J E C T

Creating a student profile

In this project you will work together to create a student profile for each person in your team.

1. Form a team with four or five students.

   In your team, you need:

Position	Job	Student Name
Student 1 Leader	See that everyone speaks English. See that everyone participates.	
Student 2 Secretary	Complete the student profile with help from the team.	
Student 3	Give personal information for introductions.	
Students 4 and 5	Introduce student to other groups.	

2. Choose one student in your group to do a profile on.

3. Complete a student profile sheet by asking questions. Each student in the group asks three or more questions. (See page 17 for help.)

4. Write the information on the profile sheet. (See pages 6–9 for help.)

5. Practice introducing the student to the other groups. Use the profile sheet.

6. Repeat with other student profiles if you have time.

PRONUNCIATION

Practice the /h/ sound at the beginning of words. Listen and repeat.

he	his	here	husband	home
hair	how	who	height	her

LEARNER LOG

Circle what you learned and write the page number where you learned it.

1. I can talk about places and names.
   Yes   Maybe   No   Page _1–3_

2. I can find countries on a map.
   Yes   Maybe   No   Page _3_

3. I can introduce people.
   Yes   Maybe   No   Page _4–5_

4. I can describe people.
   Yes   Maybe   No   Page _6–7_

5. I can talk about families.
   Yes   Maybe   No   Page _10–12_

6. I can use the verb *be*.
   Yes   Maybe   No   Page _4–5_

7. I can talk about things I like.
   Yes   Maybe   No   Page _13–14_

8. I can tell the time.
   Yes   Maybe   No   Page _15–16_

Did you answer *No* to any questions? Review the information with a partner.

Rank what you like to do best from 1 to 6. 1 is your favorite activity. Your teacher will help you.

☐ practice listening

☐ practice speaking

☐ practice reading

☐ practice writing

☐ learn new words (vocabulary)

☐ learn grammar

In the next unit I want to practice more
_____*(Answers will vary.)*_____ .

Unit 1 Pronunciation and Learner Log

 Pronunciation (*optional*): 10–15 min.
(*Audio CD Track 14*)

Practice the /h/ sound at the beginning of words. Listen and repeat.

Play the recording and pause after each word.

For additional pronunciation practice: (The following words should be used for pronunciation practice, not for vocabulary instruction.)

Write the following examples on the board:

help   happy
host   home
hostess   homeless
have   has   had

His host is happy.   Who is her husband?
Her height is 5′6″.   Here is help.
Help the homeless.

You may find it helpful to contrast the following pairs of words:

hear   ear
hair   air
his   is
heat   eat

Learner Log:

Presentation 1: 15–20 min.

Explain that the Learner Log helps students think about what they learned in this unit. You may need to demonstrate how the Learner Log works with a few examples on the board. Some instructors may want to read the exercises aloud and work through this first log with the students. Other instructors with stronger readers may want to have the students work through it by themselves.

Circle what you learned and write the page number where you learned it.
Students research the answers individually. When they've finished, they should share their answers with a partner. These results need not be shared with the class.

Practice 1: 10–15 min.

Rank what you like to do best from 1 to 6. 1 is your favorite activity. Your teacher will help you. Students may need help with ranking only this first time. Results should be shared with the class in order to demonstrate to students how people learn differently.

Evaluation 1: 10–20 min.

In the next unit I want to practice more ____. Students should fill in the blank with assistance from a partner or from you. They may focus on a skill (e.g., listening), on a vocabulary area (e.g., numbers), on grammar, and so on. Don't limit them to a single answer. Emphasize that the purpose of completing the sentence is to improve their self-assessment skills. Ask volunteers to share answers with the class.

Instructor's Notes for Unit 1 Team Project, Pronunciation, and Learner Log

_____
_____
_____
_____
_____
_____
_____
_____
_____
_____
_____
_____

LESSON PLAN

Objective:
Identify places to make purchases
Key vocabulary:
department store, clothing store, convenience store, shoes, books, dictionary, shirt, CD player, bread, cheese, fruit

Pre-Assessment: Use the *Stand Out* ExamView® Pro *Test Bank* for Unit 2. *(optional)*

Warm-up and Review: 5–10 min.

Ask the students if they like shopping. Ask the students if they like money. Ask them what they would buy if they had a million dollars. They won't need to understand the sentence construction to answer this question. Accept all answers.

Introduction: 5–10 min.

State objective: *Today and in this unit, we will learn about shopping and money.*

Presentation 1: 20–30 min.

Ask the students what items or supplies they need to bring to school. Start them off by saying you need a pencil or pen. Show them your pencil or pen. Ask them what else they need.

Ask the students to open their books and look at the pictures in exercise A. Tell them that Van is preparing to start school. Ask them what a student needs for school.

A Read about Van.

Do this as a class. Be sure the students understand all the vocabulary. Ask the students to help you list other things Van might need. Write the class list on the board. This is basically a repeat of what you just asked the students about themselves. Also repeat the vocabulary.

B Write Van's shopping items under the correct stores below.

Do this with the class.

Practice 1: 10–15 min.

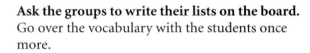

C What other things can you buy at each store? Make a list with a group.

Ask students to form groups and discuss the question before making a group list. To expand its list, a group will then send a representative to one other group, look at their list, and add one more item to be purchased from each store. To extend this activity, send representatives to other groups.

Evaluation 1: 10 min.

Ask the groups to write their lists on the board. Go over the vocabulary with the students once more.

Pronunciation:

An optional pronunciation activity is found on the final page of this unit. This pronunciation activity may be introduced during any lesson in this unit, especially if students need practice with the two sounds of /th/. Go to pages 40/40a for Unit 2 Pronunciation.

STANDARDS CORRELATIONS

CASAS: 1.3.8, 1.3.9, 4.8.1
SCANS: **Resources** Allocates Materials and Facility Resources
Interpersonal Participates as a Member of a Team, Teaches Others New Skills, Exercises Leadership
Information Acquires and Evaluates Information, Organizes and Maintains Information, Interprets and Communicates Information, Uses Computers to Process Information (optional)
Technology Applies Technology to Task (optional)
Basic Skills Reading, Listening, Speaking

Thinking Skills Creative Thinking, Decision Making, Problem Solving, Seeing Things in the Mind's Eye
EFF: **Communication** Read with Understanding, Speak So Others Can Understand, Listen Actively, Observe Critically
Decision Making Solve Problems and Make Decisions
Interpersonal Guide Others, Advocate and Influence, Cooperate with Others
Lifelong Learning Reflect and Evaluate, Learn through Research, Use Information and Communications Technology (optional)

UNIT 2

Let's Go Shopping

GOALS

- Talk about where to buy goods
- Count money and read receipts
- Identify clothing
- Use possessive adjectives
- Use adjectives to describe things
- Write checks
- Use *this, that, these,* and *those*

LESSON 1 ## Shopping

GOAL ▶ Talk about where to buy goods   *Vocabulary*

A **Read about Van.**

Van starts school on Monday. She wants a dictionary,  sneakers,

new shirts, a CD player, and food for lunches.

B **Write Van's shopping items under the correct stores below.**

Martin's Department Store	24–7 Convenience Store	Sam's Food Mart	Hero's Books	Victory Shoes	Shop and Dress for Less
dictionary	*bread*	*bread*	*dictionary*	*sneakers*	*sneakers*
sneakers	*cheese*	*cheese*			*shirts*
CD player	*oranges*	*oranges*			

C **What other things can you buy at each store? Make a list with a group.**

D Listen to Van and her husband. Draw a circle around where she goes.

Goods	Types of stores	
1. CD player	(department store)	convenience store
2. shoes	shoe store	(department store)
3. shirts	clothing store	(department store)
4. dictionary	(bookstore)	department store
5. bread, cheese, and fruit	supermarket	(convenience store)

E In a group ask, "Where do you shop for clothes?" Make a list.

(Answers will vary.)

_____   _____   _____

_____   _____   _____

F Make a bar graph. How many students shop in different types of stores?

EXAMPLE:

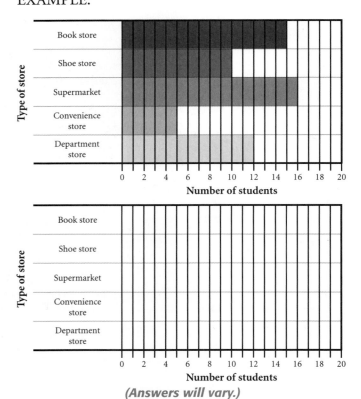

(Answers will vary.)

G **Active Task:** Go to a mall or on the Internet. Find the names of three clothing stores. Report to the class.

Presentation 2: 5–10 min.

Remind the students that different stores sometimes sell the same items. Show students the overlap among the group lists they wrote on the board. Review focused listening. Help students see that, although they will hear many words in the listening exercise to follow, they should listen only for mention of items and the names of the stores where they can be bought. Review the items and kinds of stores in exercise D to make sure students know what to listen for.

Practice 2: 15–25 min.

 D Listen to Van and her husband. Draw a circle around where she goes.
(Audio CD Track 15)

Play the recording. If students have trouble with focused listening, you may wish to ask them to listen for only a single item or store name. Play the recording as many times as needed. Shorter classes can do this for homework. If they don't have the recording, students can look at the listening script in the back of their books and do this as listening comprehension.

Evaluation 2:

Observe the listening activity.

Presentation 3: 5 min.

Ask students to get into groups of three or four students. Assign each group one of the stores listed on page 21.

Practice 3: 10–30 min.

Ask the students in groups to make a list of all the items they can think of that can be purchased at those stores. Put a time limit on this part of the exercise. Ask each group to submit its finished list to you. Read from the lists and then say: *I need _____ (a new pen, etc.). Where should I go?* Some students will notice the overlap between lists. Write on the board items that can fit into one or more categories. Ask a few students where they would go to shop for these items. For example, if you wrote *shoes* on the board, you might ask a student where he or she buys shoes: *at a department store, shoe store, or clothing store?*

Evaluation 3:

Observe the activity.

Application: 10–15 min.

E In a group ask, "Where do you shop for clothes?" Make a list.

Ask students in groups to make a list of all the places they shop for clothes.

F Make a bar graph. How many students shop in different types of stores?

Look at the example graph and have students answer questions about the data presented there. Write on the board: *How many students shop in _____?* Ask students in groups to decide which stores they will ask the rest of the class about. Show them how to get the attention of the class, phrase a question, and ask for a vote. Each group should ask the class at least one question. If you want students to know about additional types of stores for their graphs, mention them now. Graphs can be designed on the computer (optional). For more help with using graphs, see Teaching Hints.

 G Active Task: Go to a mall or on the Internet. Find the names of three clothing stores. Report to the class.

Refer to the *Activity Bank 1 CD-ROM*, Unit 2 Worksheet 1, for more vocabulary practice in an information gap activity. *(optional)*

LESSON PLAN

Objectives:
Count money and read receipts
Key vocabulary:
tennis shoes, vacuum, bread, peanut butter, jelly, apples, pound, potato chips, dollar, bills, coins, quarter, nickel, penny, dime, bilingual, tax, how much, washing machine, total, receipt

Warm-up and Review: 10–15 min.

Ask the students which stores they used for their bar graphs in the previous lesson. Ask them to share their bar graphs with the class.

Introduction: 3–5 min.

Write *How much?* on the board. Ask the students how much a dictionary might cost.

State objective: *Today you will learn to count money and to read receipts.*

Presentation 1: 20–30 min.

A Look at the receipts. What are the totals? What is the tax?

Review the receipts by asking questions. Make sure you ask about the totals and the tax.

B How much is the total for the shirts, sneakers, bilingual dictionary, and food together with tax? Total____

Work with the class to figure out the total. If you wish, turn this into a competition to see who comes up with the correct total first. Do the math

on the board to verify that all students know how to do it. You may also ask them for the total before taxes and for totals for different combinations of purchases.

Practice 1: 15–20 min.

C Listen and circle what you hear.

(Audio CD Track 16)
This listening exercise will prepare students for the focused listening that follows.

D Listen and write the prices.

(Audio CD Track 17)
Review focused listening with the students. See Teaching Hints.

Evaluation 1: 10–15 min.

Review answers as a class. This is a good place to point out the difference in pronunciation between numbers like 15 and 50 (optional).

STANDARDS CORRELATIONS

CASAS: 1.1.6, 1.3.9, 1.6.4
SCANS: Resources Allocates Money
Interpersonal Participates as a Member of a Team, Teaches Others New Skills, Exercises Leadership, Works with Cultural Diversity
Information Acquires and Evaluates Information, Organizes and Maintains Information, Interprets and Communicates Information
Systems Understands Systems

Basic Skills: Arithmetic, Listening, Speaking
Thinking Skills Problem Solving
EFF: Communication Speak So Others Can Understand, Listen Actively, Observe Critically
Decision Making Use Math to Solve Problems and Communicate, Solve Problems and Make Decisions
Interpersonal Guide Others, Resolve Conflict and Negotiate, Cooperate with Others

LESSON 2 — Van's purchases

GOAL ▶ Count money and read receipts   **Life Skill**

A Look at the receipts. What are the totals? What is the tax?

Martin's	
SHIRTS 2 @ $17.98 –	$35.96
SNEAKERS –	$22.99
TAX –	$4.72
TOTAL –	$63.67

Hero's Books	
BILINGUAL DICTIONARY–	
	$21.95
TAX –	$ 1.76
TOTAL –	$23.71

Sam's Food Mart	
BREAD –	$ 2.30
CHEESE –	$ 2.75
ORANGES @ 60¢	
A POUND –	$ 1.20
POTATO CHIPS –	$ 2.60
TOTAL –	$8.85

B How much is the total for the shirts, sneakers, bilingual dictionary, and food together with tax? Total ___$96.23___

C Listen and circle what you hear.

EXAMPLE: $12.50 $ 2.15   ⟨$22.50⟩ $22.15

1. $35.15   ⟨$34.15⟩ $34.50 $45.50
2. $13.00 $30.00   ⟨$33.00⟩ $43.00
3. $.57 $57.00   ⟨$15.70⟩ $17.00
4. $19.75 $17.90 $79.00   ⟨$77.95⟩

D Listen and write the prices.

       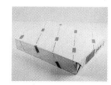      

vacuum	washing machine	paper	candy bar	telephone
$98.99	$ 450	$ 6.50	$ 1.25	$ 80

E Practice asking about prices. Look at exercise D on page 23 for information.

EXAMPLE:
Student A: Excuse me, how much is the **_vacuum_**?
Student B: It's $98.99.
Student A: Thank you.

F Look at the money. Write the words with the pictures.

a one-dollar bill	a five-dollar bill	a ten-dollar bill	a twenty-dollar bill
a quarter	a dime	a nickel	a penny

a one-dollar bill   *a quarter*   *a five-dollar bill*   *a nickel*

a penny   *a ten-dollar bill*   *a dime*   *a twenty-dollar bill*

G What bills and coins do you need for these items? Tell a partner and the class.

$63.99 $45.50 $23.71

(Answers may vary slightly.)

H **Active Task:** Bring receipts from home and show the class.

Presentation 2: 10–15 min.

Review the answers again to exercise D by asking students how much the items cost. Help them understand that they can answer by using dollars and cents (as in *5 dollars and 12 cents*) or simply the numbers (as in *5, 12*). Stress that they can't mix the two alternatives (as in *5 dollars and 12*).

Preview the dialog in exercise E. Show students how to substitute information. This practice can also be extended to the items on the receipts in exercise A, if you wish. If so, be sure to review *It's* versus *They're* to help students use the singular and plural correctly.

Practice 2: 15–20 min.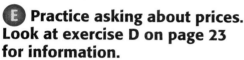

E **Practice asking about prices. Look at exercise D on page 23 for information.**

Alternative practice for exercise E: Write an item from exercise D on a notecard or piece of paper. Make enough cards so three or four students can have cards with the same information on them. Tell the students to keep their item a secret until they are asked. They must do the dialog in exercise E with several students, using the information on the card as a prompt. Instruct students to say *I'm sorry. I don't know* if they don't have the card with the price. When they find two or three other students with the same information they have finished the activity. See Teaching Hints for ideas on extending dialog practice.

Evaluation 2: 10–15 min.

Ask for volunteers to demonstrate in front of the class.

Presentation 3: 10–15 min.

F **Look at the money. Write the words with the pictures.**

Do this activity with the class. Review all bills. This would be a good time to display real bills and coins. Also, be prepared to discuss who or what is pictured on the bills and coins.

Practice 3: 15–30 min.

G **What bills and coins do you need for these items? Tell a partner and the class.**

Ask students to work individually at first, then to compare items in pairs. Bring in real ads if you wish to extend this activity even more (optional).

Evaluation 3: 10–15 min.

Discuss different monetary combinations with the students.

Application: 15–20 min.

Ask the students in groups to make a list of things the group would buy if it had $100. Students will need to negotiate so that the group as a whole agrees on what to buy.

H **Active Task: Bring receipts from home and show the class.**

Refer to the *Activity Bank 1 CD-ROM*, Unit 2 Worksheet 2, for additional practice counting money. *(optional)*

Instructor's Notes for Lesson 2

_____

_____

_____

_____

_____

_____

_____

_____

_____

_____

```
LESSON PLAN
Objective:
Identify clothing
Key vocabulary:
socks, suit, baseball cap, T-shirt, tennis
shoes, tie, blouse, hat, coat, sweater,
skirt, dress, credit, cheap, expensive
```

Warm-up and Review: 15–20 min. `1.5+`

Review the receipts students brought in for the **active task from the last lesson.** Write *How much is the___?* on the board. Ask the students again where they shop for clothes. Ask them if the stores they name are cheaper than others are. Help them understand the words *cheap* and *expensive.*

Introduction: 2 min. `1.5+`

State objective: *Today we will learn about different kinds of clothing.*

Presentation 1: 15–20 min. `1.5+`

Look at the picture at the top of the page with the students. Take them through the vocabulary. Look around the room and point to a student wearing an article of clothing similar to one in the picture. Then say, *Felipe wears a T-shirt,* for example.

Ⓐ Write the correct letter under each type of clothing.

Practice 1: 10–15 min. `1.5+`

Ⓑ Write the clothing in the chart. Work in a group. Add other clothing words that you know.

Ask the students to do this activity in groups. When they finish, explain that there are different ways to classify the same information. Then ask the groups to classify clothing by casual or formal, by above and below the waist, and by singular versus plural.

Evaluation 1: 5–10 min. `1.5+`

Ask group representatives to write their classifications on the board.

STANDARDS CORRELATIONS

CASAS: 1.2.1, 1.3.1, 1.3.9, 7.2.3
SCANS: **Resources** Allocates Money
Interpersonal Participates as a Member of a Team, Teaches Others New Skills, Exercises Leadership
Information Acquires and Evaluates Information, Organizes and Maintains Information, Interprets and Communicates Information
Technology Applies Technology to Task (optional)
Basic Skills Reading, Arithmetic, Listening, Speaking

Thinking Skills Creative Thinking, Decision Making, Problem Solving
EFF: **Communication** Read with Understanding, Speak So Others Can Understand, Listen Actively, Observe Critically
Decision Making Use Math to Solve Problems and Communicate, Solve Problems and Make Decisions
Interpersonal Guide Others, Cooperate with Others
Lifelong Learning Learn through Research, Use Information and Communications Technology (optional)

LESSON 3 Buying new clothes

GOAL ▶ Identify clothing

Vocabulary

A Write the correct letter under each type of clothing.

a. suit   g. socks

b. T-shirt   h. baseball cap

c. ties   i. tennis shoes

d. hat   j. blouse

e. sweater   k. coat

f. dress   l. skirt

SHOP AND DRESS FOR LESS

g $12

c $22

a $285

k $84

e $36

h $12

b $17

i $33

d $38

f $48

j $24

l $35

B Write the clothing in the chart. Work in a group. Add other clothing words that you know.

(Answers may vary. Some suggestions listed below.)

Women's	Men's	Both	
dress	ties	socks	sweater
blouse	suit	baseball cap	tennis shoes
skirt		T-shirt	
hat		coat	

Where is Gabriela?
What is her problem?

C **Read about Gabriela's problem.**

Gabriela is worried. She needs new clothes for her job. She has $75 in cash, and she has a credit card. Is it a good idea to use a credit card?

D **Look at the ad on page 25. What can Gabriela buy with $75? What is the total before tax? Write the items and their prices. Then talk in a group.**

(Answers will vary.) _____ _____

_____ _____ _____

E **Active Task:** At home, find an ad in the newspaper or on the Internet. What clothing can you buy for $100?

Presentation 2: 15–20 min.

Look at the picture with the students and ask the questions. If you have a credit card, show it to the students.

 C Read about Gabriela's problem.

Discuss credit cards with the class as best you can at this level. Take a poll to find out how many students have credit cards and if they think they are good, OK, or bad.

Practice 2: 15–20 min.

D Look at the ad on page 25. What can Gabriela buy with $75? What is the total before tax? Write the items and their prices. Then talk in a group.

Ask the students in groups to see how many different combinations of articles they can buy with $75.

Evaluation 2: 5–15 min.

Receive and discuss group reports.

Presentation 3: 10–15 min.

Write *How much is the T-shirt?* **and** *How much are the socks?* **on the board.** Ask students why you use *is* in the first question and *are* in the second. Do the same thing with *It is $17* and *They are $12.*

Write the following dialog on the board.
Student A: *Excuse me, how much are (is) the _____?*
Student B: *They are (It is) _____ .*
Student A: *Thank you.*

Make sure the students know how to substitute information in the dialog.

 Refer to *Stand Out Grammar Challenge 1,* **Unit 2, page 11 for more practice with spelling plural nouns.**

Practice 3: 10–15 min.

Ask the students to work in pairs and use the information on page 25 for the dialog.

Evaluation 3: 10–15 min.

Ask for volunteers to demonstrate the dialog in front of the class.

Application: 10–15 min.

Ask students in groups to make a list of the clothing they see people wearing in their group. Ask them to add other items they could be wearing today to their list.

 E Active Task: At home, find an ad in the newspaper or on the Internet. What clothing can you buy for $100?

Refer to the *Activity Bank 1 CD-ROM,* **Unit 2 Worksheet 3, for additional practice reading and listening to conversations about clothing. The listening is on** *AB1 CD-ROM* **Track 3.** *(optional)*

Instructor's Notes for Lesson 3

_____
_____
_____
_____
_____
_____
_____
_____
_____
_____
_____
_____
_____
_____
_____
_____
_____

> ## LESSON PLAN
>
> **Objective:**
> Use possessive adjectives to
> show ownership
> **Key vocabulary:**
> white, red, black, brown, green, blue,
> orange, yellow, blouse, dress, belt,
> shorts, slacks

Warm-up and Review: 10–15 min.

Write *same* and *different* on the board as you did in the previous unit. Find two students wearing similar clothes (e.g., T-shirts or jeans) but of different colors. Ask how the clothes are the same and how they are different. Allow for all answers, including size, material, color, logo, etc. Be sure to use *his* or *her* when appropriate. You may also wish to create a Venn diagram on the board to depict the similarities and differences.

Introduction: 5–10 min.

State objective: *Today you will learn to use possessive adjectives and colors to describe clothing.*

Presentation 1: 15–20 min.

A Say the clothes and colors with your teacher.

Add more colors to the chart, if you like. Use articles of student clothing to show colors. Ask questions using *his* or *her*. For example, ask *What color is Roberto's polo shirt?* Students respond *It's red.* Say to them: *That's right. His shirt is red.* Write the exchange on the board. Help the students see when to use *are* and *is.*

Practice 1: 20–25 min.

B Complete the chart with the words from the picture. Can you add any other clothing words?

Show the students how to fill in the chart.

Ask student pairs to practice asking each other color questions based on the examples you have written on the board.

Evaluation 1: 5–10 min.

Review colors with the students to gauge their grasp of them.

Refer to *Stand Out Grammar Challenge 1,* Unit 2, page 14 for more practice. *(optional)*

STANDARDS CORRELATIONS

CASAS: 0.1.2, 1.3.9, 7.2.3
SCANS: Interpersonal Participates as a Member of a Team, Teaches Others New Skills, Exercises Leadership
Information Acquires and Evaluates Information, Organizes and Maintains Information, Interprets and Communicates Information
Basic Skills Writing, Listening, Speaking

Thinking Skills Seeing Things in the Mind's Eye
EFF: Communication Speak So Others Can Understand, Listen Actively, Observe Critically
Decision Making Solve Problems and Make Decisions
Interpersonal Guide Others, Resolve Conflict and Negotiate, Cooperate with Others

 **What color is your shirt?**

GOAL ▶ Use possessive adjectives

Grammar

 Say the clothes and colors with your teacher.

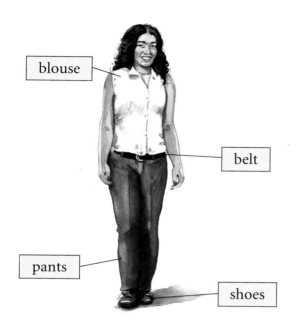

blouse

belt

pants

shoes

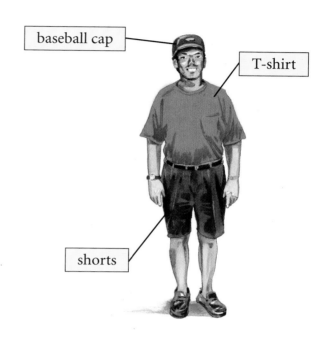

baseball cap

T-shirt

shorts

Colors

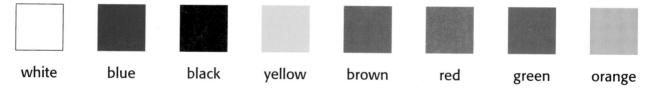

white   blue   black   yellow   brown   red   green   orange

B   **Complete the chart with the words from the picture. Can you add any other clothing words?**

(Answers may vary.)

Singular	Plural	Plural only
T-shirt	T-shirts	pants
blouse	blouses	shorts
belt	belts	
shoe	shoes	
baseball cap	baseball caps	

C Study the chart with your teacher. Use the words in the box to complete the chart.

his	her
my	our
your	their
its	

Pronoun	Possessive adjectives
I	_____**My**_____ shirt is blue.
	_____**My**_____ shoes are black.
you	_____**Your**_____ baseball cap is blue.
	_____**Your**_____ shorts are brown.
he	_____**His**_____ belt is black.
	_____**His**_____ sandals are brown.
she	_____**Her**_____ blouse is pink.
	_____**Her**_____ shoes are white.
it	_____**Its**_____ label is red.
	_____**Its**_____ doors are green.
we	_____**Our**_____ house is white.
	_____**Our**_____ books are blue.
they	_____**Their**_____ school is in Center City.
	_____**Their**_____ children are happy.

D Look at page 27. Then answer the questions below.

EXAMPLE:
What color are Roberto's shorts?
His shorts are brown.

1. What color is Gabriela's blouse?
   Her blouse is white.

2. What color are Gabriela's and Roberto's belts?
   Their belts are black.

3. What color are Gabriela's pants?
   Her slacks are blue.

4. What color is Roberto's T-shirt?
   His T-shirt is red.

5. What color are Gabriela's and Roberto's shoes?
   Their shoes are brown.

Presentation 2: 10–15 min.

C Study the chart with your teacher. Use the words in the box to complete the chart.

Some students might be confused by the fact that the possessive adjective does not reflect whether the noun is singular or plural. Try to clarify. Also, make sure they understand that the *be* verb is affected by the noun.

Practice 2: 10–15 min.

D Look at page 27. Then answer the questions below.

This activity is similar to what students did orally in Practice 1, except now they are using possessive adjectives.

Have the students in pairs practice orally as well, with one student asking the questions and the other looking only on page 27. This then becomes an information gap activity.

Evaluation 2: 5–10 min.

Briefly quiz students on possessive adjectives.

Presentation 3: 15–20 min.

Preview *Activity Bank 1 CD-ROM,* Unit 2 Worksheet 4 with the students. This activity allows students to describe people by their clothing and other items using possessive adjectives. This is another classifying activity where the students put items into a Venn diagram using *his, her,* and *their.*

Note: Please refer to page 2 of Worksheet 4 for assistance working with Venn diagrams and, specifically, this worksheet.

Refer to *Stand Out Grammar Challenge 1,* Unit 2, pages 13–14 for more practice. *(optional)*

Practice 3: 15–20 min.

Ask the students to do the Venn diagram activity with a partner. Use Worksheet 4.

Evaluation 3: 10–15 min.

Ask students to report on their Venn diagrams by forming sentences orally. Students may complete written sentences for homework or in class if time.

Application: 10–15 min.

E **Talk to a partner and describe the clothes of students in the class. Then write the sentences.**

F **With a different partner, describe students by their clothes and guess who they are.**

Model the exercise for the students by describing a student's clothes. Ask the class for the student's name.

G **Look around the classroom. In groups, make a list of clothes by color.**

After students have written items in the chart, have the groups make sentences with possessive adjectives. Ask a member of each group to read the sentences to the class.

Refer to the *Activity Bank 1 CD-ROM* Unit 2 for additional practice on possessive adjectives (Worksheet 5), as well as reading practice and listening practice about colors and clothes (Worksheet 6). The listening is on *AB1 CD-ROM* Track 4. (*optional*)

Instructor's Notes for Lesson 4

E **Talk to a partner and describe the clothes of students in the class. Then write the sentences.**

My (shirt) is *(Answers will vary.)* _____ .   Her (blouse) is *(Answers will vary.)* _____ .

His (shirt) is *(Answers will vary.)* _____ .   Their (shirts) are *(Answers will vary.)* _____ .

Your (shirt) is *(Answers will vary.)* _____ .   Our (shirts) are *(Answers will vary.)* _____ .

F **With a different partner, describe students in the class by their clothes and guess who they are.**

EXAMPLE:
Student A: Her blouse is blue.
Student B: It's Amy!

G **Look around the classroom. In groups, make a list of clothes by color.**

Red	Blue	Green	Orange
(Answers will vary.)			

LESSON 5 A big TV or a small TV?

GOAL ▶ Use adjectives to describe things

Vocabulary

A Look at the pictures. Write the correct adjective under each picture.

Do you want a small CD player or a large CD player?

_____small_____   _____large_____

Do you want a new car or a used car?

_____new_____   _____used_____

Do you want a large blouse or a medium blouse?

_____medium_____   _____large_____

Do you want an old house or a new house?

_____new_____   _____old_____

Do you want a striped shirt or a checked shirt?

_____checked_____   _____striped_____

Do you want a small shirt or a medium shirt?

_____small_____   _____medium_____

B Complete the chart. Write the new words.

Size	Age	Pattern
small	used	striped
large	old	checked
medium	new	

LESSON PLAN

Objective:
Use adjectives to describe things
Key vocabulary:
little, big, old, new, used, striped, checked, small, medium, large, age, pattern, size

Warm-up and Review: 10–15 min.

Ask students to read the sentences they wrote for exercise E in the previous lesson. Make sure they are using the correct form of the verb *be*. Correct them where necessary.

Introduction: 5–10 min.

State objective: *Today we will learn to use adjectives to describe things.*

Presentation 1: 20–30 min.

Ⓐ Look at the pictures. Write the correct adjective under each picture.

Do this activity with the students. Show the students that adjectives can give more information about things. Also show them that, in English, when the adjective is with a noun, it always goes before the noun. Then ask students to work with a partner to read and answer the questions together using the adjectives.

Practice 1: 10–15 min.

Ⓑ Complete the chart. Write the new words.

Ask students to complete the exercise in small groups. Have them figure out the exercise without your guidance.

Evaluation 1: 5–10 min.

Write the three categories on the board. Have a volunteer come up to fill in one category. Discuss answers as a class. Repeat with the other two categories.

Presentation 2: 15–20 min.

Look at the art and discuss the questions in the question box as a class.

 C Listen to the conversation with your books closed. What does Tatsuya want to buy? *(Audio CD Track 18)*

Play the recording one or two times. Ask the students to open their books and read along with the recording.

D Practice the conversation with a partner.

Ask the students to practice, helping them with rhythm to some extent.

Present the dialog as described in Teaching Hints. Show the students how to substitute information in preparation for exercise E.

Practice 2: 10–15 min.

E Practice new conversations using the information below.

See Teaching Hints for alternative ways to practice dialogs (or conversations).

Evaluation 2: 10–15 min.

Ask volunteers to demonstrate in front of the class.

Presentation 3: 15–25 min.

Explain to students how to do Worksheet 7 for Practice 3 found on the *Activity Bank 1 CD-ROM* Unit 2. Make sure to remind the students about adjective placement. Worksheet 7 is composed of two pages. The first is the activity and the second is the answer key.

 Refer to *Stand Out Grammar Challenge 1*, Unit 2, page 14 for more practice. *(optional)*

Practice 3: 30–40 min.

Have the students work in groups on the activity. Since this activity involves critical thinking, some students will find it difficult. They will need to read more than one statement to answer most questions.

Evaluation 3: 10–15 min.

Review answers as a class.

Application: 20–30 min.

F Write a new conversation with a partner.

This dialog should not be exactly the same as exercise C, although it can be loosely patterned after it. One way to keep students from following the dialog too closely is to ask students to close their books. Ask for volunteers to demonstrate their new dialog in front of the class.

Refer to the *Activity Bank 1 CD-ROM,* Unit 2 Worksheet 8, for additional practice using adjectives in a dialog. *(optional)*

Instructor's Notes for Lesson 5
_____
_____
_____
_____
_____
_____
_____
_____
_____
_____
_____
_____
_____

Where is Tatsuya?
What does he want?

C **Listen to the conversation with your books closed. What does Tatsuya want to buy?**

Tatsuya: Excuse me, I want a TV.
Salesperson: A big TV or a small TV?
Tatsuya: I want a large TV for my bedroom.
Salesperson: Okay, how about this one?

Tatsuya: Yes, that's good. How much is it?
Salesperson: It's $135.00.
Tatsuya: I'll take it!

D **Practice the conversation with a partner.**

E **Practice new conversations using the information below.**

Student A is the customer. Student B is the salesperson.	Student B is the customer. Student A is the salesperson.
1. Blouse: medium / small	1. Car: used / new
2. CD player: large / small	2. House: old / new
3. Refrigerator: new / used	3. Sweater: striped / checked
4. Shirt: small / medium	4. Blouse: large / medium

F **Write a new conversation with a partner.**

LESSON 6 Cash, check, or charge?

GOAL ▶ **Write checks**

Life Skill

```
                                                            #001
Van Nguyen
23 Parker Street, Apt. 305                  Date July 10, 2003
San Francisco, CA 94160

Pay to the   Martin's Department Store              $  63.67
order of
     sixty-three dollars and------------67/100          ____ Dollars

Bank of California

For  clothes for school              Van Nguyen
:011000111 : 005 0000   00X0
```

How much is the check for?
What is it for?

(A) **Read about banks with your teacher.**

It is a good idea to put your money in the bank. It is not a good idea to carry a lot of cash with you. When you want to use your money, you can take the money out of the bank, or you can write a check. Many people buy things in the United States with cash, checks, or credit cards.

(B) **Circle *True* or *False*.**

1. People use checks to buy things in the United States.   (True)   False

2. It is not a good idea to put money in the bank.   True   (False)

3. It is a good idea to carry a lot of cash with you.   True   (False)

(C) **Write a check for a new TV to Al's Big Screen for $350.00.**

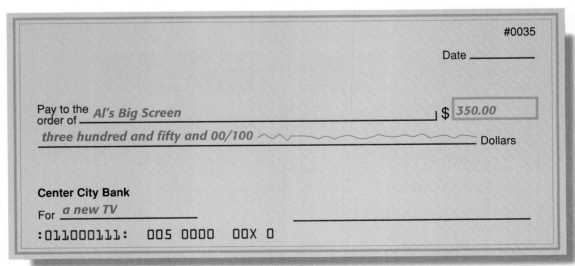

```
                                                            #0035

                                                  Date _____

Pay to the   Al's Big Screen                          $  350.00
order of _____
     three hundred and fifty and 00/100 ~~~~~~~~~~~~~~~ Dollars

Center City Bank

For  a new TV                        _____
:011000111:   005 0000   00X 0
```

LESSON PLAN

Objectives:
Write checks; identify different payment methods
Key vocabulary:
cash, check, on sale, off, regular, coupon, with, without

Warm-up and Review: 10–15 min.

Ask a few more students to demonstrate the dialogs they created in the previous lesson.

Introduction: 1 min.

Ask the students how they might purchase things in a store. Write *cash* on the board, followed by *credit card* and *checks*.

State objective: *Today you will learn how to write checks.*

Presentation 1: 15–20 min.

Review the check at the top of the page with the students. Ask how much the check is for and what it is for. Find out if any students have a bank account. Help them appreciate the advantages of an account. Mention that one advantage is that account holders can pay bills by check through the mail.

A Read about banks with your teacher.

You may want students to first read silently and then listen as you read aloud. Next, have students read aloud with you as a class.

Practice 1: 5–10 min.

B Circle *True* or *False*.

Read the sentence in the text which answers the question if students need assistance.

C Write a check for a new TV to Al's Big Screen for $350.00.

Evaluation 1: 5–10 min.

Examine student checks. Remind students to add the current date. Refer to Useful Words in the appendix for help with writing dates.

Refer to *Stand Out Grammar Challenge 1*, Unit 2, page 16 for more practice. *(optional)*

STANDARDS CORRELATIONS

CASAS: 1.3.1, 1.8.2
SCANS: Resources Allocates Money
Interpersonal Participates as a Member of a Team, Teaches Others New Skills, Exercises Leadership, Works with Cultural Diversity
Information Acquires and Evaluates Information, Organizes and Maintains Information, Interprets and Communicates Information
Systems Understands Systems
Technology Applies Technology to Task (optional)
Basic Skills Reading, Writing, Arithmetic, Listening, Speaking

Thinking Skills Decision Making, Problem Solving
Personal Qualities Responsibility, Self-Management
EFF: Communication Read with Understanding, Speak So Others Can Understand, Observe Critically
Decision Making Use Math to Solve Problems and Communicate, Solve Problems and Make Decisions, Plan
Interpersonal Guide Others, Advocate and Influence, Cooperate with Others
Lifelong Learning Take Responsibility for Learning, Learn through Research, Use Information and Communications Technology (optional)

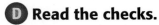

Presentation 2: 5–10 min.

D Read the checks.

Study the checks with the students. Look at every part of each check to ensure that the students can read them. Ask the questions in the boxes.

Practice 2: 10–15 min.

E Ask your partner. Listen and write the answers.

Ask partners to follow the instructions by covering the checks in their books and asking the three questions. Then students write the answers in the chart.

Evaluation 2:

Observe the partner exchange.

Presentation 3: 10–15 min.

On the *Activity Bank 1 CD-ROM* for Unit 2 you will find Worksheet 9 with several checks over three pages for students to fill out. The information for writing the checks is listed at the top of page 1. A check ledger is at the bottom of page 1. Students are asked to take the information from the checks they have written and enter it into the ledger. Then they add up the amounts of the checks and enter the total.

Practice 3: 15–20 min.

Ask the students to do the three pages of Worksheet 9.

Evaluation 3: 10–15 min.

Review the checks and ledgers together as a class.

Application: 10–15 min.

Ask students in groups to consider when to use credit cards, checks, and cash. Make a three-column chart on the board, each column headed by one of the three forms of payment. Ask groups to make a similar chart and decide on appropriate occasions for using each form of payment.

F Active Task: Visit a bank or look on the Internet and find the names of three banks where you can open a checking account.

Refer to the *Activity Bank 1 CD-ROM*, Unit 2 Worksheet 10 (two pages), for an information gap activity on writing checks. *(optional)*

Instructor's Notes for Lesson 6

_____

_____

_____

_____

_____

_____

_____

_____

_____

_____

_____

_____

_____

_____

_____

_____

_____

_____

_____

_____

_____

_____

D **Read the checks.**

Check 1

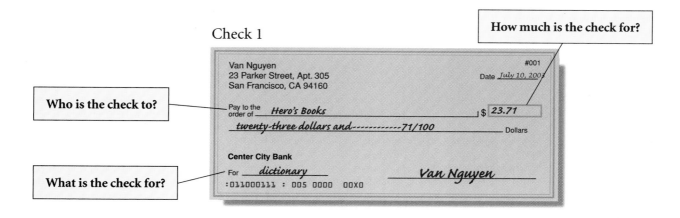

How much is the check for?

Who is the check to?

What is the check for?

Check 2

E **Ask your partner. Listen and write the answers.**

1. Student A covers checks and asks questions.
2. Student B covers checks and asks questions.

Check #	Who is the check to?	What is the check for?	How much is the check for?
Check #1	Hero's Books	dictionary	$23.71
Check #2	Sam's Food Mart	lunches	$12.30

F **Active Task:** Visit a bank or look on the Internet and find the names of three banks where you can open a checking account.

GOAL ▶ Use *this, that, these,* and *those*

Grammar

Where is Roberto?
Who is talking to Roberto?

  A **Listen to the first part of the conversation. What does Roberto want to buy?**

this orange cap   *that red umbrella*

This

That

  B **Listen to the next part of the conversation. What does Roberto want to buy?**

those blue jeans   *these white socks*

These

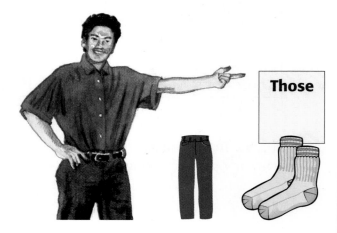

Those

LESSON PLAN

Objective:
Use *this, that, these,* and *those* to
show preference in making purchases
Key vocabulary:
cap, umbrella, socks, jeans, radio, pen,
dishes, baseball, tickets

Warm-up and Review: 10–15 min.

Ask students in groups to make sentences about items in the classroom. Direct them to describe the items by using adjectives. Then ask group representatives to quiz the rest of the class by reciting a sentence that describes but doesn't name the item. The class will try to identify the item by its description. For example, one sentence might say, *This thing is big and green.* The class would guess chalkboard. Write this exchange on the board.

Introduction: 1 min.

State objective: *Today, you will learn to use "this," "that," "these," and "those" to express preference.*

Presentation 1: 15–20 min.

Present *this, these, that,* **and** *those* **to students by asking them about items in the classroom.** Ask: *What is this?* Help students respond appropriately, as in "That's a clock." Write the four key words on the board and work on them with students until you feel confident that they understand the meaning.

Ask students to open their books and look at the picture of Roberto. Ask the questions in the box and any others you consider appropriate.

Look at the pictures in exercises A and B. Ask the class which ones they like better. Allow them to answer by identifying the color.

Practice 1: 10–15 min.

After students close their books, play the recording from exercise A. Ask them to identify what Roberto wants to buy. Then ask them to open their books.

Ⓐ Listen to the first part of the conversation. What does Roberto want to buy? *(Audio CD Track 19)*

Play the recording.

Ⓑ Listen to the next part of the conversation. What does Roberto want to buy? *(Audio CD Track 19)*

Play the recording.

Evaluation 1: 5–10 min.

Check the answers as a class.

STANDARDS CORRELATIONS

CASAS: 0.1.2, 1.2.2, 1.2.4
SCANS: Resources Allocates Money
Interpersonal Participates as a Member of a Team, Teaches Others New Skills, Serves Clients/Customers, Exercises Leadership
Information Acquires and Evaluates Information, Organizes and Maintains Information, Interprets and Communicates Information
Basic Skills Arithmetic, Listening, Speaking

Thinking Skills Creative Thinking, Decision Making, Problem Solving
Personal Qualities Sociability
EFF: Communication Speak So Others Can Understand, Listen Actively
Decision Making Use Math to Solve Problems and Communicate, Solve Problems and Make Decisions
Interpersonal Guide Others, Cooperate with Others
Lifelong Learning Reflect and Evaluate

Presentation 2: 15–20 min.

C Study the chart with your teacher.

 Refer to *Stand Out Grammar Challenge 1,* Unit 2, page 12 for more practice. *(optional)*

Practice 2: 15–20 min.

D Look at the pictures on page 34 and fill in the missing words below.

You may want to focus on pronunciation of /th/ in these words at this point. (This will also be practiced in the pronunciation exercise on page 40 at the end of this unit.)

E Ask your partner 5 questions about the pictures on page 34.

Be sure that students understand that they will be playing the role of Roberto, so they should respond appropriately with *this, that, these,* and *those.*

Evaluation 2: 5–10 min.

Review all the answers in the book and, as a spot check, allow students to ask you the questions.

GOAL ▶ Use *this, that, these,* and *those*   **Grammar**

C Study the chart with your teacher.

	Near the speaker	Far from the speaker
Singular	this	that
Plural	these	those

D Look at the pictures on page 34 and fill in the missing words below.

EXAMPLE:
Roberto: "**This** cap is orange and ***that*** cap is yellow."

1. _____*That*_____ cap is yellow and _____*this*_____ cap is orange.

2. _____*That*_____ umbrella is _____*red*_____ and _____*this*_____ umbrella is green.

3. _____*Those*_____ jeans are blue and _____*these*_____ jeans are _____*black*_____.

4. _____*These*_____ socks are _____*white*_____ and _____*those*_____ socks are yellow .

E Ask your partner five questions about the clothes in your classroom. Use *this, that, these, those.*

EXAMPLE:
Student A: What color is that shirt?   *Student B:* What color are these pants?
Student B: It's blue.   *Student A:* They're black.

F **Read the conversation.**

Salesperson: Can I help you?
Roberto: How much is this radio, please?
Salesperson: It's $8.65.

Roberto: How about that radio?
Salesperson: It's $48.
Roberto: I'll take this radio, please.

G **Practice new conversations with the pictures below.**

this/these   that/those

pen $0.89

pen $8.00

TV $225.50

TV $115.00

dishes $58.98

dishes $28.99

movie tickets $17.98

baseball
tickets $22.00

Presentation 3: 15–20 min.

 Read the conversation.

Present the dialog and show students how to substitute information for exercise G. See Teaching Hints for help with presenting dialogs. Remind students to use the correct form of *be*.

 Refer to *Stand Out Grammar Challenge 1,* Unit 2, page 12 for more practice. *(optional)*

Practice 3: 10–15 min.

 Practice new conversations with the pictures below.

Evaluation 3: 15–20 min.

Ask for volunteers to demonstrate in front of the class.

Application: 15–20 min.

Write *Let's buy this one.* on the board. Ask students in groups to pretend they are Roberto and choose which item in exercise G they want to buy. Ask them to use the phrase from the board.

Then have students add up the total cost of all items they have chosen and report to the class.

 Refer to the *Activity Bank 1 CD-ROM,* Unit 2 Worksheet 11, for additional practice using *this, that, these,* and *those.* *(optional)*

Instructor's Notes for Lesson 7

REVIEW

Objectives:
All previous objectives
Key vocabulary:
All previous Unit 2 vocabulary

Warm up and Review: 10–15 min.

List the following on the board: *department store, supermarket, shoe store, bookstore,* and *electronics store.* Discuss as a class what you can buy in each store.

Introduction: 3–5 min.

State objective: *Today we will review all that we have done in the past unit in preparation for the application project to follow.* Ask students as a class to try to recall all the goals of this unit without looking at their books. Then remind them of the goals they haven't mentioned.

Unit Goals: Talk about where to buy goods, Count money and read receipts, Identify clothing, Use possessive adjectives, Use adjectives to describe things, Write checks, Use "this," "that," "these" and "those."

Presentation 1, Practice 1, and Evaluation 1:

Do the Learner Log on page 40. Notes are adjacent to the page.

Presentation 2: 5–10 min.

Review adjectives and their placement in a sentence.

Practice 2: 10–15 min.

Ⓐ Listen and write the answers in column 1. *(Audio CD Track 20)*

Review question with students before the listening is played.

Ⓑ Complete columns 2 and 3 with your ideas.

Students can do this activity as a group or individually. After they finish, ask them to write sentences about a few of the items on this page. Write an example on the board: *The new, big, black boom box is $98.45 in the department store.* Don't worry about adjective order here.

Evaluation 2: 10–15 min.

Observe activities and review student charts.

STANDARDS CORRELATIONS

CASAS: 1.2.4, 1.3.9, 1.6.4, 1.8.2, 7.1.1, 7.1.4, 7.4.1, 7.4.9
SCANS: Information Acquires and Evaluates Information, Organizes and Maintains Information, Interprets and Communicates Information
Basic Skills Reading, Writing, Listening, Speaking
Thinking Skills Decision Making, Problem Solving
Personal Qualities Responsibility, Self-Esteem, Sociability, Self-Management

EFF: Communication Speak So Others Can Understand, Listen Actively, Observe Critically
Decision Making Solve Problems and Make Decisions, Plan
Interpersonal Cooperate with Others
Lifelong Learning Take Responsibility for Learning, Reflect and Evaluate

Review

A Listen and write the answers in column 1.

B Complete columns 2 and 3 with your ideas.
(Answers may vary in columns 2 and 3. Suggested answers below.)

Item	1. How much is it?	2. Where can you buy it?	3. Describe it.
	$98.45	department store	black and white
	$168.00	department store	small and red
	$18.95	book store	large and blue
	$28.98	shoe store	large and brown
	$456.78	department store	small and gray
	$33.99	clothing store	medium and green
	$17.00	clothing store	small and red
	$24.50	clothing store	large and striped

C Look at the receipt. What is the total? Fill in the correct amounts on the check.

Martin's Department Store	
Men's shirts 2@ $27.98	$ *55.96*
Men's pants	$ 65.49
Tax	$ 4.48
Total	$ *125.93*

Gabriela Ramirez   #001

Date *July 10, 2003*

Pay to the order of *Martin's Department Store* _____ $ [ ]

_____ Dollars

Center City Bank

For _____

Gabriela Ramirez

:011000111 : 005 0000 00X0

one hundred and twenty-five and 93/100   *$125.93*

D Describe the pictures. Use *his, her,* or *their*.

EXAMPLE:
What color is Eva's hat? **_Her hat is blue._**

1. What color is Duong's cap? _____ *His cap is red* _____.

2. What color is Duong's shirt? _____ *His shorts are brown* _____.

3. What color are Eva's pants? _____ *Her pants are green* _____.

4. What color are Eva's and Duong's shoes? _____ *Their shoes are brown* _____.

Presentation 3: 5–15 min.

Review with students each part of a check and possessive adjectives.

Practice 3: 5–15 min.

C Look at the receipt. What is the total? Fill in the correct amounts on the check.

D Describe the pictures. Use *his, her,* or *their.*

 Refer to *Stand Out Grammar Challenge 1,* Unit 2, pages 13–14 for review practice. *(optional)*

Evaluation 3: 10 min.

Some classes may have completed this as homework. Review as a class.

Application: 1-2 days

The Team Project Activity on the following page is the application activity to be done on the next day of class.

 Post-Assessment: Use the *Stand Out* ExamView® Pro *Test Bank* for Unit 2. *(optional)*

Note: With the ExamView® Pro *Test Bank* CD-ROM you can design a post-assessment that focuses on what students have learned. It is designed for three purposes:

- To help students practice taking a test similar to current standardized tests.
- To help the teacher evaluate how much the students have learned, retained, and acquired.
- To help students see their progress when they compare their scores to the pre-test they took earlier.

Instructor's Notes for Unit 2 Review

Unit 2 Application Activity

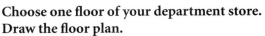

> **TEAM PROJECT: PLANNING A DEPARTMENT STORE**
>
> Objective:
> Project designed to apply all the objectives of this unit.
> Product:
> a department store plan

Introduction:

Each group designs a department store floor plan which identifies different retail sections. The groups list the items they will sell and also prepare a skit to present to the class. This project can extend over two days.

Stage 1: 5–10 min.

Form a team with four or five students.

Students decide who will lead which steps as described on the student page. Provide well-defined directions on the board for how students should proceed. Explain to them that every task is to be done by each student. Students don't go to the next stage until the previous one is complete.

Stage 2: 25–30 min.

Choose a name for your department store.

This works better when they choose a name they create, not one that already exists.

Stage 3: 20–30 min.

Choose one floor of your department store. Draw the floor plan.

Supply students with paper, rulers, and other items needed to make the floor plan. You can use the *Activity Bank 1 CD-ROM*, Unit 2 Worksheet 12.

Stage 4: 30–40 min.

Make a list of ten things you sell, with their prices.

Ask students to make a list of items and prices. They can research on the Internet (optional). Have the students practice asking for prices in their groups. You can use *AB1* Unit 2 Worksheet 13.

Stage 5: 35–40 min.

Prepare a skit.

Students can create receipts and checks as props if time permits or use *Activity Bank 1 CD-ROM* Unit 2 Worksheet 14 (two pages).

Stage 4: 30–40 min.

Practice the skit and present it to the class.

Consider videotaping these presentations. Students will prepare better for formal presentations if they are to be videotaped. Another approach is for students to videotape themselves and polish their presentations.

After the presentations, post department store floor plans and information.

STANDARDS CORRELATIONS

CASAS: 1.2.1, 1.2.4, 1.3.9, 4.6.1, 4.8.1, 4.8.5
SCANS: **Resources** Allocates Time, Allocates Money, Allocates Material and Facility Resources
Interpersonal Participates as a Member of a Team, Teaches Others New Skills, Serves Clients/Customers, Exercises Leadership, Works with Cultural Diversity
Information Acquires and Evaluates Information, Organizes and Maintains Information, Interprets and Communicates Information, Uses Computers to Process Information
Systems Understands Systems, Monitors and Corrects Performance, Improves and Designs Systems
Technology Applies Technology to Task (optional)
Basic Skills Reading, Writing, Arithmetic, Listening, Speaking

Thinking Skills Creative Thinking, Decision Making, Problem Solving, Seeing Things in the Mind's Eye, Knowing How to Learn, Reasoning
Personal Qualities Responsibility, Self-Esteem, Sociability, Self-Management
EFF: **Communication** Read with Understanding, Convey Ideas in Writing, Speak So Others Can Understand, Listen Actively, Observe Critically
Decision Making Use Math to Solve Problems and Communicate, Solve Problems and Make Decisions, Plan
Interpersonal Guide Others, Resolve Conflict and Negotiate, Advocate and Influence, Cooperate with Others
Lifelong Learning Take Responsibility for Learning, Reflect and Evaluate

TEAM PROJECT

Planning a department store

In this project you will plan a department store, decide what to sell, and present it to the class.

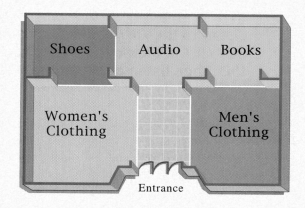

Shoes — Audio — Books

Women's Clothing — Men's Clothing

Entrance

1. Form a team with four or five students.

   In your team, you need:

Position	Job	Student Name
Student 1 Leader	See that everyone speaks English. See that everyone participates.	
Student 2 Architect	With help from the team, draw the floor plan.	
Student 3 Sales manager	List the sales prices.	
Student 4 Writer	With help from the team, prepare a skit to present to the class.	

2. Choose a name for your department store.

3. Choose one floor of your department store. Draw the floor plan.

4. Make a list of ten things you sell, with their prices. Where are they located on your floor plan?

5. Prepare a skit in which a person in your group talks to a salesperson and buys some things. You can also make checks and receipts if you want. People in your group can be: a salesperson, a cashier, a customer or customers, and a manager.

6. Practice the skit and present it to the class.

PRONUNCIATION

Listen to the /th/ sound in these words. Circle the words which sound like /th/ in *thank you*. Underline the words which sound like /th/ in *this*. Then listen again and repeat.

(think) these (thirty) those (theater) brother (thing)
mother clothing with (bath) (three) father (path)

LEARNER LOG

Circle what you learned and write the page number where you learned it.

1. I know where to shop.
   Yes Maybe No   Page _21–22_

2. I can identify clothing.
   Yes Maybe No   Page _25–26_

3. I can read receipts.
   Yes Maybe No   Page _23_

4. I can count money.
   Yes Maybe No   Page _24_

5. I can write a check.
   Yes Maybe No   Page _32–33_

6. I can describe things.
   Yes Maybe No   Page _30–31_

7. I can use possessive adjectives.
   Yes Maybe No   Page _28–29_

8. I can use *this, that, these,* and *those*.
   Yes Maybe No   Page _34–36_

Did you answer *No* to any questions? Review the information with a partner.

Rank what you like to do best from 1 to 6. 1 = your favorite activity. Your teacher will help you.

☐ practice listening

☐ practice speaking

☐ practice reading

☐ practice writing

☐ learn new words (vocabulary)

☐ learn grammar

In the next unit I want to practice more

(Answers will vary.)

_____.

Unit 2 Pronunciation and Learner Log

Pronunciation (optional): 10–15 min.
(Audio CD Track 21)

Listen to the /th/ sound in these words. Circle the words which sound like /th/ in *thank you*. Underline the words which sound like /th/ in *this*. Then listen again and repeat.

Play the recording and pause after each word.

For additional pronunciation practice:

The following list of words should be used for pronunciation practice, not for vocabulary instruction.

Many students have difficulty with voiced and unvoiced /th/ sounds. Write the words below on the board. Have students practice the words to note the difference. Teach students the difference between voiced and unvoiced sounds by putting your hand lightly on your throat and saying a word from the first column and then one from the second. Indicate that they should do the same. Point out the vibration that occurs with the first column of (voiced) words.

voiced /th/	*unvoiced /th/*
then	*thin*
they	*thank*
that	*math*
other	*cloth*
another	*teeth*

Write the following pairs on the board. Have students practice these pairs to notice the difference between the /th/ sound and /s/, /z/, and /d/ sounds. Ask students to copy the pairs of words and read one from each pair to their partner.

The partner should then point to the word that he or she hears.

thank–sank	*thank–dank*
math–mass	*math–mad*
they–say	*they–day*
thin–sin	*thin–din*
then–Zen	*then–den*

(You'll find more review of /th/ in Unit 6.)

Learner Log

Presentation 1: 10–15 min.

If needed, review the purpose of the Learner Log.

Circle what you learned and write the page number where you learned it. Students research the answers individually. When they've finished, they should share their answers with a partner. These results need not be shared with the class.

Practice 1: 10–15 min.

Rank what you like to do best from 1 to 6. 1 = your favorite activity. Your teacher will help you. Results should be shared with the class in order to demonstrate to students how people learn differently.

Evaluation 1: 5–10 min.

In the next unit I want to practice more ——————. Students should fill in the blank with assistance from a partner or from you. They may focus on a skill (e.g., listening), on a vocabulary area (e.g., numbers), on grammar, and so on. Don't limit them to a single answer. Emphasize that the purpose of completing the sentence is to improve their self-assessment skills.

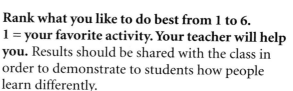

Instructor's Notes for Unit 2 Team Project, Pronunciation, and Learner Log

_____

_____

_____

_____

_____

_____

_____

_____

LESSON PLAN

Objective:
Identify eating habits and meals
Key vocabulary:
eggs, toast, orange juice, pizza, salad, potato chips, apples, corn, chicken, tea, rice, vegetables, size, meal, noodles, eggrolls, spaghetti, roast beef, tacos, healthy, hot, cold, breakfast, lunch, dinner

Pre-Assessment: Use the *Stand Out* ExamView® Pro *Test Bank* for Unit 3. (optional)

Warm-up and Review: 10–20 min.

Write the word *favorite* **on the board.** Tell the students what your favorite meal is. Write the words *breakfast*, *lunch*, and *dinner* on the board and above them write *meals*. Ask the students what their favorite meal is and take a class poll.

Introduction: 1 min.

State objective: *Today and in this unit you will learn about food and eating habits.*

Presentation 1: 15–20 min.

Ask students to open to this page and talk about the picture of Dave. Ask the questions in the box and any additional ones that you consider appropriate. See how much vocabulary the students know by asking them to identify the foods in the picture. Make a list of the foods on the board and help them with those they don't know.

A Read about Dave.

Do the reading as a class. Review the meal vocabulary the students learned in the Warm-up and Review.

Practice 1: 10–15 min.

B Write the names of the food from the picture in the chart below.

Ask the students in pairs or in groups to classify the vocabulary. Then ask the pairs or groups to get together with other pairs or groups to see if they have classified the foods in the same way. In different cultures, foods for meals may differ, so accept any answer.

Evaluation 1: 5–10 min.

Discuss differences in food preferences with the class.

Pronunciation:

An optional pronunciation activity is found on the final page of this unit. This pronunciation activity may be introduced during any lesson in this unit, especially if students need practice contrasting the sounds of /j/ and /y/. Go to pages 60/60a for Unit 3 Pronunciation.

STANDARDS CORRELATIONS

CASAS: 1.1.3, 1.3.8, 6.7.2, 7.2.3, 7.2.6
SCANS: **Resources** Allocates Materials and Facility Resources
Interpersonal Participates as a Member of a Team, Teaches Others New Skills, Exercises Leadership
Information Acquires and Evaluates Information, Organizes and Maintains Information, Interprets and Communicates Information, Uses Computers to Process Information (optional)
Technology Applies Technology to Task (optional)

Basic Skills Reading, Listening, Speaking
Thinking Skills Problem Solving, Seeing Things in the Mind's Eye
EFF: **Communication** Read with Understanding, Speak So Others Can Understand, Listen Actively, Observe Critically
Decision Making Solve Problems and Make Decisions
Interpersonal Guide Others, Cooperate with Others
Lifelong Learning Use Information and Communications Technology (optional)

UNIT 3

Food

GOALS

- Talk about eating habits and meals
- Read and follow instructions
- Read a menu and order food
- Use count and non-count nouns
- Use the simple present
- Compare prices
- Read a recipe

LESSON 1 — What's for lunch?

GOAL ▶ Talk about eating habits and meals

Vocabulary

A **Read about Dave.**

I'm Dave Chen. I'm an English teacher in Florida. I like to eat! I eat a big breakfast in the morning, a small lunch at noon, and a big dinner around six o'clock.

Where is Dave? What kind of food does he eat?

B **Write the names of the food from the picture in the chart below.**

(Answers may vary. Suggested responses are below.)

Breakfast	Lunch	Dinner
orange juice	*pizza*	*chicken*
toast	salad	corn
scrambled eggs	chips	apples

C What time do you eat breakfast? Make a bar graph with your class.

beans and rice

tacos

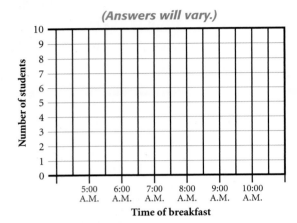

(Answers will vary.)

Number of students

10
9
8
7
6
5
4
3
2
1
0

5:00 A.M. 6:00 A.M. 7:00 A.M. 8:00 A.M. 9:00 A.M. 10:00 A.M.

Time of breakfast

fried noodles

egg rolls

roast beef

spaghetti

D What do you eat for breakfast, lunch, and dinner? Ask your teacher for words you don't know.

Breakfast	Lunch	Dinner
(Answers will vary.)		

E Ask your partner what he or she eats for breakfast, lunch, and dinner.

EXAMPLE:
Student A: What do you eat for dinner?   *Student B:* I eat spaghetti and salad for dinner.

F Tell the class about your partner.

Presentation 2: 10–15 min.

Explain the bar graph in exercise C to the students. Help students know that people eat differently in different places in the world. Take a poll to determine the data for the graph. This graph can also be reproduced on the computer. See Teaching Hints for suggestions.

 C **What time do you eat breakfast? Make a bar graph with your class.**

Practice 2: 10–15 min.

D **What do you eat for breakfast, lunch, and dinner? Ask your teacher for words you don't know.**

Ask students to do this exercise individually. Allow them to ask questions or use dictionaries if necessary.

E **Ask your partner what he or she eats for breakfast, lunch, and dinner.**

Evaluation 2:

Observe the activity.

Presentation 3: 15–20 min.

Make the following charts on the board:

Hot	Cold

Healthy	Not very healthy

I like it.	I don't like it.

Drinks	Food

Make sure the students understand the chart headings.

Practice 3: 15–20 min.

After they have formed groups, ask the students to make group charts like the ones on the board and to classify foods according to all opinions in the group.

Evaluation 3: 10–15 min.

Ask volunteers to fill in the charts on the board. Compare and discuss answers.

Application: 15–20 min.

F **Tell the class about your partner.**

Ask students to discuss their partner's food preferences and meal schedules.

Refer to the *Activity Bank 1 CD-ROM*, Unit 3 Worksheet 1 (two pages),for additional practice with food vocabulary and meals. *(optional)*

Instructor's Notes for Lesson 1

_____

_____

_____

_____

_____

_____

_____

_____

_____

_____

_____

_____

_____

_____

LESSON PLAN

Objective:
Read and follow instructions
Key vocabulary:
lunch truck, vending machines, peanuts, mints, gum, chocolate bar, fruit bar, trail mix, pretzels, cookies, granola bar, code, selection, snack

Warm-up and Review: 5–10 min.

Ask students to walk around the room and ask individuals what their favorite foods are. Ask them to spend about five minutes doing this. As a class, decide on the overall favorite food.

Introduction: 3–5 min.

Ask students where they can buy food. They will say *supermarket.* Have them discuss other options, such as a *lunch truck* and a *vending machine.*

State objective: *Today we will follow directions on vending machines and talk more about different kinds of food.*

Presentation 1: 20–30 min.

Ask students what foods vending machines might contain. Ask them if they have ever seen machines with sandwiches. Ask the students to open their books and look at the picture and brief description at the top of the page. Ask the questions next to the picture. Review the imperatives with the students and make sure they understand their meanings. Also go over any other vocabulary they may need help with. Prepare students for focused listening. See Teaching Hints.

Practice 1: 10–15 min.

A Look at the vending machine. Listen and write a number by each sentence when you hear it. *(Audio CD Track 22)*

Play the recording two or three times.

Have students practice giving the directions to a partner. Then ask them to cover up exercise A and look only at the picture above.

B Can you give a partner directions without looking at the sentences?

Ask students to practice this with the same partner.

Evaluation 1: 5–10 min.

Ask for volunteers to give directions to the class.

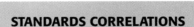

STANDARDS CORRELATIONS

CASAS: 1.3.6, 1.3.8, 2.2.1, 6.1.1
SCANS: Resources Allocates Money
Interpersonal Participates as a Member of a Team, Teaches Others New Skills, Exercises Leadership
Information Acquires and Evaluates Information, Organizes and Maintains Information, Interprets and Communicates Information
Systems Understands Systems
Basic Skills Reading, Arithmetic, Listening, Speaking

Thinking Skills Decision Making, Problem Solving
Personal Qualities Self-Management
EFF: Communication Read with Understanding, Speak So Others Can Understand, Listen Actively, Observe Critically
Decision Making Use Math to Solve Problems and Communicate, Solve Problems and Make Decisions, Plan
Interpersonal Guide Others, Cooperate with Others
Lifelong Learning Reflect and Evaluate, Learn through Research

LESSON 2 **Using a vending machine**

GOAL ▶ **Read and follow instructions**

Life Skill

Natasha gets her lunch every day after class from a vending machine at school.

What is in the vending machine? Do you eat from a vending machine sometimes?

A **Look at the vending machine. Listen and write a number by each sentence when you hear it.**

_2_ Put your dollar bills in this slot.

_4_ Take your change.

_3_ Choose the number.

_1_ Decide what you want.

B **Can you give a partner the directions without looking at the sentences?**

C Work in pairs. Ask questions about the prices of items and explain how to use the vending machine.

D How much money do you need? Complete the chart.

Selection	Total	Code
Ex. potato chips, peanuts, and gum	$2.50	C1, B2, A3
1. pretzels and a chocolate bar	$2.00	A2, B1
2. granola bar and mints	$1.50	C3, B3
3. cookies, trail mix, and gum	$2.45	A1, C2, A3
4. peanuts, pretzels, and cookies	$3.15	B2, A2, A1

E **Active Task:** Go to a vending machine in your school or neighborhood. Write down the instructions and bring them to class.

Presentation 2: 15–20 min.

C Work in pairs. Ask questions about the prices of items and explain how to use the vending machine.

Do this activity with the students. Review all the vocabulary words and help them with pronunciation.

Practice 2: 10 min.

D How much money do you need? Complete the chart.

Have the students work individually or in pairs to complete the chart.

Write *We need* _____. on the board. Ask the students *how much money* they need for each combination of items. Then ask them to practice this exchange with a partner.

Evaluation 2:

Observe the activity.

Presentation 3: 15–20 min.

Write the following dialog on the board:
Student A: *I need a quick snack.*
Student B: *Me, too. You can buy a granola bar at the vending machine.*
Student A: *Sounds great. How much is it?*
Student B: *It's 85 cents.*
Student A: *Thanks.*

Present the dialog and practice it, showing the students how to substitute other information. See Teaching Hints for presenting dialogs.

Practice 3: 15–20 min.

Ask the students to practice the dialog with **several different students.** See Teaching Hints for alternate ways to practice dialogs.

Evaluation 3: 10–15 min.

Ask for volunteers to come up and demonstrate the dialog.

Application: 10–15 min.

Tell the students that they have $3.00 and they need to spend it on snacks for a few days. Ask

them in groups to decide what they will buy from the vending machine and report to the class.

E Active Task: Go to a vending machine in your school or neighborhood. Write down the instructions and bring them to class.

Refer to the *Activity Bank 1 CD-ROM,* Unit 3 Worksheet 2 (two pages), for additional practice identifying foods in a vending machine and following instructions. *(optional)*

Instructor's Notes for Lesson 2

_____

_____

_____

_____

_____

_____

_____

_____

_____

_____

_____

_____

_____

_____

_____

_____

_____

_____

_____

LESSON PLAN

Objectives:
Read a menu and place an order
Key vocabulary:
cheeseburger, cola, sandwiches, beverages, side orders, fruit cup, ham sandwich, milk, hot dog, French fries, mustard, selection, section, price, order

Practice 1: 15–20 min.

B **Listen to the orders. Write the order for each student below.** *(Audio CD Track 23)*

Do each order separately a few times so students can absorb all the information.

Evaluation 1: 10–15 min.

Review the table entries with students.

Warm-up and Review: 10–15 min.

Ask the students to report on the application activity from the previous lesson. What do they like for snacks? Ask them again what they like to eat for lunch and discuss the topic as a class.

Introduction: 1 min.

State objective: *Today you will learn how to read a menu and place an order.*

Presentation 1: 15–20 min.

A **Study the menu on the lunch truck with your teacher.**

Go over all the vocabulary words with the students and help them with pronunciation where needed. Ask many questions about the menu. For example, *How much are cheeseburgers?* and *What costs $2.25?* Point out the different sections and ask which items are in which sections.

STANDARDS CORRELATIONS

CASAS: 1.3.8, 2.6.4
SCANS: Resources Allocates Money
Interpersonal Teaches Others New Skills
Information Acquires and Evaluates Information, Organizes and Maintains Information, Interprets and Communicates Information

Basic Skills Reading, Arithmetic, Listening, Speaking
EFF: Communication Read with Understanding, Speak So Others Can Understand, Listen Actively, Observe Critically
Interpersonal Guide Others

LESSON 3 **Buying lunch**

GOAL ▶ Read a menu and order food

Vocabulary

A Study the menu on the lunch truck with your teacher.

Sebastien buys his lunch every day from the lunch truck.

B Listen to the orders. Write the order for each student below.

1. Sebastien's order

Selection	Section	Price
cola	beverages	$1.99
cheeseburger	sandwiches	$2.70
	Total	$4.69

2. Tran's order

Selection	Section	Price
ham sandwich	sandwiches	$2.70
green salad	side orders	$2.00
	Total	$4.70

3. Miyuki's order

Selection	Section	Price
hot dog	sandwiches	$2.25
French fries	side orders	$1.60
milk	beverages	$2.00
	Total	$5.85

C **Practice the conversation with the class.**

Sebastien: Hi! I want a cheeseburger.
Server: A cheeseburger?
Sebastien: Yes, please. No onions. And a soda, please.
Server: OK, that's a cheeseburger and a soda.
Sebastien: That's right, thanks.

D **Practice the conversation again with new information.**

1. Ham sandwich with no tomato, French fries, and milk.

   Student A: Hi! I want a _____ *(Answers will vary.)* _____.

2. Hot dog with no mustard, fruit cup, and water.

   Student B: Hi! I want a _____ *(Answers will vary.)* _____.

E **Make your own conversations with a different partner. Use the menu on the lunch truck.**

F **Active Task:** Go to a lunch truck or cafeteria and order your lunch in English.

Presentation 2: 10–15 min.

C Practice the conversation with the class.

Present the dialog as described in Teaching Hints.

Practice 2: 10–15 min.

D Practice the conversation again with new information.

Make sure the students understand how to substitute the information. Refer to Teaching Hints for alternate ways to practice a dialog.

Evaluation 2: 10–15 min.

Ask for volunteers to demonstrate in front of the class.

Presentation 3: 10–15 min.

3

Prepare the students for a competition. First divide the class into two, three, or four teams. Then assign each team a section of the board where they will write. Finally, ask each team to choose one student to run to the board and write the answer to a question.

Practice 3: 20–30 min.

3

The students in this game will be taking an order from you and totaling it. Ask them to refer to the menu on page 45.

Speaking at a normal rate, place an order. Ask for at least three items. The students will then tally the score and a representative of the team will write it on the board. The team that writes the correct answer first receives a point. Do this as many times as you would like. Make sure all students participate.

Evaluation 3:

Observe the game.

Application: 15–30 min.

E Make your own conversation with a different partner. Use the menu on the lunch truck.

Review exercise C and ask students to make their own dialog to present to the class.

Alternate activity: Ask the students in groups to make a menu and then invite students from other groups to read the menu and then place an order. Use *Activity Bank 1 CD-ROM*, Unit 3 Worksheet 3 for placing orders. *(optional)*

F Active Task: Go to a lunch truck or cafeteria and order your lunch in English.

Have students discuss the experience in class.

Refer to the *Activity Bank 1 CD-ROM*, Unit 3 Worksheet 4, for additional activities related to reading menus including prices and food items.
(optional)

Instructor's Notes for Lesson 3

_____

_____

_____

_____

_____

_____

_____

_____

_____

_____

_____

_____

_____

_____

LESSON PLAN

Objective:
Use count and non-count nouns to talk about food and quantity
Key vocabulary:
cucumbers, tomatoes, avocados, cookies, carrots, peanut butter, yogurt, mustard, apples, beef, bread, bag, bottle, pound, gallon, can, jar, box, package, container, each, quantity

Warm-up and Review: 10–15 min.

Ask any students who didn't perform their new dialogs on the previous day to do so now. Ask students to report if they did the previous Active Task by placing a lunch order in English.

Introduction: 1 min.

State objective: *Today we will learn how to use count and non-count nouns to talk about food.*

Presentation 1: 10–20 min.

Make a transparency or ask the students to look only at the picture on this page and not at the story. Ask the questions in the box and any others you consider appropriate.

A Read Duong's story.
Do this as a class. Help the students with any vocabulary that troubles them.

B Answer the questions. Fill in the circle for *True* or *False*.
Do this as a class.

Practice 1: 10–15 min.

C With a group, make a list of food for sandwiches that you can buy at the supermarket.
After the groups make their lists, ask a representative from each group to visit another group and see if he or she can add to their list.

Evaluation 1: 10–15 min.

Ask one group to start a list on the board. Ask each group to add anything the first group didn't include. Then review the vocabulary together.

STANDARDS CORRELATIONS

CASAS: 1.1.7, 1.2.1, 1.3.8
SCANS: Interpersonal Participates as a Member of a Team, Teaches Others New Skills, Exercises Leadership **Information** Acquires and Evaluates Information, Organizes and Maintains Information, Interprets and Communicates Information, Uses Computers to Process Information (optional) **Systems** Understands Systems **Technology** Applies Technology to Task (optional) **Basic Skills** Reading, Arithmetic, Listening, Speaking

Thinking Skills Creative Thinking, Decision Making, Problem Solving
Personal Qualities Sociablity
EFF: Communication Read with Understanding, Speak So Others Can Understand, Listen Actively, Observe Critically **Decision Making** Use Math to Solve Problems and Communicate, Solve Problems and Make Decisions **Interpersonal** Guide Others, Cooperate with Others **Lifelong Learning** Reflect and Evaluate, Learn through Research, Use Information and Communications Technology (optional)

How much are the oranges?

| GOAL ▶ | Use count and non-count nouns | *Grammar* |

Where is Duong?
What is he eating?

A **Read Duong's story.**

My name is Duong. I'm from Vietnam. I study at North Creek Adult School. It is very expensive to eat out every day so I bring my lunch to school. My wife and I go to the store every Saturday. We buy bread and meat for my sandwiches.

B **Answer the questions. Fill in the circle for *True* or *False*.**

	True	False
1. Duong buys his lunch at school.	○	●
2. Duong and his son go to the store every Saturday.	○	●
3. Duong and his wife buy bread and meat for sandwiches.	●	○

C **With a group, make a list of food for sandwiches that you can buy at the supermarket.**

(Answers will vary.)

_____ _____ _____

_____ _____ _____

_____ _____ _____

D Study the advertisement with your teacher.

MORE GROCERY SAVINGS FROM FOOD CITY

Bread $1.98	Ground Beef $2.25 a pound	Peanut Butter $3.25
Cucumbers $.68 each		

Spaghetti $1.25 per package — Tomatoes $.68 a pound — Milk $3.25 per gallon — Avocados $1.25 each

Oranges $.69 each — Cookies $2.75 — Mustard $1.89 — Potato chips $2.75

Apples $1.49 a pound — Cola $2.69 — Carrots $1.00 a pound — Yogurt $.79

E Look at the advertisement. Which food items can you count? Your teacher will help.

Count nouns	Non-count nouns
cucumbers	bread
tomatoes	ground beef
avocados	peanut butter
oranges	spaghetti
cookies	milk
potato chips	mustard
apples	cola
carrots	yogurt

F Ask your partner about the prices of the food.

EXAMPLES:
Student A: How much is the peanut butter?
Student B: It's $3.25.

Student B: How much are the oranges?
Student A: They are 69 cents each.

Presentation 2: 20–30 min.

D **Study the advertisement with your teacher.**

Go over the new vocabulary and help the students understand. Ask such questions as *What costs $3.05 a gallon?* Help the students notice which items end with an *s*. Explain that nouns with a plural form are count nouns. Nouns which do not have a plural form are non-count nouns. (*Yogurt* is a non-count noun which can be used in the plural to refer to "containers" of yogurt.)

 Refer to *Stand Out Grammar Challenge 1*, Unit 3, pages 17 and 23 for more practice. *(optional)*

E **Look at the advertisement. Which things can you count? Your teacher will help.**

Practice 2: 10–15 min.

F **Ask a partner about the prices of the food.**

Before the students do this activity, make sure you review the forms of *be* with them.

Evaluation 2:

Observe the activity.

Presentation 3: 10–15 min. ⓵⁵⁺

ⓖ Study the following words for food containers. Write the correct word under each picture.

Do this activity with the students and make sure that they understand the vocabulary.

Practice 3: 15–20 min. ③

ⓗ What other food goes into each kind of container?

Have students fill out this list in groups. You can also bring in a newspaper with ads to help the students become even more familiar with containers and their contents. Looking up ads on the Internet should also prove useful.

Ask group representatives to announce their group's list. Suggest they do so in such sentences as, *We have a can of soup and a bottle of oil.*

Evaluation 3: 5–10 min. ③

Listen to the announcements.

Application: 15–30 min. ⓵⁵⁺

ⓘ What food do you need today? Make a shopping list of 6 items.

Ask students to put a quantity to each item if they can. For example, *3 jars of mustard.*

Report to a partner saying, *I need _____.*

Refer to *Stand Out Grammar Challenge 1,* Unit 3, page 18 for more practice. *(optional)*

Refer to the *Activity Bank 1 CD-ROM,* Unit 3 Worksheet 5, for additional practice with container vocabulary and count and non-count nouns. *(optional)*

Instructor's Notes for Lesson 4

G **Study the following words for food containers. Write the correct word under each picture.**

bag	bottle	can	jar	box	package

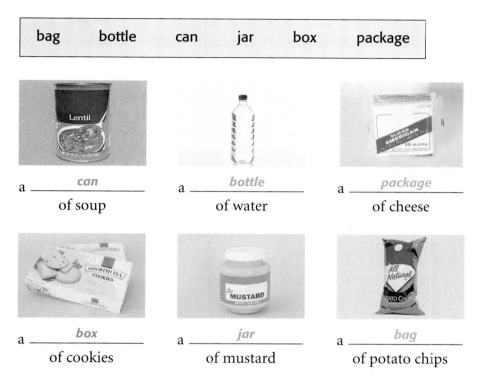

a ___can___ of soup

a ___bottle___ of water

a ___package___ of cheese

a ___box___ of cookies

a ___jar___ of mustard

a ___bag___ of potato chips

H **What other food goes into each kind of container?**

(Answers will vary.)

Container	Food	
can	coffee, beans	
bottle	cola, juice	
package	sugar, tea	
box	pasta, crackers	
jar	jelly, mayonnaise	
bag	rice, beans	

I **What food do you need today? Make a shopping list of six items.**

(Answers will vary.)

_____   _____

_____   _____

_____   _____

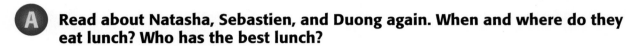

LESSON 5 Who has the best lunch?

GOAL ▶ Use the simple present

Grammar

A **Read about Natasha, Sebastien, and Duong again. When and where do they eat lunch? Who has the best lunch?**

Natasha gets her lunch every day from a vending machine at school. Sebastien buys his lunch every day from the lunch truck. Duong brings his lunch every day in a paper bag and eats after class.

B **Study the chart with your teacher.**

Simple present		
Subject	**Verb**	**Example sentence**
I, you, we, they	bring	I **bring** my lunch.
	eat	You **eat** after class.
	get	We **get** our lunch from the store.
	buy	They **buy** lunch at the cafeteria.
he, she, it	brings	He **brings** his lunch.
	gets	She **gets** her lunch from the store.
	eats	It **eats** dog food.

C **Do you bring or buy lunch? Write a complete sentence.**
(Answers will vary.)
_____

D **Talk to four students in the class. Ask: Do you bring or buy lunch? Write sentences.**

EXAMPLE:
I buy bread and fruit at the convenience store.

1. *(Answers will vary.)* _____
2. _____
3. _____
4. _____

LESSON PLAN

Objective:
Use the simple present and the negative simple present to express habits and preferences

Key vocabulary:
what, where, when, ground beef, spaghetti, milk, carrots, tomatoes, peanut butter, cola, avocados, bring, advertisement, buy, get

Warm-up and Review: 10–15 min.

Ask the students how much milk they buy every week. Discuss other quantities with them by asking questions that will encourage them to use container vocabulary from the last lesson.

Introduction: 2–5 min.

Ask the students if they eat lunch and where they eat it.

State objective: *Today you will learn to use the simple present and the negative simple present to talk about eating habits.*

Presentation 1: 20–25 min.

Ask the students what they remember from previous lessons about Natasha, Sebastien, and Duong.

Draw this chart on the board:

	Natasha	Sebastien	Duong
When?			
Where?			
What?			

A **Read about Natasha, Sebastien, and Duong again. When and where do they eat lunch? Who has the best lunch?**

Fill in the chart as a class. The students will have to refer to earlier pages to complete *what*.

B **Study the chart with your teacher.**

This should be review for the students. Make sure they understand the vocabulary and third person singular.

Refer to *Stand Out Grammar Challenge 1*, Unit 3, page 19 for more practice. *(optional)*

Practice 1: 10–15 min.

C **Do you bring or buy lunch? Write a complete sentence.**

Ask the students to add what they bring for lunch or where they buy it.

D **Talk to four students in the class. Ask: Do you bring or buy lunch? Write sentences.**

Students should first copy the sentences the four other students had written for exercise C. Then ask the students to transform those 4 sentences to third person singular and say them to a group. For example, *She buys a sandwich from the lunch truck* or *He brings his lunch from home.*

Evaluation 1:

Observe and listen carefully to the activities.

STANDARDS CORRELATIONS

CASAS: 1.2.1
SCANS: **Information** Acquires and Evaluates Information
Basic Skills Reading, Writing, Listening, Speaking
EFF: **Communication** Read with Understanding, Convey Ideas in Writing, Speak So Others Can Understand, Listen Actively, Observe Critically

Interpersonal Cooperate with Others
Lifelong Learning Reflect and Evaluate

Presentation 2: 10–15 min.

E Read the advertisement with your teacher.

Review the vocabulary and ask questions to ensure comprehension. Ask questions like: *How much is the spaghetti?* and *What item costs $3.20 a gallon?*

Prepare the students for focused listening. See Teaching Hints. Explain that they will be listening for the specific vocabulary in exercise F. Review that vocabulary with them.

Practice 2: 10–15 min.

F Listen to Duong and his wife talk about the advertisement. What do they buy? Write *Yes* or *No*. *(Audio CD Track 24)*

Play the recording. Show the students how to find the listening script in their books to self-check or peer correct.

G Write the sentences about what Duong and Minh buy.

At this point the students are only working with the affirmative, so show them how they will convert their *yes* answers in exercise F.

Evaluation 2: 10–15 min.

Ask the students to write their sentences on the board. Review as a class.

E Read the advertisement with your teacher.

PUENTE MARKET

COLA $2.99 a bottle — Spaghetti 99¢ a package — MIRALAGO PASTA

Carrots $1.25 a pound — Ground Beef $1.99 a pound

Peanut Butter $3.25 a jar — GOOBERS BEST CREAMY — MILK $3.20 a gallon

Tomatoes $.60 a pound — Avocados $.99 each

F Listen to Duong and his wife talk about the advertisement. What do they buy? Write *Yes* or *No*.

Yes/No	Item
Yes	ground beef
no	spaghetti
no	milk
yes	carrots
yes	tomatoes
no	peanut butter
yes	cola
yes	avocados

G Write sentences about what Duong and Minh buy.

EXAMPLE: ***They buy ground beef.*** *(Answers may vary. Suggestions below.)*

1. *They buy carrots and tomatoes.*
2. *They buy cola.*
3. *They buy avocados.*

Study the chart with your teacher.

Negative simple present			
Subject	**do + not**	**Base**	**Example sentence**
I you we they	do not (don't)	bring eat get buy	I don't bring sandwiches for lunch.
he she it	does not (doesn't)	bring eat get buy	He doesn't eat pizza for dinner.

I **Write sentences about what Duong and Minh don't buy.** *(Answers may vary.)*

1. **They don't buy** *spaghetti* _____ .

2. *They don't buy milk* _____ .

3. *They don't buy peanut butter* _____ .

J **Write three things that you and your partner don't like and don't buy.**

I don't buy _____*(Answers will vary.)*_____ . _____ _____ _____	My partner doesn't like _*(Answers will vary.)*_ _____ _____ _____
I don't like _____*(Answers will vary.)*_____ . _____ _____ _____	My partner doesn't buy _*(Answers will vary.)*_ _____ _____ _____

Presentation 3: 15–20 min.

 H Study the chart with your teacher.

Make sure the students see that the combination of *do* or *does* and *not* is followed by the base form of the verb and not a conjugated form.

I Write sentences about what Duong and Minh don't buy.

Ask the students to refer to the previous page to write these sentences. Write a few third-person plural examples on the board. Then ask volunteers to come up and change the subjects in these sentences from *they* to *Duong* or *Minh*, making them third-person singular.

Refer to *Stand Out Grammar Challenge 1,* Unit 3, pages 19–20 for more practice. *(optional)*

Practice 3: 15–20 min.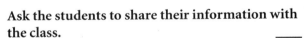

J Write three things that you and your partner don't like and don't buy.

Encourage use of contractions. Explain that we use "do not" or "does not" in formal writing. We use don't and doesn't in conversation and informal writing.

Evaluation 3: 10–15 min.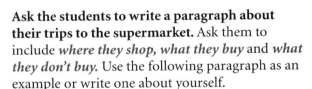

Ask the students to share their information with the class.

Application: 20–30 min.

Ask the students to write a paragraph about their trips to the supermarket. Ask them to include *where they shop, what they buy* and *what they don't buy.* Use the following paragraph as an example or write one about yourself.

> *I shop at Alden's Market. I buy a lot of vegetables. I like green beans and lettuce. I don't like mushrooms. I go to the supermarket every week.*

If you have time, have the students share their paragraph with a friend who will transform it into the third person. These paragraphs can be written on the computer. See Teaching Hints. *(optional)*

Refer to the *Activity Bank 1 CD-ROM,* Unit 3 Worksheet 6 (two pages), for more simple present practice. *(optional)*

Instructor's Notes for Lesson 5

_____

_____

_____

_____

_____

_____

_____

_____

_____

_____

_____

_____

_____

_____

_____

_____

_____

_____

_____

_____

_____

LESSON PLAN

Objectives:
Compare prices and read labels
Key vocabulary:
cheap, cheaper, expensive, ketchup, coffee, ice cream, cereal, corn flakes, ounce

Warm-up and Review: 10–15 min.

Ask volunteers to read their paragraphs to the class from the previous lesson.

A **Look at Duong's shopping list. Look at the advertisement on page 48 for Food City and the advertisement on page 51 for Puente Market. Which store is cheaper? Talk in a group.**

Have student groups compare answers and see if they agree.

Introduction: 1 min.

State objective: *Today you will learn to compare prices and read quantity in ounces.*

Presentation 1: 10–15 min.

B **Study the graph. Fill in the missing information.**

Do this activity with the students. Make sure that they understand how the graph works. Ask them comprehension questions. Be sure to introduce *cheaper* at this point.

Prepare the students for the dialog. Practice for it by quizzing them on the information in the graph. Review the plural and singular forms of *be*.

Practice 1: 10 min.

C **Use the graph to practice comparing prices.**

Evaluation: 1: 5–10 min.

Ask for volunteers to demonstrate a brief dialog in front of the class.

STANDARDS CORRELATIONS

CASAS: 1.1.7, 1.2.1, 1.2.2, 1.2.4
SCANS Resources Allocates Money, Allocates Materials and Facility Resources
Interpersonal Participates as a Member of a Team, Teaches Others New Skills, Exercises Leadership, Works with Cultural Diversity
Information Acquires and Evaluates Information, Organizes and Maintains Information, Interprets and Communicates Information, Uses Computers to Process Information (optional)
Systems Understands Systems
Technology Applies Technology to Task (optional)

Basic Skills Reading, Writing, Arithmetic, Listening, Speaking
Thinking Skills Creative Thinking, Decision Making, Problem Solving, Seeing Things in the Mind's Eye
Personal Qualities Self-Management
EFF: Communication Read with Understanding, Speak So Others Can Understand, Listen Actively, Observe Critically
Decision Making Use Mathematics in Problem Solving and Communication, Solve Problems and Make Decisions
Interpersonal Guide Others, Resolve Conflict and Negotiate, Advocate and Influence, Cooperate with Others
Lifelong Learning Learn through Research, Use Information and Communications Technology (optional)

6 Which store is cheaper?

GOAL ▷ **Compare prices**

Life Skill

A Look at Duong's shopping list. Look at the advertisement on page 48 for Food City and the advertisement on page 51 for Puente Market. Which store is cheaper for Duong? Talk in a group.

> Shopping list
>
> ground beef
> tomatoes
> avocados
> carrots

B Study the graph. Fill in the missing information.

	($2.25)							
$2.25	($1.99)							
$2.00								
$1.75								
$1.50			($1.25)			($1.25)		
$1.25				($1.00)	($0.99)			
$1.00								
$.75							($0.60)	($0.68)
$.50								
	ground beef		carrots		avocados		tomatoes	

KEY

▨ Puente

▨ Food City

C Use the graph to practice comparing prices.

EXAMPLE:
Student A: I need some ground beef. Where is it cheaper?
Student B: It's cheaper at Puente Market.

Student B: I need some carrots. Where are they cheaper?
Student A: They're cheaper at Food City.

D Look at the three bottles. How much is each bottle? Look at the unit price for each bottle. Which bottle is cheaper by the ounce?

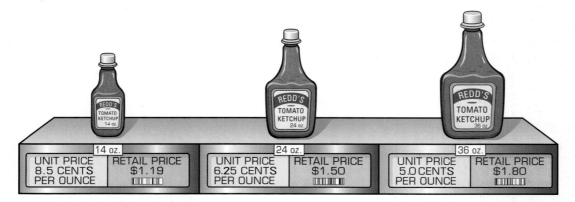

| 14 oz. |
| UNIT PRICE 8.5 CENTS PER OUNCE | RETAIL PRICE $1.19 |

| 24 oz. |
| UNIT PRICE 6.25 CENTS PER OUNCE | RETAIL PRICE $1.50 |

| 36 oz. |
| UNIT PRICE 5.0 CENTS PER OUNCE | RETAIL PRICE $1.80 |

E Look at the pictures above and practice.

EXAMPLE:
Student A: How much is the fourteen-ounce bottle?
Student B: It's one dollar and nineteen cents.
          That's eight point five cents an ounce.

> oz = ounce
>
> lb = pound
>
> 16 oz = 1 lb
>
> 8 pints = 1 gallon

F Look at the chart and compare prices. Ask your partner: Which can of coffee is cheaper by the ounce?

Coffee	Ice Cream	Cereal
8 oz $1.99 24.9 cents per ounce	1 pint $0.81 $6.48 per gallon	15 oz $2.19 14.6 cents per ounce
1 lb $2.99 18.7 cents per ounce	half gallon $1.99 $3.98 per gallon	20 oz $2.49 12.5 cents per ounce
24 oz $3.99 16.7 cents per ounce	1 gallon $3.49 $3.49 per gallon	25 oz $4.49 18 cents per ounce

G **Active Task:** As a class, choose one type of food. Choose two stores in your neighborhood or go to the Internet. Compare prices and tell the class which store is cheaper.

Presentation 2: 15–20 min.

D Look at the three bottles. How much is each bottle? Look at the unit price for each bottle. Which bottle is cheaper by the ounce?

Help the students understand that the best deal is described by the price per ounce. Refer to the box defining weights to help the students understand.

Ask comprehension questions to confirm that the students understand.

Preview the exchanges in exercises E and F. Practice a few times with the students.

Practice 2: 15–20 min.

E Look at the pictures above and practice.

See Teaching Hints for alternative ways to practice dialogs.

F Look at the chart and compare prices. Ask your partner: Which can of coffee is cheaper by the ounce?

Make sure the students practice all the items in the chart.

Evaluation 2: 5–10 min.

Ask individual students questions that were asked in the practice.

Presentation 3: 5–10 min.

Activity Bank 1 CD-ROM, **Unit 3 Worksheet 7 incorporates both comparison shopping and price per ounce information.** It allows the students to choose the best deal for given situations. Explain the worksheet to the students.

Practice 3: 20–30 min.

Ask the students in groups to do Worksheet 7. To encourage group work, you may decide to give only one worksheet to each group. Be sure to monitor their progress.

After the groups complete their worksheets, ask them to compare theirs to other groups'. There isn't necessarily one right answer.

Shorter classes may wish to complete this for homework.

Evaluation 3: 10–15 min.

Go over the answers with the class.

Application: 10–15 min.

Ask the students in groups to look at the advertisements on page 48 and 51 again. Ask them to decide on one meal for their family (group) and decide which store would be best to shop at and how much they will spend.

Have groups report to the class and list food items and expenses on the board.

G Active Task: As a class, choose one type of food. Choose two stores in your neighborhood or go to the Internet. Compare prices and tell the class which store is cheaper.

Refer to the *Activity Bank 1 CD-ROM,* Unit 3 Worksheet 8 for more work on comparison shopping including a listening activity. This listening is on *AB1 CD-ROM* Track 5. *(optional)*

Instructor's Notes for Lesson 6

_____

_____

_____

_____

_____

_____

_____

_____

_____

_____

_____

LESSON PLAN

Objectives:
Read a recipe and learn the imperative
Key vocabulary:
mashed potatoes, peel, mix, add, drain, chop, whip, boil, cook, bake, ingredients, blender, instructions

Warm-up and Review: 20–30 min.

Write the word *ingredients* **on the board.** Then under the word, list all the ingredients to a dish that the students might be familiar with. For example, if you have Mexican students, you could write *corn tortillas, beef, cheese, lettuce,* and *jalapenos.* Ask the students to guess what dish you have in mind. Ask students in groups to list ingredients for a dish of their choice. Then ask the groups to quiz the class.

Alternative activity: Pantomime baking a cake from taking the eggs out of the refrigerator to taking the final cake out of the oven and cutting it. After the students guess what you have made, do it again. This time, use words to describe actions in the imperative. As you say the words, have a student write them on the board.

Introduction: 1 min.

State objective: *Today we will learn to read recipes.*

Presentation 1: 15–20 min.

A Read the recipe for mashed potatoes with your class.

Ask the students to identify the ingredients. Review all the vocabulary words they need help with. Then pantomime making the potatoes, following the recipe. After students see what you are doing, ask them to underline the words on the recipe card in their books that express action. Ask the students to say the words with you as you do the pantomime again.

Practice 1: 10–15 min.

B Read the recipe and write the correct number next to each picture. Then match the pictures with the words.

C What other food words can go with these verbs?

Ask the students to complete then discuss the answers to exercise C with a group.

Evaluation 1: 5–10 min.

Review the activity as a class.

STANDARDS CORRELATIONS

CASAS: 1.1.1, 1.1.4
SCANS: **Resources** Allocates Materials and Facility Resources
Interpersonal Participates as a Member of a Team, Teaches Others New Skills, Exercises Leadership, Works with Cultural Diversity
Information Acquires and Evaluates Information, Organizes and Maintains Information, Interprets and Communicates Information, Uses Computers to Process Information (optional)
Systems Understands Systems
Technology Applies Technology to Task (optional)
Basic Skills Reading, Writing, Listening, Speaking
Thinking Skills Creative Thinking, Decision Making, Problem Solving, Seeing Things in the Mind's Eye, Knowing How to Learn, Reasoning

Personal Qualities Responsibility, Self-Esteem, Sociability, Self-Management, Integrity/Honesty
EFF: **Communication** Read with Understanding, Convey Ideas in Writing, Speak So Others Can Understand, Listen Actively, Observe Critically
Decision Making Use Math to Solve Problems and Communicate, Solve Problems and Make Decisions, Plan
Interpersonal Guide Others, Resolve Conflict and Negotiate, Advocate and Influence, Cooperate with Others
Lifelong Learning Take Responsibility for Learning, Reflect and Evaluate, Learn through Research, Use Information and Communications Technology (optional)

LESSON 7 — Following instructions

GOAL ▶ **Read a recipe**

Vocabulary

A **Read the recipe for mashed potatoes with your class.**

> Mashed potatoes: Serves 6.
>
> **Ingredients:** 6 potatoes, 2 tablespoons of
> butter or margarine, 1 teaspoon of salt, garlic salt
> to taste, 1/4 cup of milk. **Instructions:** Peel and chop
> potatoes. Boil water. Add potatoes to boiling water.
> Cook for 10 minutes. Drain. Mix all ingredients.
> Whip with a whisk or a blender.

B **Read the recipe and write the correct number next to each picture. Then match the pictures with the words.**

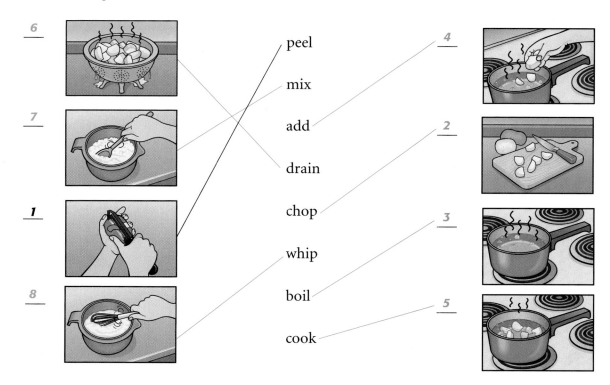

6   peel

7   mix

1   add

8   drain

    chop

    whip

    boil

    cook

4

2

3

5

C **What other food words can go with these verbs?** *(Answers will vary. Suggestions below.)*

boil __**eggs, rice**__   peel __*apples, oranges*__   chop __*celery, carrots*__

add __*water, soup*__   cook __*fish, noodles*__   whip __*cream, eggs*__

D **Study the charts with your teacher.**

Imperative verbs		
(You)	**Base**	**Example sentence**
	drain	Drain the water.
	chop	Chop the potatoes.
	peel	Peel the potatoes.

Negative imperative verbs			
(You)	**do + not**	**Base**	**Example sentence**
	do not	boil	Do not boil the water.
	(don't)	use	Do not use if seal is broken.
		cook	Do not cook in microwave.

E **Choose the correct food for each instruction.**

EXAMPLE:

Use by September 3.

○ spaghetti   ● beef   ○ salt

1. Use within 5 days after opening.

   ● spaghetti sauce   ○ carrots   ○ mustard

2. Heat slowly.

   ○ ice cream   ○ peanut butter   ● soup

3. Refrigerate after opening.

   ● milk   ○ potato chips   ○ sugar

  F **Active Task:** Find an easy recipe from a cookbook or from the Internet. Tell the class.

Presentation 2: 10–15 min.

D Study the charts with your teacher.

Show the students how all the verbs on the previous page are in the imperative.

Refer to *Stand Out Grammar Challenge 1*, Unit 3, page 22 for more practice. *(optional)*

E Choose the correct food for each instruction.

Do this activity as a class. Also ask the students to underline the imperative to make sure that they understand. Show the students that most instructions are in the imperative, not just instructions in recipes. Ask students to give more examples of warnings or instructions found on food labels.

Practice 2: 15–20 min.

Write on the board all the imperatives for making mashed potatoes from the previous page. Ask students with their books closed to practice giving instructions to a partner and practice writing those instructions down.

Evaluation 2: 5–10 min.

Ask the students to find out how they did by turning back to page 55.

Presentation 3: 5–10 min.

Review the imperative again with the students. Make sure they understand that its construction is used when giving instructions.

Practice 3: 20–30 min.

Ask students in groups to choose between making spaghetti, an omelet, or soup. Then ask them to write a recipe for the dish they chose. Be sure they follow the pattern established on page 55. There is a template available for recipes on the *Activity Bank 1 CD-ROM*, Unit 3 Worksheet 9 (optional).

Evaluation 3: 10–15 min.

Ask a few groups to share their recipes with the class.

Application: 20–30 min.

Ask the students in groups to write a recipe for any dish the group decides on and to share it with the class.

F Active Task: Find an easy recipe from a cookbook or from the Internet. Tell the class.

Refer to the *Activity Bank 1 CD-ROM*, Unit 3 Worksheet 10, for more practice listening to and reading recipes and the imperative. The listening is on *AB1 CD-ROM* Track 6.

Instructor's Notes for Lesson 7

_____

_____

_____

_____

_____

_____

_____

_____

_____

_____

_____

_____

_____

_____

_____

_____

_____

REVIEW

Objectives:
All previous objectives
Key vocabulary:
All previous Unit 3 vocabulary

Warm-up and Review: 10–15 min.

Ask the students in groups to write a recipe as they did in the previous application and to share it with the class. Then ask them to make a shopping list for the ingredients and estimate how much each ingredient will cost.

Introduction: 3–5 min.

State objective: *Today we will review all that we have done in the past unit in preparation for the application project to follow.*

Ask students as a class to try to recall all the goals of this unit without looking at their books. Then remind them of the goals they haven't mentioned.

Unit Goals: Talk about eating habits and meals, Read and follow instructions, Read a menu and order food, Use count and non-count nouns, Use the simple present, Compare prices, Read a recipe.

Presentation 1, Practice 1, and Evaluation 1:

Do the Learner Log on page 60. Notes are adjacent to the page.

Presentation 2: 5–10 min.

Review *breakfast*, *lunch*, and *dinner* with the students. Ask them questions about their eating habits. For example, *Do you like big or small meals? What time do you eat?* Write *decide*, *choose*, *put*, and *take* on the board and review their meanings.

Practice 2: 20–30 min.

A Write the names of these foods. Are they for breakfast, lunch, or dinner?
Make sure students understand that they can place the same food in more than one column.

B Talk to a partner about what he or she eats for breakfast, lunch, and dinner.

C You are in your school cafeteria. Order some of the food items from exercise A. Make a conversation with your partner.

D Give instructions on how to use a vending machine. Match the verbs with the instructions below.

Evaluation 2: 5–10 min.

Review exercises A and D.

STANDARDS CORRELATIONS

CASAS: 1.1.1, 1.1.4, 1.1.7, 7.1.1, 7.1.4, 7.4.1, 7.4.9
SCANS: Interpersonal Participates as a Member of a Team, Teaches Others New Skills, Exercises Leadership, Works with Cultural Diversity
Information Acquires and Evaluates Information, Organizes and Maintains Information, Interprets and Communicates Information
Basic Skills Reading, Writing, Arithmetic, Listening, Speaking
Thinking Skills Creative Thinking, Decision Making, Problem Solving

Personal Qualities Responsibility, Self-Esteem, Self-Management
EFF: Communication Read with Understanding, Convey Ideas in Writing, Speak So Others Can Understand, Listen Actively, Observe Critically
Decision Making Solve Problems and Make Decisions, Plan
Interpersonal Guide Others, Resolve Conflict and Negotiate, Advocate and Influence, Cooperate with Others
Lifelong Learning Take Responsibility for Learning, Reflect and Evaluate

Review

A Write the names of these foods. Are they for breakfast, lunch, or dinner?

Breakfast	Lunch	Dinner
milk	hamburger	rice
orange juice	taco	hot dog
apple	sandwich	spaghetti
	French fries	mashed potatoes
(All answers may vary.)	salad	beans
		soup

B Talk to a partner about what he or she eats for breakfast, lunch, and dinner.

C You are in your school cafeteria. Order some of the food items from exercise A. Make a conversation with your partner.

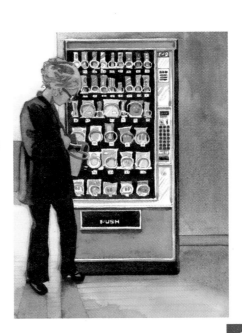

D Give instructions on how to use a vending machine. Match the verbs with the instructions below.

1. __c__ what you want.   a. Take
2. __d__ the number.   b. Put
3. __b__ your dollar bills in the slot.   c. Decide
4. __a__ your change.   d. Choose

Review

E **Complete the chart.**

Food	Count	Non-count	Container/Measurement
cereal		x	*box*
tomatoes	x		*pound*
cookies	x		*package*
mustard		x	*jar*
potato chips	x		*bag*
soup		x	*can*
water		x	*bottle*

(Containers may vary. Suggested answers above.)

F **Write four kinds of food you like and four kinds of food you don't like. Write complete sentences.**

1. **_I like_** *(Answers will vary.)* _____

2. _____

3. _____

4. _____

5. **_I don't like_** _____

6. _____

7. _____

8. _____

G **Write four kinds of food your partner doesn't like. Write complete sentences.**

1. *(Answers will vary.)* _____

2. _____

3. _____

4. _____

Presentation 3: 5–10 min.

All shorter classes can do Practice 3 for homework.

Help the students understand what to do with exercises E, F, and G. Review count and non-count nouns. Review the simple present negative.

Refer to *Stand Out Grammar Challenge 1,* Unit 3, pages 17–18 for more practice. *(optional)*

Practice 3: 30–45 min.

E Complete the chart.

Tell students they need only indicate whether the nouns in the food column are count or non-count by marking the appropriate box with an **X.** However, they will have to write the container type.

F Write four kinds of food you like and four kinds of food you don't like. Write complete sentences.

G Write four kinds of food your partner doesn't like. Write complete sentences.

Evaluation 3: 10–15 min.

Ask volunteers to write their answers on the board. Review as a class. Shorter classes may wish to complete work at home and review the following class day.

Application: 1–2 days

The Team Project Activity on the following page is the application activity to be done on the next day.

Post-Assessment: Use the *Stand Out* ExamView® Pro *Test Bank* for Unit 3. *(optional)*

Note: With the ExamView® Pro *Test Bank* CD-ROM you can design a post-assessment for Unit 3 that focuses on what students have learned. It is designed for three purposes:

• To help students practice taking a test similar to current standardized tests.

• To help the teacher evaluate how much students have learned, retained, and acquired.

• To help students see their progress when they compare their scores to the pre-test they took earlier.

Instructor's Notes for Unit 3 Review

_____

_____

_____

_____

_____

_____

_____

_____

_____

_____

_____

_____

_____

_____

_____

_____

_____

_____

_____

_____

_____

Unit 3 Application Activity

> ## TEAM PROJECT: WRITING A SECRET RECIPE
>
> Objective:
> Project designed to apply all the objectives of this unit.
> Products:
> A recipe and a list of ingredients

Introduction:

Student teams of four or five members will write a recipe and compile a shopping list. This project can extend over two days.

Stage 1: 5–10 min.

Form a team with four or five students.

The students decide who will fill which team position, as described on the student page. Provide well-defined steps for how students should proceed on the board. Explain to them that all the students do every task. Students don't go to the next stage until the previous one is complete.

Stage 2: 20–30 min.

Student 2 writes a recipe.

Use *Activity Bank 1 CD-ROM*, Unit 3 Worksheet 11 to make the recipe on the template. Make sure that the team works together and that the chef directs the work. Make sure no title is given.

Stage 3: 35– 40 min.

Make a shopping list with quantities and prices.

Student 3 leads this discussion and the production of the list. This can be done on the template provided (*Activity Bank 1 CD-ROM*, Unit 3 Worksheet 12). It can also be done directly on the computer in a spreadsheet format where the amounts are calculated. See Teaching Hints.

Stage 4: 20–30 min.

Give the recipe card and the shopping list to other groups. Ask them to guess what the name of the recipe is.

Ask the students to make a descriptive and appetizing menu entry for the dish they are preparing, but not to give away the name of the dish.

Presentation: 20–30 min.

Ask a couple of members of each group to stand and read the recipe and shopping list.

Have the other students name or guess the name of the recipe.

If time, ask students to compile recipes on the computer using a template. Print out the class recipe book for all.

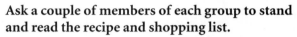

STANDARDS CORRELATIONS

CASAS: 1.1.7, 1.3.8, 3.5.2, 4.6.1, 4.8.1, 4.8.5, 6.1.1
SCANS: Resources Allocates Time, Allocates Money, Allocates Material and Facility Resources, Allocates Human Resources
Interpersonal Participates as a Member of a Team, Teaches Others New Skills, Exercises Leadership, Works with Cultural Diversity
Information Acquires and Evaluates Information, Organizes and Maintains Information, Interprets and Communicates Information, Uses Computers to Process Information
Systems Understands Systems, Monitors and Corrects Performance, Improves and Designs Systems
Technology Applies Technology to Task (optional)
Basic Skills: Reading, Writing, Arithmetic, Listening, Speaking

Thinking Skills Creative Thinking, Decision Making, Problem Solving, Seeing Things in the Mind's Eye, Knowing How to Learn, Reasoning
Personal Qualities Responsibility, Self-Esteem, Sociability, Self-Management
EFF: Communication Read with Understanding, Convey Ideas in Writing, Speak So Others Can Understand, Listen Actively, Observe Critically
Decision Making Use Math to Solve Problems and Communicate, Solve Problems and Make Decisions, Plan
Interpersonal Guide Others, Resolve Conflict and Negotiate, Advocate and Influence, Cooperate with Others
Lifelong Learning Take Responsibility for Learning, Reflect and Evaluate

T E A M
P R O J E C T

Writing a secret recipe

In this project you will write a recipe and make a shopping list.

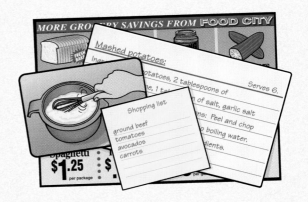

1. Form a team with four or five students.

   In your team, you need:

Position	Job	Student Name
Student 1 Leader	See that everyone speaks English. See that everyone participates.	
Student 2 Chef	With help from the team, write a recipe.	
Student 3 Shopping manager	With help from the team, make a shopping list.	
Student 4 Budget manager	Advise your team on prices of food items.	

2. Choose a recipe and put it on an index card or on a piece of paper. Include the servings, ingredients, and instructions, but don't write its name! (See page 55 for help.)

3. Make a shopping list of the food you need. Include quantities and prices. (See page 49 for help.)

4. Give the recipe card and the shopping list to other groups. Ask them to guess what the recipe is for.

PRONUNCIATION

Can you hear the sounds /j/ and /y/ in these words? Listen and repeat.

| jar | jelly | juice | package | orange | margarine |
| yes | yogurt | use | mayonnaise | menu | papaya |

LEARNER LOG

Circle what you learned and write the page number where you learned it.

1. I can talk about meals and food.
   Yes   Maybe   No   Page _41–42_

2. I can use a vending machine.
   Yes   Maybe   No   Page _43–44_

3. I can read a menu.
   Yes   Maybe   No   Page _45–46_

4. I can place an order.
   Yes   Maybe   No   Page _46_

5. I can read an advertisement.
   Yes   Maybe   No   Page _48, 51_

6. I can use count and non-count nouns.
   Yes   Maybe   No   Page _47–49_

7. I can comparison shop.
   Yes   Maybe   No   Page _53–54_

8. I can read a recipe.
   Yes   Maybe   No   Page _55–56_

Did you answer *No* to any questions? Review the information with a partner.

Rank what you like to do best from 1 to 6. 1 is your favorite activity. Your teacher will help you.

☐ practice listening

☐ practice speaking

☐ practice reading

☐ practice writing

☐ learn new words (vocabulary)

☐ learn grammar

In the next unit I want to practice more
(Answers will vary.) _____.

Unit 3 Pronunciation and Learner Log

Pronunciation (optional): 10–15 min.
(Audio CD Track 25)

Can you hear the sounds /j/ and /y/ in these words? Listen and repeat.

Play the recording and pause after each word.

For additional pronunciation practice: (The following words should be used for pronunciation practice, not for vocabulary instruction.)Write the following examples on the board. Show the students how the /y/ sound continues softly (a continuant) and how the /j/ sound (the stop /d/ followed by the continuant /zh/) is produced by a short burst of air.

jell–yell	*jewel–you'll*
jam–yam	*jet–yet*
joke–yoke	*juice–use*

Ask students to copy the pairs of words and read one from each pair to a partner. The partner should then point to the word that he or she hears. Model the pairwork if needed.

Learner Log

Presentation 1: 10–15 min.

If needed, review the purpose of the Learner Log.

Circle what you learned and write the page number where you learned it. Students research the answers individually. When they've finished, they should share their answers with a partner. These results need not be shared with the class.

Practice 1: 10–15 min.

Rank what you like to do best from 1 to 6. 1 is your favorite activity. Your teacher will help you. Results should be shared with the class in order to demonstrate to students how people learn differently.

Evaluation 1: 10–15 min.

In the next unit I want to practice more _____. Students should fill in the blank with assistance from a partner or from you. They may focus on a skill (e.g., listening), on a vocabulary area (e.g., numbers), on grammar, and so on. Don't limit them to a single answer. Emphasize that the purpose of completing the sentence is to improve their self-assessment skills. Have volunteers share responses. Discuss answers.

Instructor's Notes for Unit 3 Team Project, Pronunciation, and Learner Log

_____

_____

_____

_____

_____

_____

_____

_____

_____

_____

_____

_____

_____

_____

_____

_____

_____

_____

_____

_____

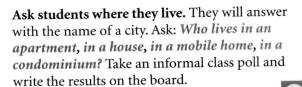

LESSON PLAN

Objective:
Identify basic housing
Key vocabulary:
house, apartment, mobile home,
condominium, housing

Pre-Assessment: Use the *Stand Out ExamView® Pro Test Bank* for Unit 4. (optional)

Warm-up and Review: 10–15 min.

Ask students where they live. They will answer with the name of a city. Ask: *Who lives in an apartment, in a house, in a mobile home, in a condominium?* Take an informal class poll and write the results on the board.

Introduction: 3–5 min.

State objective: *Today and in this unit we will learn about different types of homes and other things about housing.*

Presentation 1: 10–15 min

(A) Read the information about housing in Corbin. Then complete the chart and fill in the total.

Help students understand how a pie chart works. Read the statistics aloud and ask the class to repeat. You may also want to make a simplified pie chart on the board. Run a line through it to show *50%*, then another to show *25%*. If time permits,

make a slightly more complex pie chart that shows *10%*, *20%*, *30%*, and *40%*.

Practice 1: 10–15 min.

(B) What other types of housing do you have in your town or city?

Have students make a list of different types of housing and collect their ideas on the board.

Evaluation 1: 2–3 minutes

Review student answers.

Pronunciation:

An optional pronunciation activity is found on the final page of this unit. This pronunciation activity may be introduced during any lesson in this unit, especially if students need practice contrasting the sounds of *air* and *ear*. Go to pages 80/80a for Unit 4 Pronunciation.

STANDARDS CORRELATIONS

CASAS: 1.4.1, 6.7.4
SCANS: **Resources** Allocates Money
Interpersonal Participates as a Member of a Team, Teaches Others New Skills, Exercises Leadership, Works with Cultural Diversity
Information Acquires and Evaluates Information, Organizes and Maintains Information, Interprets and Communicates Information
Technology Applies Technology to Task (optional)
Basic Skills Reading, Arithmetic, Listening, Speaking

Thinking Skills Creative Thinking, Decision Making, Problem Solving, Seeing Things in the Mind's Eye, Reasoning
EFF: **Communication** Read with Understanding, Speak So Others Can Understand, Listen Actively, Observe Critically, **Decision Making** Solve Problems and Make Decisions
Interpersonal Guide Others, Resolve Conflict and Negotiate, Advocate and Influence, Cooperate with Others
Lifelong Learning Reflect and Evaluate, Learn through Research, Use Information and Communications Technology (optional)

GOALS

- Identify types of housing
- Talk about rooms in a home
- Read and interpret classified ads

- Use the present continuous
- Use prepositions of location
- Understand a family budget
- Make a family budget

LESSON 1

What type of home do you have?

GOAL ▶ Identify types of housing

Vocabulary

 A Read the information about housing in Corbin. Then complete the chart and fill in the total.

Housing Statistics: Corbin, CA

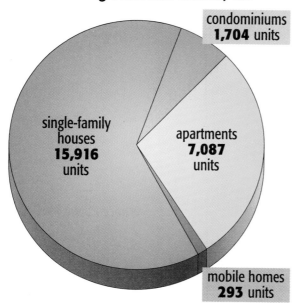

- condominiums **1,704** units
- single-family houses **15,916** units
- apartments **7,087** units
- mobile homes **293** units

Type of housing	Number of units
	15,916
	7,087
	1,704
	293
Total number of housing units:	25,000

B What other types of housing do you have in your town or city?

C   What types of homes are in your town? Make groups of five or six students and complete the chart.

What's your name?	What type of housing do you live in?
(Answers will vary.)	*(Answers will vary.)*

D   Now put the information into a pie chart. Look at the example on the left, then complete the chart on the right with your group's information.

EXAMPLE:

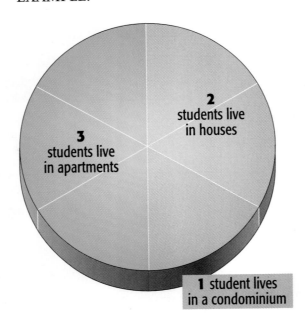

3 students live in apartments

2 students live in houses

1 student lives in a condominium

Where do we live?

E   Write two sentences about your group's pie chart.

EXAMPLE: *Two students in my group live in single-family houses.*

1.   *(Answers will vary.)* _____

2.   _____

Presentation 2: 10–15 min.

Review the question in exercise C with the students. Show the students how they will complete the chart by practicing with a few students.

Practice 2: 10–15 min.

C **What types of homes are in your town? Make groups of 5 or 6 students and complete the chart.**

Evaluation 2: 5–10 min.

Ask for volunteers to re-create the chart in front of the class.

Presentation 3: 15–20 min.

Ask students in groups to write the four kinds of homes or housing on a piece of paper. Make sure all the groups have the same 4 types of housing.

Practice 3: 15–20 min.

Ask the students in their groups to discuss and agree upon the price of rent for each of the homes in their neighborhood.

Have each group send a representative to the board and write their figures on the board. Work with the students to agree upon a final amount for each type of home. You will have to take a vote several times until you come up with an answer all will be happy with. If you have a current newspaper handy or have time to research on the Internet, you can give them a conclusive answer after you have made a guess as a class about each housing type.

Evaluation 3:

Observe the activity.

Application: 10–15 min.

D **Now put the information into a pie chart. Look at the example on the left, then complete the chart on the right with your group's information.**

Check that students understand how to divide the pie chart into segments according to the number of people in their group who live in each type of housing.

E **Write 2 sentences about your group's pie chart.**

Have a student in each group read the sentences aloud.

Refer to the *Activity Bank 1 CD-ROM*, Unit 4 Worksheet 1, for additional reading and listening activities related to housing types. The listening is on *AB 1 CD-ROM* Track 7. (optional)

Instructor's Notes for Lesson 1

_____
_____
_____
_____
_____
_____
_____
_____
_____
_____
_____
_____
_____
_____
_____
_____
_____
_____
_____
_____
_____

LESSON PLAN

Objective:
Talk about rooms in a house
Key vocabulary:
bedrooms, sleep, shower, entertain,
bathrooms, family room, living room,
dining room, front door, yard, kitchen,
hall

Warm-up and Review : 5–10 min.

Ask students what kind of home they live in and how many bedrooms they have. Ask students to write all the kinds of rooms in a home they can think of. Don't allow dictionary use at this stage. The idea is to see what they already know. Then ask students to report. Write the vocabulary on the board.

Introduction: 1 min.

State objective: *Today we are going to learn about rooms in a house and other places around the house.*

Presentation 1: 5–10 min.

Look at the picture with the students. Ask the questions in the boxes. Review the principles of focused listening with the class. (See Teaching Hints.) Tell students that they will listen to a conversation with Saud and a real estate agent. They need to listen only for the number of bedrooms and bathrooms Saud needs.

Practice 1: 15–20 min.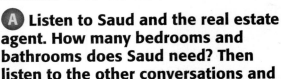

A Listen to Saud and the real estate agent. How many bedrooms and bathrooms does Saud need? Then listen to the other conversations and fill in the information below. *(Audio CD Track 26)*

Play the recording a few times. If students have trouble with focused listening, play each conversation separately and check the answers together.

Evaluation 1:

Observe the listening activities.

Presentation 2: 10–15 min.

Write the vocabulary on the board from the box at the bottom of the page and practice pronunciation with the students. Ask them to close their books. Read the statements in exercise B aloud and ask students to identify each room. Advise students to listen for one or two key words that might help them identify rooms.

Practice 2: 10–15 min.

B Where in the house do people do these things? With a group, write the names of the rooms. Use the words from the box.

Ask students to open their books and complete the exercise in small groups.

Evaluation 2: 5–10 min.

Have groups share answers to the exercise. Name a few rooms and have students say the activity that families do there.

STANDARDS CORRELATIONS

CASAS: 1.4.1, 7.2.3
SCANS: **Interpersonal** Participates as a Member of a Team, Teaches Others New Skills
Information Acquires and Evaluates Information, Organizes and Maintains Information, Interprets and Communicates Information

Basic Skills Listening, Speaking, Seeing Things in the Mind's Eye
EFF: **Communication** Speak So Others Can Understand, Listen Actively, Observe Critically
Interpersonal Guide Others, Cooperate with Others

LESSON 2 Describing your home

GOAL ▶ Talk about rooms in a home

A Listen to Saud and the real estate agent. How many bedrooms and bathrooms does Saud need? Then listen to the other conversations and fill in the information below.

Name	No. of bedrooms	No. of bathrooms
1. Saud	3	1
2. Silvia	2	2
3. Tien	4	2
4. Felipe	1	1

Where is Saud? Why is he there?

B Where in the house do people do these things? With a group, write the names of the rooms. Use the words from the box.

Activity	Room
People sleep in this room.	bedroom
People take showers in this room.	bathroom
People watch TV in this room.	living room/family room
People eat dinner in this room.	dining room/kitchen
People make dinner in this room.	kitchen
People go from room to room here.	hall
People entertain in this room.	living room/family room
People enter a home here.	front door
Children play outside here.	yard

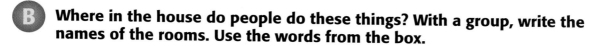

bedroom   bathroom   yard   dining room   hall
kitchen   living room*   front door   family room*

* Many people have one room and they call it both family room and living room.

C Study the picture with your teacher. Write the correct letter next to each word.

_g_ garage   _c_ swimming pool   _a_ bathroom   _i_ family room

_k_ kitchen   _f_ hall   _b_ balcony   _d_ front porch

_h_ bedroom   _l_ deck   _j_ stairs

_n_ front yard   _e_ back yard   _m_ driveway

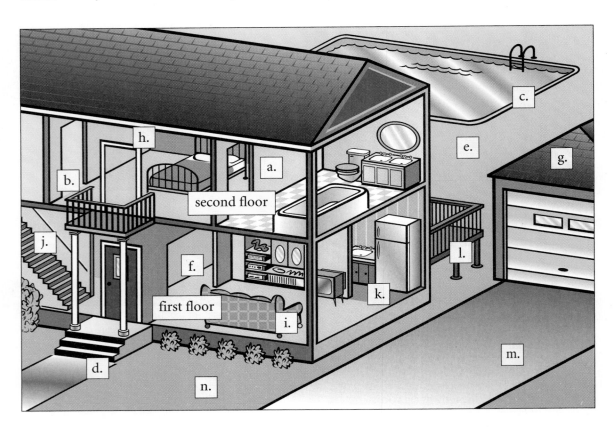

D Ask your partner about his or her home. *(Answers will vary.)*

1. What kind of home do you have?

2. How many bedrooms do you have?

3. How many bathrooms do you have?

4. Do you have a front or back yard?

5. Do you have a garage or a carport?

6. Do you have a balcony?

carport

Presentation 3: 5–10 min.

C Study the picture with your teacher. Write the correct letter next to each word.

Identify the new vocabulary. Help students with pronunciation.

Practice 3: 15–20 min.

Inside or outside? Have students ask and answer questions about the picture.

Student A: Where is the kitchen?

Student B: It's inside the house, on the first floor.

Evaluation 3: 10–15 min.

Check exercise C in student books and observe the activity.

 ## Application: 10–15 min.

D Ask your partner about his or her home.

Show students how to make a grid and fill it in. Let them do this activity with several partners. You may want to use the grid from the *Activity Bank 1 CD-ROM*, Unit 4 Worksheet 2.*(optional)*

 Alternative Activity: Ask the students to make a Venn diagram with a partner about their rooms at home. Show them how this is done. A template for Venn diagrams is available on the *Activity Bank 1 CD-ROM*, Worksheet 3. A transparency could be made of the sample Venn diagram on page 2 of Worksheet 3.

Partner A	Both	Partner B
dining room	*small kitchen two bedrooms*	*basement*

 Refer to the *Activity Bank 1 CD-ROM*, Worksheet 4, for additional practice reading and listening about rooms of a house. The listening is on *AB 1 CD-ROM* Track 8. *(optional)*

Instructor's Notes for Lesson 2

LESSON PLAN

Objectives:
Read and interpret classified ads
Key vocabulary:
pets, utilities, public transportation,
air conditioning, pool, garage, cable,
classified ads, deposit, furnished

Warm-up and Review: 10–15 min.

Have students repeat the application activity
from the last lesson with a different partner
(**exercise D**). Again, you may wish to have students
either speak to multiple partners using a grid or
make a Venn diagram and report to the class.

Introduction: 1 min.

Ask students to look at exercise A and explain
that it shows a classified ad.

State objective: *Today we are going to learn to
read and interpret a classified ad.*

Presentation 1: 10–15

A Read this ad from a newspaper.

Go through the ad with students. Ask pertinent
comprehension questions like those in exercise C,
but don't let students know you are doing exercise
C. Write *bed* on the board and ask them what it
means. Most will reply it is what you sleep on.
Help them see that, in the ad, *bed* serves as an
abbreviation for bedroom. Write *Utilities* on the
board. Ask students what the word means. Clarify

after they answer by discussing the box on
the page.

Practice 1: 15–20 min.

**B Draw a line from the word to
its abbreviation. What do these
words mean?**

Ask students to do this activity in pairs.

**C Answer these questions about the
ad in exercise A. Add one more
question of your own.**

Again, ask students to pair up for this activity.

Evaluation 1: 10–15 min.

Review the answers to exercises B and C.

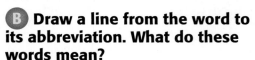

STANDARDS CORRELATIONS

CASAS: 1.4.1, 1.4.2
SCANS: **Interpersonal** Participates as a Member of a
Team, Teaches Others New Skills, Exercises Leadership
Information Acquires and Evaluates Information,
Organizes and Maintains Information, Interprets and
Communicates Information, Uses Computers to Process
Information (optional)
Technology Applies Technology to Task (optional)
Basic Skills Reading, Listening, Speaking

Thinking Skills Creative Thinking, Decision Making,
Problem Solving
EFF: **Communication** Read with Understanding, Speak So
Others Can Understand, Listen Actively, Observe Critically
Decision Making Solve Problems and Make Decisions
Interpersonal Guide Others, Resolve Conflict and
Negotiate, Advocate and Influence, Cooperate with Others
Lifelong Learning Reflect and Evaluate, Learn through
Research, Use Information and Communications
Technology (optional)

GOAL ▶ Read and interpret classified ads

Life Skill

 A Read this ad from a newspaper.

APT FOR RENT
2 bed, 1 bath apt,
818 Sundry Ave. #19.
$750, furn a/c
all utls pd 1 mth dep.
call 555-7744

B Draw a line from the word to its abbreviation. What do these words mean?

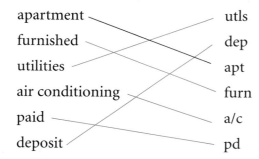

apartment   utls
furnished   dep
utilities   apt
air conditioning   furn
paid   a/c
deposit   pd

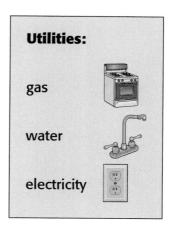

Utilities:

gas

water

electricity

C Answer these questions about the ad in exercise A. Add one more question of your own.

1. Is it a house or an apartment? _____*an apartment*_____

2. How many bedrooms does it have? _____*2 bedrooms*_____

3. Is it furnished or unfurnished? _____*furnished*_____

4. Does it have air conditioning? _____*yes*_____

5. Are the utilities paid? _____*yes*_____

6. How much is the rent? _____*$750.00*_____

7. How much is the deposit? _____*$750.00/1 month's rent*_____

8. What's the address? _____*818 Sundry Ave., #19*_____

9. What's the phone number? _____*555-7744*_____

10. _____*(Questions and answers will vary.)*_____ ?

a.
3 bed, 2 bath apt.,
a/c, balcony,
★ $800, ★
call Lien
at 555-7744

b.
2 bed, 3 bath apt.
a/c, elect. pd.
call Margaret
for more
information
555-5678

c.
FOR RENT
$700 a month.
1 bed, 1 bath apt.
n/pets. call Fred
at 555–7164

d.
ca. Phn 554-5711
d. 3 bed, 3 bath apt. p
c. with pool, utls pd. u
6 nr schools, call c
555-5987 5

 D **Listen and write the letter from the classified ads above.**

1. ___d___

2. ___a___

3. ___b___

4. ___c___

E **Put a check by things about your home.** *(Answers will vary.)*

_____ pets allowed   _____ cable TV

_____ utilities paid (if you rent)   _____ air conditioning

_____ near a school   _____ near a park

_____ near public transportation   _____ garage

F **In a group, write a classified ad about your home.**

(Answers will vary.)

_____

_____

_____

_____

 G **Active Task:** Go to a newspaper or look on the Internet and find a home to rent or buy that is good for your family.

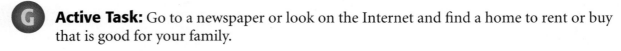

Presentation 2: 10–15 min.

Review the classified ads with students by asking comprehension questions similar to those posed in the previous exercise. Prepare the students for focused listening by giving them clues and seeing if they can identify which ad you are talking about. See Teaching Hints on focused listening.

Practice 2: 10–15 min.

D Listen and write the letter from the classified ads above. *(Audio CD Track 27)*

Play the recording several times. Ask students to list the abbreviations that they see in the 4 ads on a separate sheet of paper. Then ask them to write out the full versions of what the abbreviations stand for without looking at the previous page.

This is a good place to provide real newspapers with classified ads. Help students find where those ads are usually located. Also ask them to identify abbreviations in three or four ads and report to the class (optional).

Evaluation 2: 5–10 min.

Have students look at each other's work and then review as a class.

Presentation 3: 10–15 min.

Find Worksheet 5 on Unit 4 of the *Activity Bank 1 CD-ROM* for Practice 3. Show students how to complete the worksheet by filling in the grid about classified ads.

Practice 3: 20–30 min.

Ask students to read and complete the worksheet in pairs.

Evaluation 3: 10–15 min.

Have the students change partners and peer-edit their work.

Application: 5–10 min.

E Put a check by things about your home.

Lead the students through this activity.

F In a group, write a classified ad about your home.

Ask student groups to choose one member's home at a time and to write a classified ad about the home using the information from exercise E. This can also be done on a computer. There is a template for making a classified page of a newspaper on the *Activity Bank 1 CD-ROM,* Unit 4 Worksheet 6.

G Active Task: Go to the newspaper or look on the Internet and find a home to rent or buy that is good for your family.

Instructor's Notes for Lesson 3

_____

_____

_____

_____

_____

_____

_____

_____

_____

_____

_____

_____

_____

_____

_____

_____

_____

_____

LESSON PLAN

Objectives:
Use the present continuous and ask
for information about housing
Key vocabulary:
rent

Warm-up and Review: 10–15 min.

Ask students to come up with questions to ask if they call someone about renting an apartment.
Write on the board, *How much is the rent?*
Students won't be likely to construct such questions correctly, but encourage them to try. Then write your corrected versions of their questions on the board. Ask students to turn back to exercise C on page 65 and look at the questions again. Write each question on the board for use in Practice 1.

Introduction: 10–15 min.

State objective: *Today we will learn to make phone calls and get information. We will also learn about the present continuous.*

Presentation 1: 15–20 min.

Look at the picture at the top of the page with students. Ask the questions in the boxes and additional ones that will help students practice. Then ask the class to close books and get ready for the conversation.

A Listen to the conversation first with your books closed. Then read and listen.
(Audio CD Track 28)
Play the recording. Before and after students listen, ask them what information Carmen is

seeking. Help students use proper intonation and present the dialog in preparation for Practice 1.

Practice 1: 10–15 min.

B With a partner, make new conversations using the information below.
This conversation would be very easy to expand beyond pair work. Show students how to substitute information in the last exchange by using the questions you wrote on the board from both the Warm-up questions on the board and the ads on page 66. See Teaching Hints for additional ways to practice dialogs.

Evaluation 1: 10–15 min.

Ask for volunteers to demonstrate in front of the class.

STANDARDS CORRELATIONS

CASAS: 1.4.2
SCANS: **Interpersonal** Participates as a Member of a Team, Teaches Others New Skills
Information Acquires and Evaluates Information, Organizes and Maintains Information, Interprets and Communicates Information

Basic Skills Reading, Writing, Listening, Speaking
EFF: **Communication** Convey Ideas in Writing, Speak So Others Can Understand, Listen Actively, Observe Critically

Making an appointment

GOAL ▶ Use the present continuous   *Grammar*

What is Carmen doing?
Who is she talking to?

  A **Listen to the conversation first with your book closed. Then read and listen.**

Ms. Rollings: Hello.
Carmen: Hello. I am calling about the apartment for rent.
Ms. Rollings: Yes, it's still available.
Carmen: Can I see it?
Ms. Rollings: Of course, you can come to see it right now.
Carmen: I'm looking after my grandson right now. How about at 6 P.M?
Ms. Rollings: OK. What's your name?
Carmen: Carmen.
Ms. Rollings: See you at 6 P.M., Carmen.

B **With a partner, make new conversations using the information below.**

Type of home	What are you doing?
house	I'm looking after my grandson.
apartment	I'm working.
condominium	I'm cleaning my house.
mobile home	I'm making dinner.

Study the chart with your teacher.

Present continuous			
Subject	**be**	**Base + ing**	**Example sentence**
I	am	call + ing	I am calling about the apartment.
you	are	work + ing	You are working right now.
he, she, it	is	talk + ing	He is talking now.
we, they	are	look + ing	We are looking for a new house.

D **Look at the pictures and write a sentence about each one.**

    1. eat   2. read   3. sleep   4. bark

1. *They are eating.*
2. *He is reading.*
3. *He is sleeping.*
4. *It is barking.*

 Write answers to the questions.

1. What are you doing right now?

(Answers will vary.)

2. What is your teacher doing right now?

(Answers will vary.)

3. What is your sister or brother or friend doing?

(Answers will vary.)

Presentation 2: 15–20 min.

C Study the chart with your teacher.

Ask the students questions about themselves and about where they are living, etc. Make sure you go over the chart in detail.

 Refer to *Stand Out Grammar Challenge 1*, Unit 4, pages 26–27 for more practice. *(optional)*

Practice 2: 10–15 min.

Look at the pictures in exercise D with the class and decide on the right verbs.

D Look at the pictures and write a sentence about each one.

E Write answers to the questions.

Evaluation 2: 5–10 min.

Check student sentences.

Presentation 3: 10–15 min.

 Note: This dialog, chart, and information on the present continuous are on the *Activity Bank 1 CD-ROM*, Unit 4 Worksheets 7 and 8. Show students how to substitute information in the dialog.

If the worksheets are not available, write and present the following dialog. See Teaching Hints for help in dialog presentation.

Ms. Rollings: *Hello.*
Carmen: *Hello. My name is <u>Carmen</u>. I'm calling about the house you have for rent.*
Ms. Rollings: *Of course. It's still available.*
Carmen: *Great. When can I see it?*
Ms. Rolling: *What are you doing right now?*
Carmen: *Right now, <u>I'm watching my niece</u>.*
Ms. Rollings: *Oh, can you come tomorrow about this time?*
Carmen: *I think so.*
Ms. Rollings: *The <u>house</u> is beautiful. <u>I'm painting the inside</u> right now.*
Carmen: *That's great. I'll see you tomorrow. Good-bye.*
Ms. Rollings: *OK, good-bye.*

Write the following information on the board:

What does Carmen say?	What does Ms. Rollings say?
I'm watching my niece.	I'm painting.
I'm working.	I'm cleaning the kitchen.
I'm cleaning my house.	I'm repairing the doors.
I'm making dinner.	I'm writing an ad.

Practice 3: 15–20 min.

Have the students practice the dialog with a partner. See Teaching Hints for alternative ways to practice dialogs.

Evaluation 3: 10–15 min.

Ask for volunteers to demonstrate different dialog versions in front of the class.

Application: 15–30 min.

Ask the students to make their own dialog. They will need to use ideas from the earlier dialog. Print out Worksheet 8 from the *Activity Bank 1 CD-ROM*, which also includes the present continuous, to help them write this dialog in pairs.

Refer to the *Activity Bank 1 CD-ROM*, Unit 4 Worksheet 9, for additional practice with the present continuous. *(optional)*

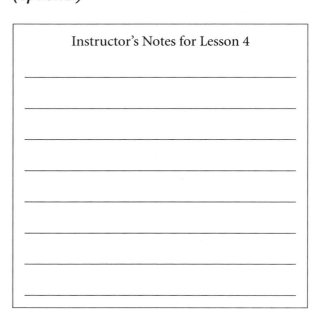

Instructor's Notes for Lesson 4

LESSON PLAN

Objectives:
Use prepositions of location and identify furniture

Key vocabulary:
lamp, mirror, dresser, night stand, cabinets, stove, sink, counter, china cabinet, rug, walls, toilet, sink, towel rack, tools, trash can, coffee table, end table, TV, painting, in, on, under, next to, between, over

Warm-up and Review: 10–15 min.

Ask students in groups to make a list of furniture without using a dictionary or their books. This will tell you how much students already know. Ask one group to put its list on the board. Then ask the other groups to add to the list any other items.

Introduction: 1 min.

State objective: *Today we are going to learn to use prepositions of location and identify furniture in a home.*

Presentation 1: 10–15 min.

Go over the pictures at the top of the page in exercise A. Help students with pronunciation.

A **Write the words under the correct room. Tell your partner about your decisions.**

Ask students to do this exercise quickly and then ask them to compare answers.

Practice 1: 15–20 min.

B **In a group, make a list of other things you see in the rooms. Use a dictionary or ask your teacher for help.**

Evaluation 1: 10–15 min.

Ask groups to report.

STANDARDS CORRELATIONS

CASAS: 7.2.3
SCANS: **Resources** Allocates Materials and Facility Resources
Interpersonal Participates as a Member of a Team, Teaches Others New Skills, Exercises Leadership, Works with Cultural Diversity
Information Acquires and Evaluates Information, Organizes and Maintains Information, Interprets and Communicates Information, Uses Computers to Process Information (optional)
Technology Applies Technology to Task (optional)

Basic Skills Listening, Speaking
Thinking Skills Creative Thinking, Decision Making, Problem Solving
EFF: **Communication** Speak So Others Can Understand, Listen Actively, Observe Critically
Interpersonal Guide Others, Resolve Conflict and Negotiate, Advocate and Influence, Cooperate with Others
Lifelong Learning Reflect and Evaluate, Learn through Research (optional), Use Information and Communications Technology (optional)

LESSON 5

Where do you put the refrigerator?

GOAL ▶ **Use prepositions of location**

Grammar

A Write the words under the correct room. Tell your partner about your decisions.

EXAMPLE: The bed goes in the bedroom.

1. bed   2. car   3. chair   4. refrigerator   5. bathtub   6. sofa

bedroom ____*bed*____

kitchen ___*refrigerator*___

dining room _____*chair*_____

bathroom ____*bathtub*____

garage _____*car*_____

living room _____*sofa*_____

B In a group, make a list of other things you see in the rooms. Use a dictionary or ask your teacher for help.

(Answers may vary. Suggestions below.)

bedroom	kitchen	dining room	bathroom	garage	living room
lamp	*stove*	*table*	*toilet*	*ladder*	*TV*
end table	*sink*	*cabinet*	*sink*	*shelves*	*armchair*
painting	*dishwasher*	*painting*	*mirror*	*rake*	*coffee table*

C Study the prepositions with your teacher.

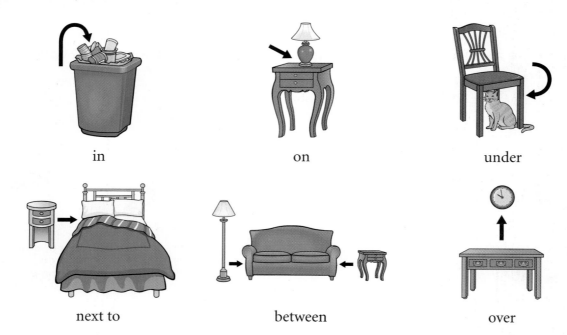

in　　　　　　　　　on　　　　　　　　　under

next to　　　　　　　between　　　　　　over

D Ask a partner where things are. Ask about: the lamp, the cat, the nightstand, the sofa, and the clock.

EXAMPLE:
Student A: Where's the trash?
Student B: It's in the trash can.

E Use the prepositions above to identify the location of things in your classroom. Your partner will guess which thing you are talking about.

EXAMPLE:
Student A: It's next to the window.
Student B: The TV.

Presentation 2: 10–15 min.

C Study the prepositions with your teacher.

Quiz students by asking them where various items are located.

Prepare for exercise D by asking the class similar questions.

Practice 2: 10–15 min.

D Ask a partner where things are. Ask about: the lamp, the cat, the nightstand, the sofa, and the clock.

Evaluation 2:

Observe the exchange activity.

Presentation 3: 10–15 min.

E Use the prepositions above to identify the location of things in your classroom. Your partner will guess which thing you are talking about.

Demonstrate this activity with a student. Then have students work in pairs or groups.

 Refer to *Stand Out Grammar Challenge 1*, Unit 4, page 31 for more practice. *(optional)*

Practice 3: 15–20 min.   **3**

F **Read and follow the directions below.**

G **Show your partner where the furniture is in your picture. Talk to your partner about it.**

Evaluation 3:   **3**

Look at student drawings.

Application: 15–20 min.   **1.5+**

Ask students to draw a diagram of their own living rooms on a sheet of paper. They should identify the location of their furniture. Then ask them to give directions to a partner to see if the partner can draw the diagram the same way without looking at the original diagram.

H **Active Task: Find a picture of a room with furniture from a magazine or on the Internet. Show your picture to the class and describe it.**

AB **Refer to the *Activity Bank 1 CD-ROM*, Unit 4 Worksheet 10 (two pages), for additional activities using prepositions of location.** *(optional)*

Instructor's Notes for Lesson 5

Read and follow the directions below.

Below is a picture of a living room. Draw a window and a door. Put a painting on the wall. Put a sofa under the painting. Put a chair between the sofa and the door. Put a coffee table in the middle of the room. Draw an end table next to the chair in the corner. Put a lamp on the end table.

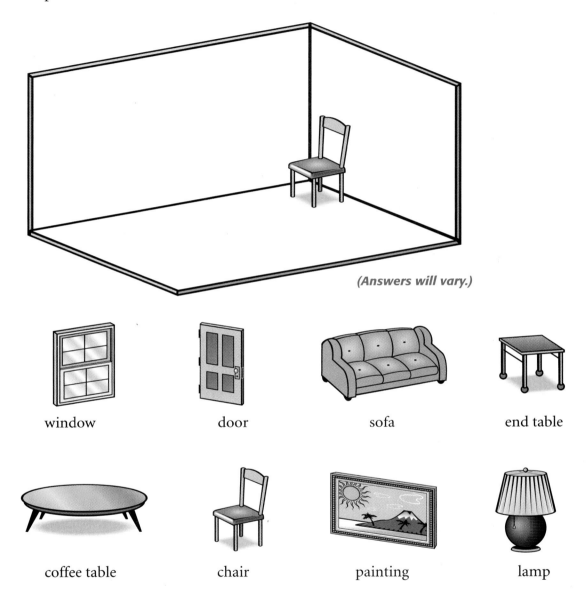

(Answers will vary.)

window	door	sofa	end table

coffee table	chair	painting	lamp

G **Show your partner where the furniture is in your picture. Talk to your partner about it.**

  Active Task: Find a picture of a room with furniture from a magazine or on the Internet. Show your picture to the class and describe it.

LESSON 6 Income and expenses

GOAL ▶ **Understand a family budget**

Life Skill

What are Roberto and Silvia talking about?

for rent: beautiful
3 bed, 2 bath hse,
nr schools, n/pets.
$1500 a month
call Marjorie at
★ **555-4545** ★

A **Read about Silvia and Roberto.**

Silvia and Roberto want to rent a new house, but it is very *expensive*. They need to *calculate* how much money they have. They also need to buy furniture for the house. Silvia and Roberto are making a family *budget* to see if they have *enough* money for a new house.

B **What do the new words mean? Talk in a group. After you talk, ask your teacher. Try to make sentences with these new words.**

expensive _____ *(Answers will vary.)* _____

calculate _____

budget _____

enough _____

72 **UNIT 4 ● Lesson 6**

LESSON PLAN

Objective:
Understand a family budget
Key vocabulary:
expensive, calculate, budget, income, insurance, budget, savings, total, expenses, enough

Warm-up and Review: 15–20 min.

Ask students to look at the classified ad. Ask comprehension questions similar to the ones you asked in previous lessons about classified ads. Ask the students to circle the abbreviations and write out what they mean. Discuss this as a class after they do the work.

Introduction: 5 min.

Write *income* **and** *expenses* **on the board.** Show students what these words mean by giving an example of someone who makes $2000 a month. Write *$2000 a month* under the word *income.* Under *expenses* write *rent $800, food $300,* etc. Show that income is more than expenses. In a second example, show that expenses are more than income.

State objective: *Today we will learn how to read a family budget.*

Presentation 1: 15–20 min.

First, ask students to cover the paragraph in exercise A. Then look with the class at the picture of Silvia and Roberto. Ask the boxed question and

any other questions you think would be helpful. Finally, ask students to uncover the paragraph and do the exercise.

Practice 1: 10–15 min.

A Read about Silvia and Roberto.
Ask the students to read this individually and try to identify what the problem is.

B What do the new words mean? Talk in a group. After you talk, ask your teacher. Try to make sentences with these new words.
Ask students to make sentences about themselves and not merely copy those in the story.

Evaluation 1: 15–20 min.

Ask volunteers to write their sentences on the board.

STANDARDS CORRELATIONS

CASAS: 1.5.1, 6.1.1
SCANS: **Resources** Allocates Money
Interpersonal Participates as a Member of a Team, Teaches Others New Skills, Exercises Leadership
Information Acquires and Evaluates Information, Organizes and Maintains Information, Interprets and Communicates Information, Uses Computers to Process Information (optional)
Systems Understands Systems, Monitors and Corrects Performance
Technology Applies Technology to Task (optional)

Basic Skills Reading, Arithmetic, Listening, Speaking
Thinking Skills Creative Thinking, Decision Making, Problem Solving
Personal Qualities Responsibility, Self-Management
EFF: **Communication** Read with Understanding, Speak So Others Can Understand, Listen Actively, Observe Critically
Decision Making Use Math to Solve Problems and Communicate, Solve Problems and Make Decisions, Plan
Interpersonal Guide Others, Resolve Conflict and Negotiate, Advocate and Influence, Cooperate with Others
Lifelong Learning Reflect and Evaluate

Presentation 2: 10–15 min.

C Look at Roberto and Silvia's income and expenses. What is their total income? What are their total monthly expenses if they rent the home for $1500?

Review the budget with the students. There are a lot of new words for the students to learn. Help them understand their meanings by referring to the budget. As a quick competition, see which student can add up the expenses first.

D Look at the words in the box. Talk about these words with your teacher.

Ask the students if they think anything in the budget is too much. Look at the phone bill. Ask the students how much they pay a month for their phone bill. On a transparency of the budget you made or on the board, cross out *$180* and write *$100*. Ask the students how much they save.

Practice 2: 15–20 min.

E Silvia and Roberto need $432 more to rent the house. What can they do? Talk in groups.

Ask groups to figure out how Roberto and Silvia can save that much money each month. Get them started by giving them $80 for the phone bill.

Evaluation 2: 10–15 min.

Ask the groups to report to the class.

Presentation 3: 10 min.

Ask the students, *What rent can you afford?* Write this sentence on the board and help them see what it means by saying things like *I have the money to pay $1000 for rent. I can afford $1000. I don't have the money to pay $2000 for rent. I can't afford it.*

Practice 3: 20–30 min.

 Ask the students to do *Activity Bank 1 CD-ROM, Unit 4 Worksheet 11.* This worksheet will help students clarify what they can and can't afford. It also prepares them for doing their own budget in the next lesson.

Evaluation 3: 10–15 min.

Observe and discuss the activities. You may not want to have students report the information in exercise C because it may be confidential.

Application: 10–15 min.

F Do you have the same expenses? What other expenses do you have?

Students can do this on a spreadsheet if they like and total the amount of expenses that they have (optional).

Refer to the *Activity Bank 1 CD-ROM, Unit 4 Worksheet 12,* for additional practice reading budgets. *(optional)*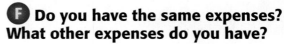

Instructor's Notes for Lesson 6

C Look at Roberto and Silvia's income and expenses. What is their total income? What are their total monthly expenses if they rent the home for $1500?

income—money you earn

expenses—money you spend

savings—money you save

budget—money you plan to spend

	Monthly income	Monthly expenses
Roberto's wages	$1800	
Silvia's wages	$1070	
Rent		$1500
Gas		$ 50
Electric		$ 125
Water		$ 32
Insurance		$ 91
Credit card		$ 150
Savings		$ 200
Phone		$ 180
Food		$ 800
Roberto's ESL class		$ 74
Other		$ 100
Total income	$2870	
Total expenses		$3302

D Look at the words in the box. Talk about these words with your teacher.

income   expenses   budget   total   insurance   savings

E Silvia and Roberto need $432 more to rent the house. What can they do? Talk in groups.

F Do you have the same expenses? What other expenses do you have?

LESSON 7 — Saving money

GOAL ▶ **Make a family budget**

Life Skill

A **Read about Roberto and Silvia's budget.**

Roberto and Silvia want to rent a new house, but they don't have the money. They decide to make changes in their budget. One of the changes is to save money on their phone bill.

B **Look at Roberto and Silvia's phone bill.**

Southwest Phone Company				
Mar 06	9:32am	Mexico	20 minutes	$35.48
Mar 13	9:00am	Mexico	32 minutes	$56.22
Mar 20	9:17am	Mexico	29 minutes	$51.27
Mar 27	9:14am	Mexico	19 minutes	$33.75

C **How much do they spend a month calling Mexico?**

```
           35.48
           56.22
           51.27
    +      33.75
  Total:  $176.72
```

D **How much is it if they talk only twenty minutes every week? How much do they save?**

```
             35.48
             35.48
             35.48
    +        35.48
  Total:    $141.92
  Savings:  $34.80
```

LESSON PLAN • Unit 4: Housing   LESSON 7 • Saving money

LESSON PLAN
Objective:
Make a family budget
Key vocabulary:
changes, test

Warm-up and Review: 10–15 min.

Ask students to report on the application activity from the previous lesson. Ask them to give you a list of the kinds of expenses. It is not necessary for them to give what the amount is here. Talk about expenses with the class.

Introduction: 1 min.

State objective: *Today we will learn more about budgets and make our own budgets.*

Presentation 1: 15–20 min.

A Read about Roberto and Sylvia's budget.

Read this as a class.

B Look at Roberto and Silvia's phone bill.

Ask questions to check for comprehension.

Practice 1: 10–15 min.

C How much do they spend a month calling Mexico?

Have students work in pairs to do calculations.

D How much is it if they talk only 20 minutes every week? How much do they save?

After students do the calculations in pairs or in groups, verify that they all have the same information. Now ask them in groups to see how they can take the same information and save an additional $30.

Evaluation 1: 10–15 min.

Ask groups to report their ideas to the class.

STANDARDS CORRELATIONS

CASAS: 1.5.1, 1.5.2
SCANS: **Resources** Money
Interpersonal Participates as a Member of a Team, Teaches Others New Skills, Exercises Leadership, Works with Cultural Diversity
Information Acquires and Evaluates Information, Organizes and Maintains Information, Interprets and Communicates Information
Systems Understands Systems, Monitors and Corrects Performance
Basic Skills Reading, Arithmetic, Listening, Speaking

Thinking Skills Creative Thinking, Decision Making, Problem Solving
EFF: **Communication** Read with Understanding, Speak So Others Can Understand, Listen Actively, Observe Critically
Decision Making Use Math to Solve Problems and Communicate, Solve Problems and Make Decisions, Plan
Interpersonal Guide Others, Resolve Conflict and Negotiate, Advocate and Influence, Cooperate with Others
Lifelong Learning Take Responsibility for Learning, Reflect and Evaluate

Presentation 2: 15–20 min.

Look at the picture. Ask questions. Look at the budget again. Review the vocabulary as you did in the previous lesson. Explain to them that this reflects the changes Roberto and Silvia plan to make. Help them understand the meaning of *actual.*

Practice 2: 10–15 min.

 E **Look at the new budget. What is the new total without savings? How much money can they put into savings?**

Ask students to do the calculations.

Evaluation 2:

Observe the activity.

Presentation 3: 10–15 min.

Review the budget vocabulary once again with the students.

Practice 3: 20–30 min.

Ask the students to write their own information next to the information on the budget in exercise F. Explain to them that they can do it on another piece of paper for confidentiality. You can also use the blank budget in the *Activity Bank 1 CD-ROM,* Unit 4 Worksheet 13. *(optional)*

Evaluation 3:

Observe the activity.

Application, (Part 1): 10–15 min.

Note: This Application has two parts. See page 76a for Part 2.

How much money can they put into savings?
Write the following exchange on the board:

Student A: *How are they saving money?*
Student B: *They are saving $25 on their electric bill.*

Teach students this exchange and have them practice it with a partner.

Silvia and Roberto want to use their savings to rent a new house.
What do you want to use your savings for?

 E Look at the new budget. What is the new total without savings? How much money can they put into savings?

Savings: $108

	Monthly income	New monthly budget
Roberto's wages	$1800	
Silvia's wages	$1070	
Rent		$1500
Gas		$ 50
Electric		$ 100
Water		$ 32
Insurance		$ 91
Credit card		$ 120
Savings		
Phone		$ 145
Food		$ 550
Roberto's ESL class		$ 74
Other		$100
Total income	$2870	
Total expenses		*$2762*

F In groups, make a budget. There are five people in your family.

	Income	Monthly expenses
Your family income	$3000	
Rent		
Gas		$ 50
Electric		$100
Water		$ 32
Food		
Life insurance		$ 91
Auto insurance		$200
Gasoline		
Phone		
Savings		
Other		
Total	$3000	

(Answers will vary.)

G Report your budget to the class. How much is the rent?

H What are your other expenses?

(Answers will vary.)

_____

_____

_____

_____

 I Active Task: Make a real budget with your family.

Application, (Part 2): 20–30 min.

F **In groups, make a budget. There are five people in your family.**

As with Team Projects, it might be useful to appoint roles for the family members.

G **Report your budget to the class. How much is the rent?**

Some groups can write their budgets on the board. Point out that rent should be about ⅓ of the family's income.

H **What are your other expenses?**

Have members from each group write other expenses on the board. Discuss new vocabulary.

I **Active Task: Make a real budget with your family.**

Ask volunteers to report their experiences to the class.

 Refer to the *Activity Bank 1 CD-ROM,* Unit 4 Worksheet 14, for additional practice with budgets and large purchases. *(optional)*

Instructor's Notes for Lesson 7

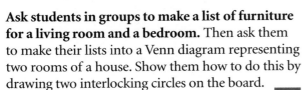

LESSON PLAN

Objective:
All previous objectives
Key vocabulary:
All previous Unit 4 vocabulary

Warm-up and Review: 10–15 min.

Ask students in groups to make a list of furniture for a living room and a bedroom. Then ask them to make their lists into a Venn diagram representing two rooms of a house. Show them how to do this by drawing two interlocking circles on the board.

Introduction: 3–5 min.

State objective: *Today we will review all that we have done in the past unit in preparation for the application project to follow.* Ask students as a class to try to recall all the goals of this unit without looking at their books. Then remind them of the goals they haven't mentioned.

Unit Goals: Identify basic housing, Talk about rooms in a house, Read and interpret classified ads, Use the present continuous and ask for information about housing, Use prepositions of location and identify furniture, Understand a family budget, Make a family budget.

Presentation 1, Practice 1, and Evaluation 1:

Do the Learner Log on page 80. Notes are adjacent to the page.

Presentation 2: 5–10 min.

Review abbreviations in classified ads by asking the students to identify them in the ad at the top of the page.

Practice 2: 15–20 min.

Ask the students to do exercises A and B in pairs and follow the instructions. Give assistance only when necessary.

A Read the classified ads.

B Write the information from the ads in the chart below. Then ask your partner questions to check your answers.

Evaluation 2: 3–5 min.

Observe student exchanges. Have a pair of students ask and answer the questions for exercise B before the class.

STANDARDS CORRELATIONS

CASAS: 1.4.1, 1.4.2, 1.5.1, 1.5.2, 7.1.1, 7.1.4, 7.4.1, 7.4.9, 7.4.10, 7.5.1
SCANS: **Resources** Allocates Money
Information Acquires and Evaluates Information, Organizes and Maintains Information, Interprets and Communicates Information
Basic Skills Reading, Writing, Arithmetic, Listening, Speaking

Personal Qualities Responsibility, Self-Management
EFF: **Communication** Read with Understanding, Speak So Others Can Understand, Listen Actively, Observe Critically
Decision Making Use Math to Solve Problems and Communicate, Solve Problems and Make Decisions, Plan
Lifelong Learning Take Responsibility for Learning, Reflect and Evaluate

Review

A Read the classified ads.

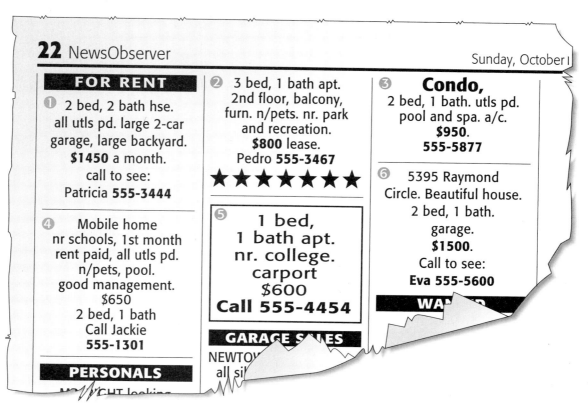

22 NewsObserver   Sunday, October I

FOR RENT

① 2 bed, 2 bath hse. all utls pd. large 2-car garage, large backyard. **$1450** a month. call to see: Patricia **555-3444**

④ Mobile home nr schools, 1st month rent paid, all utls pd. n/pets, pool. good management. $650 2 bed, 1 bath Call Jackie **555-1301**

PERSONALS

② 3 bed, 1 bath apt. 2nd floor, balcony, furn. n/pets. nr. park and recreation. **$800** lease. Pedro **555-3467**

★★★★★★★★

⑤ 1 bed, 1 bath apt. nr. college. carport $600 **Call 555-4454**

GARAGE SALES

③ **Condo,** 2 bed, 1 bath. utls pd. pool and spa. a/c. **$950**. 555-5877

⑥ 5395 Raymond Circle. Beautiful house. 2 bed, 1 bath. garage. **$1500**. Call to see: Eva **555-5600**

WANTED

B Write the information from the ads in the chart below. Then ask your partner questions to check your answers.

What type of housing is it?	How many bedrooms are there?	How many bathrooms are there?	Is it near anything?	How much is the rent?
1. *house*	2	2	*no*	*$1450*
2. *apartment*	3	1	park	*$800*
3. *condominium*	2	1	*no*	*$950*
4. *mobile home*	2	1	schools	*$650*
5. *apartment*	1	1	college	*$600*
6. *house*	2	1	*no*	*$1500*

C Look at the picture and fill in the missing prepositions.

1. The cat is _____*under*_____ the sofa.

2. The lamp is _____*next to*_____ the sofa.

3. The sofa is _____*between*_____ the end table and the lamp.

4. The book is _____*on*_____ the end table.

5. The painting is _____*over*_____ the sofa.

D Fill in the missing verbs.

1. Hi! _____*I am calling*_____ (I/call) about the apartment for rent.

2. What _____*are you doing*_____ (you/do) right now?

3. I'm busy. _____*I am working*_____ (I/work) right now.

4. Carmen and Ms. Rollings are on the phone. _____*They are making*_____ (they/make) an appointment.

5. Saud is at the rental agent's office. _____*He is looking*_____ (he/look) for a new apartment.

6. We want a new house. _____*We are reading*_____ (we/read) the classified ads right now.

E Write six words connected with making your budget.

| _____*income*_____ | _____*savings*_____ | _____*insurance*_____ |
| _____*utilities*_____ | _____*expenses*_____ | _____*total*_____ |

(Answers may vary. Suggestions above.)

Presentation 3: 5–10 min.

Review prepositions with the students by using hand signals.

Help the students understand how to do exercise C.

Review the form and use of the present continuous with the students.

Practice 3: 15–20 min.

 C Look at the picture and fill in the missing prepositions.

Refer to *Stand Out Grammar Challenge 1,* Unit 4, page 31 for more practice. *(optional)*

D Fill in the missing verbs.

 Refer to *Stand Out Grammar Challenge 1,* Unit 4, pages 26–27 for more practice. *(optional)*

E Write six words connected with making your budget.

Evaluation 3: 15–20 min.

Review answers as a class. Make note of areas for further review. Shorter classes may have completed exercises C, D, E, for homework.

Application: 1–2 days

The Team Project Activity on the following page is the application activity to be done on the next day of class.

 Post-Assessment: Use the *Stand Out* ExamView® Pro *Test Bank* for Unit 4. *(optional)*

Note: With the ExamView® Pro *Test Bank* you can design a post-assessment that focuses on what students have learned. It is designed for three purposes:
- To help students practice taking a test similar to current standardized tests.
- To help the teacher evaluate how much the students have learned, retained, and acquired.
- To help students see their progress when they compare their scores to the pre-test they took earlier.

Instructor's Notes for Unit 4 Review

Unit 4 Application Activity

> **TEAM PROJECT : PLANNING A DREAM HOME**
>
> Objective:
> Project designed to apply all the objectives of this unit.
> Products:
> floor plan of a home, classified ad

Introduction:

In a team of four or five, students will plan a home with a floor plan and make a classified ad to represent it. This project can extend over two days.

Stage 1: 5–10 min.

Form a team with four or five students. Students decide who will lead which steps as described on the student page. Provide well-defined directions on the board for how students should proceed. Explain to them that every task is to be done by each student. Students don't go to the next stage until the previous one is complete.

Stage 2: 5–10 min.

Choose a kind of home. Is it an apartment, house, condominium, or a mobile home? Ask students to choose how many bedrooms and bathrooms their dream home will have. Use *Activity Bank 1 CD-ROM*, Unit 4 Worksheet 15 to help groups to plan.

Stage 3: 20–30 min.

Make a floor plan of the home. Supply the students with paper and other materials. Use *Activity Bank 1 CD-ROM*, Unit 4 Worksheet 16.

Stage 4: 10–15 min.

Make a list of furniture for your home. Ask students to make a list of all the furniture they want in their home. Use *Activity Bank 1 CD-ROM*, Unit 4 Worksheet 17.

Stage 5: 15–25 min.

Decide where to put the furniture. Ask the students to describe to one another where the furniture goes and then draw it on their floor plans. Use *Activity Bank 1 CD-ROM*, Unit 4 Worksheet 16 again.

Stage 6: 15–20 min.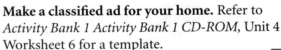

Make a classified ad for your home. Refer to *Activity Bank 1 Activity Bank 1 CD-ROM*, Unit 4 Worksheet 6 for a template.

Stage 7: 15–20 min.

Plan a presentation for the class and present your dream home. Consider videotaping these presentations. Students will prepare better for formal presentations if they are videotaped. Another approach would be for the students to videotape themselves and polish their presentations.

STANDARDS CORRELATIONS

CASAS: 1.4.1, 1.4.2, 4.8.1, 4.8.5
SCANS: **Resources** Allocates Time, Allocates Money, Allocates Material and Facility Resources
Interpersonal Participates as a Member of a Team, Teaches Others New Skills, Exercises Leadership, Works with Cultural Diversity
Information Acquires and Evaluates Information, Organizes and Maintains Information, Interprets and Communicates Information, Uses Computers to Process Information (optional)
Systems Understands Systems, Monitors and Corrects Performance, Improves and Designs Systems
Technology Applies Technology to Task (optional)
Basic Skills Reading, Writing, Arithmetic, Listening, Speaking

Thinking Skills Creative Thinking, Decision Making, Problem Solving, Seeing Things in the Mind's Eye, Knowing How to Learn, Reasoning
Personal Qualities Responsibility, Self-Esteem, Sociability, Self-Management, Integrity/Honesty
EFF: **Communication** Read with Understanding, Speak So Others Can Understand, Listen Actively, Observe Critically
Decision Making Use Math to Solve Problems and Communicate, Solve Problems and Make Decisions, Plan
Interpersonal Guide Others, Resolve Conflict and Negotiate, Advocate and Influence, Cooperate with Others
Lifelong Learning Take Responsibility for Learning, Reflect and Evaluate, Learn Through Research (optional), Use Information and Communications Technology (optional)

T E A M
P R O J E C T

Planning a dream home

In this project you will make a floor plan of a dream house, make a classified ad for it, and present it to the class.

1. Form a team with four or five students.

    In your team, you need:

Position	Job	Student Name
Student 1 Leader	See that everyone speaks English. See that everyone participates.	
Student 2 Architect	Draw a floor plan with help from the team.	
Student 3 Decorator	Place furniture in the plan with help from the team.	
Student 4 Spokesperson	With help from the team, organize a presentation to give to the class.	

2. Choose a kind of home. Is it an apartment, house, condominium, or a mobile home?

3. Make a floor plan of the home.

4. Make a list of furniture for your home. (See pages 69 and 71.)

5. Decide where to put the furniture. (See page 71.)

6. Make a classified ad for your home. (See pages 65 and 66.)

7. Plan a presentation for the class and present your dream home.

PRONUNCIATION

Listen to these words. Underline the words which sound like *air.*
Circle the words which sound like *ear.* **Then listen again and repeat.**

where   (near)   (here)   hair   (year)   wear   chair

(hear)   there   their   (clear)   stair   pair   (tear)

LEARNER LOG

Circle what you learned and write the page number where you learned it.

1. I can talk about types of housing.
   Yes   Maybe   No   Page _61–62_

2. I can talk about rooms in a home.
   Yes   Maybe   No   Page _63–64_

3. I can talk about things in a house.
   Yes   Maybe   No   Page _69–71_

4. I can understand classified ads.
   Yes   Maybe   No   Page _65–66_

5. I can use the present continuous.
   Yes   Maybe   No   Page _67–68_

6. I can use prepositions to describe location.
   Yes   Maybe   No   Page _70–71_

7. I can make a family budget.
   Yes   Maybe   No   Page _72–76_

Did you answer *No* to any questions? Review the information with a partner.

Rank what you like to do best from 1 to 6. 1 is your favorite activity. Your teacher will help you.

☐ practice listening

☐ practice speaking

☐ practice reading

☐ practice writing

☐ learn new words (vocabulary)

☐ learn grammar

In the next unit I want to practice more

_(Answers will vary.)_____.

Unit 4 Pronunciation and Learner Log

Pronunciation *(optional)*: 10–15 min.
(Audio CD Track 29)

Listen to these words. Underline the words which sound like *air*. Circle the words which sound like *ear*. Then listen again and repeat.

Play the recording and pause after each word.

For additional pronunciation practice: (The following words should be used for pronunciation practice, not for vocabulary instruction.)

Write the following word pairs on the board. Ask the students to copy the words. Read the words in bold and have the students underline the word they hear. Students should compare answers with a partner.

where–we're   share–sheer
fair–fear   pair–peer
bear–beer   lair–leer
stair–steer   rare–rear

Write the following sentences on the board for practice. Ask students to copy the sentences and then underline all the /air/ sounds and circle the /ear/ sounds. Review as a class.

There's no fair near.
Their idea is clear.
Share your fears.
We're near the stair.
Where is the bear?

Learner Log
Presentation 1: 10–15 min.

If needed, review for the students the purpose of the Learner Log.

Circle what you learned and write the page number where you learned it. Students research the answers individually. When they've finished, they should share their answers with a partner. These results need not be shared with the class.

Practice 1: 10–15 min.

Rank what you like to do best from 1 to 6. 1 is your favorite activity. Your teacher will help you. Results should be shared with the class in order to demonstrate to students how people learn differently.

Evaluation 1: 5–10 min.

In the next unit I want to practice more _____ . Students should fill in the blank with assistance from a partner or from you. They may focus on a skill (e.g., listening), on a vocabulary area (e.g., numbers), on grammar, and so on. Don't limit them to a single answer. Emphasize that the purpose of completing the sentence is to improve their self-assessment skills.

Instructor's Notes for Unit 4 Team Project, Pronunciation, and Learner Log

_____
_____
_____
_____
_____
_____
_____
_____
_____
_____
_____
_____
_____
_____

LESSON PLAN

Objective:
Identify places in the community
Key vocabulary:
neighborhood, lodging, medical care, residential, police, library, recreation, City Hall, hospital, tennis courts, dentist, doctor, hotel, motel, mobile home, apartment, playground, community, hostel, entertainment, map

Pre-Assessment: Use the *Stand Out* ExamView® Pro *Test Bank* for Unit 1 for. *(optional)*

Warm-up and Review: 10–15 min.

Ask students where they live. Help them use the preposition *in* before the name of their particular city. Ask the students what they like to do in their city. Tell them what you like to do in your city. Write *entertainment* on the board and list under it various activities you do for entertainment. Ask for students' ideas to add to the list.

Introduction: 3–5 min.

State objective: *Today and for the next several days, we are going to talk about our community.* Explain to students that a neighborhood is a small area made up of people living near one another. Write *neighborhood* on the board and state that you live in a neighborhood. Ask the students again where they live. Then explain that a community can be made up of a few or several neighborhoods.

Presentation 1: 10–15 min.

With books closed, ask students questions about different aspects of their community: *Where do you keep money? Where do you go if you have a heart attack? Where can you buy clothes? Where do you buy postage stamps?* Their answers will tell you how much students already know.

A Look at the web page from the Internet with your teacher. Talk about the different sections.

Ask students to open their books. Discuss the different buttons on the web page. Ask students to match the symbols and the section headings. They will probably need examples for some of the categories. Whether you want to discuss what a web page is or show them similar web pages is optional.

Ask students to name shopping centers in their communities. Then ask them to name nearby parks or recreation areas.

Practice 1: 10 min.

B Which of these are government offices?

Ask students in pairs or groups to figure out how they would find the answer to this question. Write the following questions on the board to extend the activity: *Where can you buy things?* and *Where can you spend money?*

Evaluation 1: 5–10 min.

Review student answers and list them on the board. Review the new vocabulary while you are doing this.

STANDARDS CORRELATIONS

CASAS: 2.5.1, 7.2.3
SCANS: **Interpersonal** Participates as a Member of a Team, Teaches Others New Skills, Exercises Leadership, Works with Cultural Diversity
Information Acquires and Evaluates Information, Organizes and Maintains Information, Interprets and Communicates Information
Systems Understands Systems, Monitors and Corrects Performance, Improves and Designs Systems

Basic Skills Listening, Speaking
EFF: **Communication** Speak So Others Can Understand, Listen Actively
Interpersonal Guide Others, Resolve Conflict and Negotiate, Cooperate with Others
Lifelong Learning Learn through Research (optional), Use Information and Communications Technology (optional)

UNIT 5

Our Community

GOALS

- Identify places in the community
- Read city maps
- Give directions
- Use prepositions of location
- Identify public agencies and services
- Use the telephone
- Use simple present and present continuous

LESSON 1 — Places in your neighborhood

GOAL ▶ Identify places in the community   *Vocabulary*

A Look at the web page from the Internet with your teacher. Talk about the different sections.

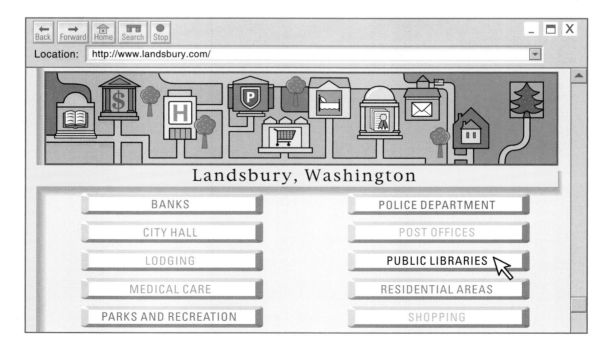

| Back | Forward | Home | Search | Stop |

Location: http://www.landsbury.com/

Landsbury, Washington

BANKS	POLICE DEPARTMENT
CITY HALL	POST OFFICES
LODGING	PUBLIC LIBRARIES
MEDICAL CARE	RESIDENTIAL AREAS
PARKS AND RECREATION	SHOPPING

B Which of these are government offices?
(Possible answers: City Hall, Parks and Recreation, Police Department, Post Offices, Public Libraries.)

GOAL ▶ **Identify places in the community**

C **Work in a group and put the words under the pictures.**

apartment	public pool	hotel	house
tennis courts	hospital	motel	playground
mobile home	doctor's office	dentist's office	hostel

Lodging

hotel

motel

hostel

Medical care

hospital

doctor's office

dentist's office

Parks and recreation

tennis courts

public pool

playground

Residential areas

apartment

mobile home

house

D **What places can you name in your community?** *(Answers will vary.)*

parks

_____

_____

banks

_____

_____

hotels

_____

_____

shopping centers

_____

_____

Presentation 2: 15–20 min.

Look at the words in the box. Review each one with the class by asking questions in a focused listening fashion. For example, *Where do you go to play with your children?* You can also add more context such as, *You and your family have a free day and . . . .* Help students listen for clues to discover which word you are aiming at. See Teaching Hints on focused listening.

Practice 2: 10–15 min.

C Work in a group and put the words under the pictures.

Evaluation 2: 5–10 min.

Ask groups to report their answers to the class. Compare answers and reinforce vocabulary.

Presentation 3: 15–20 min.

Prepare students for additional vocabulary practice by writing the following dialog on the board:
Student A: *Excuse me, I'm looking for <u>lodging</u>.*
Student B: *You're looking for <u>lodging</u>?*
Student A: *That's right. Do you know where I can go?*
Student B: *There are hotels over there.*
Student A: *Thank you so much.*

Show students how to insert other words from the box on this page into the dialog. For more help presenting dialogs, see Teaching Hints.

Practice 3: 10–15 min.

Ask students to practice the dialog with a partner by substituting information from exercise C.

See alternate ways to practice dialogs in Teaching Hints.

Evaluation 3: 10–15 min.

Ask volunteers to demonstrate in front of the class.

Application: 10–15 min.

D What places can you name in your community?

Ask student groups to list their answers. Encourage them to be specific and include the names of stores and other features of their community. On completion, ask each group to write its list on the board. Then discuss the lists as a class.

Refer to the *Activity Bank 1 CD-ROM*, Unit 5 Worksheet 1, for additional vocabulary activities about the community. *(optional)*

Pronunciation:

An optional pronunciation activity is found on the final page of this unit. This pronunciation activity may be introduced during any lesson in this unit, especially if students need practice with the sound /s/ in combination with other consonants. Go to pages 100/100a for Unit 5 Pronunciation.

Instructor's Notes for Lesson 1

_____

_____

_____

_____

_____

_____

_____

_____

_____

_____

_____

LESSON PLAN

Objectives:
Interpret maps and follow street directions
Key vocabulary:
straight ahead, block, right, left, zoo, high school, location, station, buffet

Warm-up and Review: 10–15 min.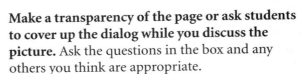

Make a big circle on the board to serve as the hub of a class clustering activity. Write *community* inside the circle. Draw lines out from the circle and make four secondary circles. Label one of them *Lodging.* Make lines from this circle to additional circles. Label these *hotels, motels,* and *hostels.*

With books closed, ask students to help you complete the cluster. Use *Medical Care, Parks and Recreation,* and *Residential Areas* for the remaining three secondary circles.

 A cluster like this can be found on the *Activity Bank 1 CD-ROM,* Unit 5 Worksheet 2. If you like, have students work in groups with the worksheet.

Introduction: 1 min.

Identify a well-known place in your community and ask students to tell you where it is located. They will probably give you the street name.

State objective: *Today you will learn to read a map and follow street directions in English.*

Presentation 1: 20–30 min.

Make a transparency of the page or ask students to cover up the dialog while you discuss the picture. Ask the questions in the box and any others you think are appropriate.

A Practice the conversation.

With books closed, ask students to listen to the dialog and identify where Gabriela wants to go. Then have the students open their books and listen again. Help students hear the proper intonation and rhythm.

B Practice these words with the teacher.

Use pantomime to demonstrate the meaning of these words and then play "Simon Says." Prepare students for exercise C by practicing the dialog as a class again.

Practice 1: 10–15 min.

C With a partner, make new conversations. Follow the example in exercise A.

See alternative ways to practice dialogs in Teaching Hints.

Evaluation 1: 5–10 min.

Ask for volunteers to present dialogs in front of the class.

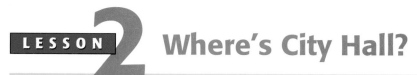

LESSON 2 — Where's City Hall?

GOAL ▶ Read city maps

Life Skill

Where is Gabriela?
What is she doing?

A **Practice the conversation.**

Alma: Excuse me, I need to find <u>City Hall</u>.
Gabriela: Of course. <u>Go straight ahead one block and turn right.</u>
Alma: <u>Straight ahead one block and turn right.</u>

Gabriela: Yes. <u>It's on the left.</u>
Alma: Thanks.
Gabriela: No problem.

B **Practice these words with the teacher.**

| left | right | straight ahead | block |

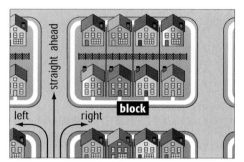

C **With a partner, make new conversations. Follow the example in exercise A.**

Place	Directions
City Hall	Go straight ahead one block and turn right. It's on the left.
Rosco's Buffet Restaurant	Go straight ahead two blocks and turn left. It's on the right.
the post office	Go straight ahead one block and turn right. Go one more block and turn left. It's on the right.
the zoo	Go straight ahead two blocks and turn right. It's on the right.
the high school	Go straight ahead two blocks and turn right. Go one more block and turn right. It's on the left.

D **Look at the map. You are in the car. Read the directions on page 83 and mark 1 to 5 in the squares on the map.**

1. City Hall
2. Rosco's Buffet Restaurant
3. the post office
4. the zoo
5. the high school

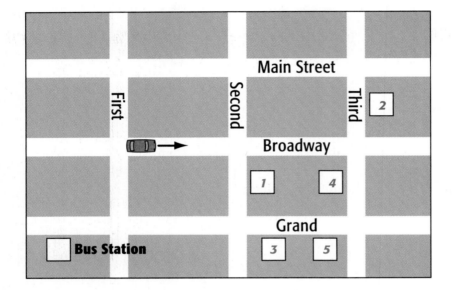

E **Where are the places? Complete the chart.**

Place	Location
Ex. the bus station	The bus station is on Grand.
City Hall	*The City Hall is on Second.*
Rosco's Buffet Restaurant	*Rosco's Buffet Restaurant is on Third.*
the post office	*The post office is on Grand.*
the zoo	*The zoo is on Third.*
the high school	*The high school is on Grand.*

 F **Active Task:** Find a map of your city on the Internet or in a local bookstore. Find similar places in your neighborhood and tell the class where they are.

Presentation 2: 10–15 min.

Study the map with students by asking such questions as *What street is next to First Street? Where is the car?* etc. Review the direction vocabulary with the class again, as you did in exercise B on the previous page.

Make an overhead or draw a similar map on the board. Find City Hall with the students by following the directions in exercise C on the previous page. This will prepare them for exercise D. After City Hall is found, see if students can give you directions to it without looking at the previous page.

Practice 2: 15–20 min.

D Look at the map. You are in the car. Read the directions on page 83 and mark 1 to 5 in the squares on the map.

Have students do this activity in pairs or groups. Then ask them to write out the directions to each of the locations without looking back at page 83. This might be difficult. Accept all attempts. They can also practice giving directions in pairs, with one student looking at page 83 to help his or her partner.

E Where are the places? Complete the chart.

Ask students to follow the example. Make sure they understand that they need to use the word **on,** not **in.** Also explain that we don't always use the word "street" in conversation, just the name.

Evaluation 2: 5–10 min.

Give directions to a prominent place nearby without naming it. See if students can identify it.

Presentation 3: 15–20 min.

Find the map on the *Activity Bank 1 CD-ROM,* Unit 5 Worksheet 3 (two pages). Read directions from exercise A to the students. Make sure the students have located the streets correctly before the practice.

Practice 3: 20–25 min.

Ask students to complete exercise B of *Activity Bank 1* Unit 5 Worksheet 3 with the building locations. This activity is a little more difficult, so it may be best to have students work in groups. An answer key is provided.

Evaluation 3: 10–15 min.

If possible, review the completed worksheet on a transparency with the students and clarify any questions they might have.

Application: 30–40 min.

Ask student groups to draw a map of the local area and to label places that they can identify. They should also draw a car somewhere on the map, then write out directions to several locations so the "driver" can reach them. For guidance, refer students again to the examples in exercise C on page 83.

F Active Task: Find a map of your city on the Internet or in your local bookstore. Find similar places in your neighborhood and tell the class where they are.

Refer to the *Activity Bank 1 CD-ROM,* Unit 5 Worksheet 4 (two pages), for a challenging map reading and information gap activity. *(optional)*

Instructor's Notes for Lesson 2

_____

_____

_____

_____

_____

_____

_____

LESSON PLAN

Objective:
Give directions
Key vocabulary:
mall, post office, movie theater, museum, park, turn around, turn left, right

Warm-up and Review: 10–15 min.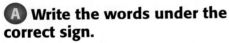

Give directions to a community landmark such as a bank, a store or a park. Ask students to identify it. Do this several times using different landmarks. You may also want to reinforce directional vocabulary by asking the class to stand. Every time you say the word *right* or *left,* they are to turn accordingly.

Introduction: 1 min.

State objective: *Today you are going to learn and practice giving street directions.*

Presentation 1: 10–15 min.

 **A Write the words under the correct sign.**

Do the exercise with the class. It is essentially review since the vocabulary is similar to that of the previous lesson.

Prepare students for focused listening. Remind them that they don't need to understand every word of the passages they will hear in exercise B. They should instead listen only for the vocabulary they practiced in exercise A. See Teaching Hints for vocabulary practice and focused listening work.

Practice 1: 10–15 min.

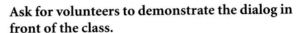 **B Listen and check the box for the words that you hear.** *(Audio CD Track 30)*

Make sure students understand what to do by going through the example with them. Play the recording as many times as needed.

Prepare students for exercise C by practicing the example dialog a few times with them. Make sure you stress the proper use of *in* and *on.*

Refer to Stand Out Grammar Challenge 1, Unit 5, page 34 for more practice. *(optional)*

C Ask four students where they live and fill in the chart below.

Evaluation 1: 10–15 min.

Ask for volunteers to demonstrate the dialog in front of the class.

STANDARDS CORRELATIONS

CASAS: 1.1.3, 1.9.4, 2.2.1, 2.2.5, 2.5.4
SCANS: **Interpersonal** Participates as a Member of a Team, Teaches Others New Skills, Exercises Leadership **Information** Acquires and Evaluates Information, Interprets and Communicates Information **Basic Skills** Listening, Speaking **Thinking Skills** Creative Thinking, Decision Making, Problem Solving

EFF: **Communication** Speak So Others Can Understand, Listen Actively, Observe Critically **Decision Making** Solve Problems and Make Decisions **Interpersonal** Guide Others, Cooperate with Others **Lifelong Learning** Take Responsibility for Learning, Reflect and Evaluate

 **LESSON 3** **Finding the right place**

GOAL ▶ **Give directions**

A Write the words under the correct sign.

| Turn around | Turn left | Go straight | Turn right |

Turn left   *Turn right*   *Go straight*   *Turn around*

 B Listen and check the box for the words that you hear.

	Turn right	Turn left	Turn around	Go straight
1. Directions to the mall.	x		x	
2. Directions to the post office.				x
3. Directions to the movie theater.	x		x	
4. Directions to the museum.	x	x		
5. Directions to the park.	x	x		x

C Ask four students where they live and fill in the chart below.

EXAMPLE:
Student A: Where do you live, Herman?
Student B: I live <u>in</u> Landsbury <u>on</u> Naple Avenue.

| <u>in</u> the city |
| <u>on</u> the street |

Student Name	City	Street
Ex. Herman	Landsbury	Naple Avenue
1. *(Answers will vary.)*		
2.		
3.		
4.		

D Draw a map from your school to your home.

> *(Answers will vary.)*

E Practice giving directions to your home with three students. Use your map.

EXAMPLE:
Student A: Can I visit you at your home?
Student B: Sure, come over any time.
Student A: Where do you live?
Student B: I live in Landsbury on Ludwig Avenue.
Student A: Can you give me directions?
Student B: Sure, look at the map. From the school, turn right on Snyder and left on Ludwig.
Student A: Thanks.

F Listen to your partner's directions and draw a map to his or her home.

> *(Answers will vary.)*

G Look at your map in exercise F and your partner's map in exercise D. Are they the same or different?

Presentation 2: 10–15 min.

On the board, draw a map from the school to a familiar landmark. Ask volunteers to give directions by looking at the map.

Practice 2: 10–15 min.

D **Draw a map from your school to your home.**

After students finish their maps, ask them in pairs to practice giving directions for getting home from school.

Evaluation 2:

Observe student practice.

Presentation 3: 10–15 min.

Review the direction vocabulary again. Ask individuals where they live and how to get there. Draw a few maps on the board based on the directions you receive.

Present the dialog in exercise E. Students should work on rhythm and intonation. See the section on presenting dialogs in Teaching Hints.

Practice 3: 20–30 min.

E **Practice giving directions to your home with three students. Use your map.**

F **Listen to your partner's directions and draw a map to his or her home.**

Evaluation 3: 10–15 min.

G **Look at your map in exercise F and your partner's map in exercise D. Are they the same or different?**

Ask a few students to report their answers.

Application: 20–30 min.

Ask students in groups to write directions for getting from school to a well-known location in the community. The best way to proceed is to have students write the directions on note cards or slips of paper. They should provide only the directions, not the name of the destination. Have them make multiple copies, one for each group in the class. Remind students that they must use the imperative when writing directions. They learned this form in a previous unit.

Refer to *Stand Out Grammar Challenge 1,* Unit 5, page 34 for more practice with the imperative. (*optional*)

Collect all the cards or papers with the directions and distribute them to the other groups. The task now is for groups to identify destinations by following the directions provided by the other groups.

Refer to the *Activity Bank 1 CD-ROM,* Unit 5 Worksheet 5, for an additional activity related to giving and following directions. (*optional*)

Instructor's Notes for Lesson 3

_____

_____

_____

_____

_____

_____

_____

_____

_____

_____

_____

_____

_____

> **LESSON PLAN**
>
> Objective:
> Use prepositions of location
> Key vocabulary:
> apparel, pets, shoes, toys, gifts,
> steakhouse

Warm-up and Review: 10–15 min.

Write *mall* on the board and ask if students know the word. Define it for them. Ask them in groups to make a list quickly of all the kinds of stores they're likely to find at a mall. After they have finished, ask groups to send a representative to other groups and try to add three or four more types of stores to their lists.

Ask one group to write its list on the board and the other groups in turn to add to the list without repeating any items.

Introduction: 5 min.

Review with students the prepositions of location they have already learned. They should know *in, under, next to, between.*

State objective: *Today we are going to learn more prepositions of location related to giving directions.*

Presentation 1: 15–20 min.

Ask students to look at the mall directory and briefly discuss different kinds of stores with them. As a class, compare the final Warm-up list with the directory. Make sure students understand the mall's numbering system by asking them to point to locations when you give the names of various stores. Also go over the categories. Ask such

questions as *Where can you eat? Where can you buy a birthday present? Where can you buy a dog?*

Practice 1: 10 min.

(A) Answer the questions about the directory above.

Ask students to do this exercise in pairs.

(B) Scan the directory. Ask your partner.

Refer to *Stand Out Grammar Challenge 1,* Unit 5, pages 34–35 for more practice. *(optional)*

Evaluation 1: 5–10 min.

Review work in student books.

STANDARDS CORRELATIONS

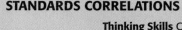

CASAS: 1.1.3, 1.3.7, 2.5.4, 7.2.6, 7.4.1
SCANS: Interpersonal Participates as a Member of a Team, Teaches Others New Skills, Exercises Leadership
Information Acquires and Evaluates Information, Organizes and Maintains Information
Systems Understands Systems
Basic Skills Reading, Listening, Speaking

Thinking Skills Creative Thinking, Decision Making, Problem Solving, Seeing Things in the Mind's Eye, Reasoning
EFF: Communication Read with Understanding, Speak So Others Can Understand, Listen Actively, Observe Critically
Decision Making Solve Problems and Make Decisions, Plan
Interpersonal Guide Others, Resolve Conflict and Negotiate, Advocate and Influence, Cooperate with Others

LESSON 4 Is it next to the music store?

| GOAL ▶ | Use prepositions of location | *Grammar* |

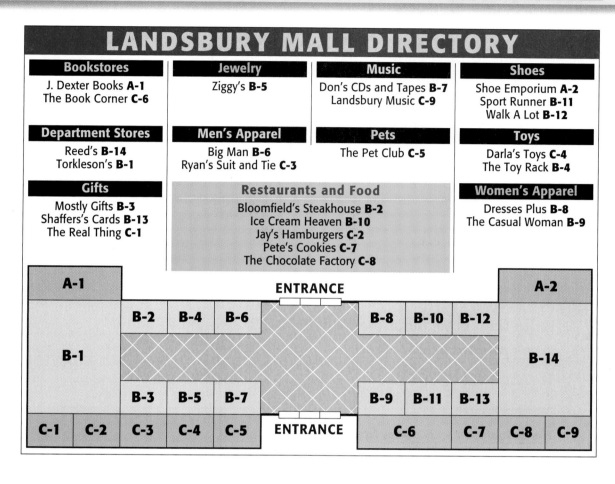

LANDSBURY MALL DIRECTORY

Bookstores	**Jewelry**	**Music**	**Shoes**
J. Dexter Books **A-1** The Book Corner **C-6**	Ziggy's **B-5**	Don's CDs and Tapes **B-7** Landsbury Music **C-9**	Shoe Emporium **A-2** Sport Runner **B-11** Walk A Lot **B-12**

Department Stores	**Men's Apparel**	**Pets**	**Toys**
Reed's **B-14** Torkleson's **B-1**	Big Man **B-6** Ryan's Suit and Tie **C-3**	The Pet Club **C-5**	Darla's Toys **C-4** The Toy Rack **B-4**

Gifts	**Restaurants and Food**	**Women's Apparel**
Mostly Gifts **B-3** Shaffers's Cards **B-13** The Real Thing **C-1**	Bloomfield's Steakhouse **B-2** Ice Cream Heaven **B-10** Jay's Hamburgers **C-2** Pete's Cookies **C-7** The Chocolate Factory **C-8**	Dresses Plus **B-8** The Casual Woman **B-9**

Mall map:

A-1 | ENTRANCE | A-2
B-2 | B-4 | B-6 | B-8 | B-10 | B-12
B-1 | | B-14
B-3 | B-5 | B-7 | B-9 | B-11 | B-13
C-1 | C-2 | C-3 | C-4 | C-5 | ENTRANCE | C-6 | C-7 | C-8 | C-9

A Answer the questions about the directory above.

1. What store is next to Big Man? _____ *The Toy Rack* _____

2. What store is next to Dresses Plus? _____ *Ice Cream Heaven* _____

3. What store is between The Pet Club and Ryan's Suit and Tie? _____ *Darla's Toys* _____

4. What store is between Landsbury Music and Pete's Cookies? _____ *The Chocolate Factory* _____

B Scan the directory. Ask your partner. *(Answers may vary. Suggestions below.)*

1. Where can you buy a dog? **The Pet Club**

2. Where can you buy a suit for a man? *Ryan's Suit and Tie*

3. Where can you buy ice cream? *Ice Cream Heaven*

4. Where can you buy tennis shoes? *Sport Runner*

5. Where can you eat a steak? *Bloomfields Steakhouse*

C Study the examples with your teacher.

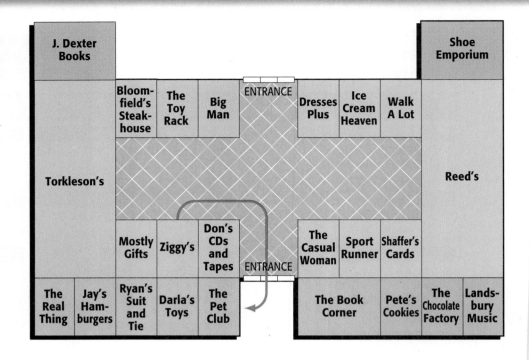

D Write sentences about the mall. Follow the examples below. *(Answers will vary.)*

Ziggy's is around the corner from the Pet Club.

1. _____

2. _____

The Casual Woman is across from Dresses Plus.

1. _____

2. _____

Landsbury Music is on the corner.

1. _____

2. _____

Sport Runner is between Shaffer's Cards and The Casual Woman.

1. _____

2. _____

The Book Corner is next to Pete's Cookies.

1. _____

2. _____

Presentation 2: 15–20 min.

C Study the examples with your teacher.

Present and quiz the students on the new vocabulary. Ask several questions about the mall. Do a little focused listening by asking the students to identify locations after you give directions using more complicated paragraphs. For example, you might say:

I need to get to the mall. There are so many things I need. I especially need a pair of shoes. I think there are 3 shoe stores in the mall. Maybe I will go to the one across from Ice Cream Heaven. That way I can eat some of their delicious ice cream later.

Help students understand that they don't need to understand everything you say to be able to identify the location.

Practice 2: 15–20 min.

Ask students to write the sentences in the following exercises independently.

D Write sentences about the mall. Follow the examples below.

Evaluation 2: 5–10 min.

Ask students to peer edit and then call on volunteers to write their sentences on the board. Don't over-correct, but make sure students use proper and correctly spelled prepositions. Also make sure they use the complete form (*across from,* for example).

Refer to the *Activity Bank 1 CD-ROM,* Unit 5 Worksheet 6, for additional activities using prepositions as well as listening to and giving directions. The listening is on *AB 1 CD-ROM* Track 9. *(optional)*

Presentation 3: 10–15 min.

Present the dialog in exercise E. Practice correct rhythm and intonation. See Teaching Hints for help with presenting dialogs.

E Practice the conversation.

Ask students to practice the dialog with a partner several times.

Remind students of how an information gap activity is conducted. Students in shorter classes may work on this activity at home with friends or family members, or they can simply write out the information for homework.

Practice 3: 15–20 min. [3]

F Student A, cover page 88 and repeat the conversation. Write the information on the directory. Student B, look at page 88 to answer.

G Student B, cover page 88 and repeat the conversation. Write the information on the directory. Student A, look at page 88 to answer.

Evaluation 3:

Observe student dialogs.

Application: 30–40 min.

Ask students in groups of four or five to design a directory of their own mall. Supply paper and additional supplies if necessary.

Instructor's Notes for Lesson 4

E **Practice the conversation.**

Student A: Excuse me. Can you help me?
Student B: Sure.
Student A: Where is The Toy Rack?
Student B: It's across from Ziggy's.

F **Student A, cover page 88 and repeat the conversation. Write the information on the directory. Student B, look at page 88 to answer.**

Where is Ice Cream Heaven?
Where is Shoe Emporium?   *(Answers will vary.)*
Where is The Pet Club?

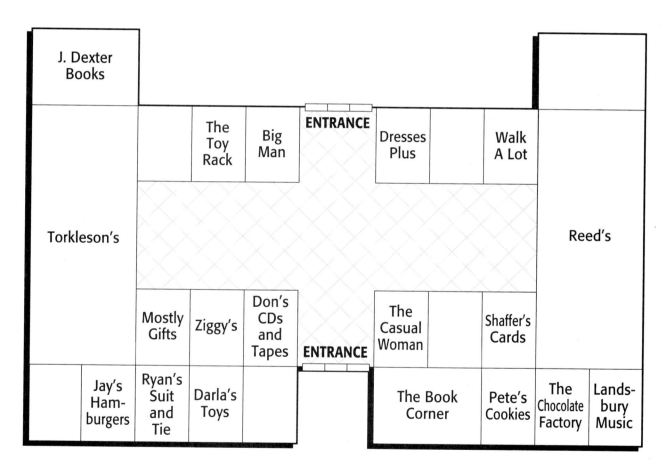

G **Student B, cover page 88 and repeat the conversation. Write the information on the directory. Student A, look at page 88 to answer.**

Where's Sport Runner?
Where's The Real Thing?   *(Answers will vary.)*
Where's Bloomfield's Steakhouse?

Making a phone call

GOAL ▶ Identify public agencies and services	Vocabulary

A What are these places? Talk about the places with your teacher.

D

A

C

E

B

F

B Listen and write the letter under the picture.

C Draw a line from the picture to the service.

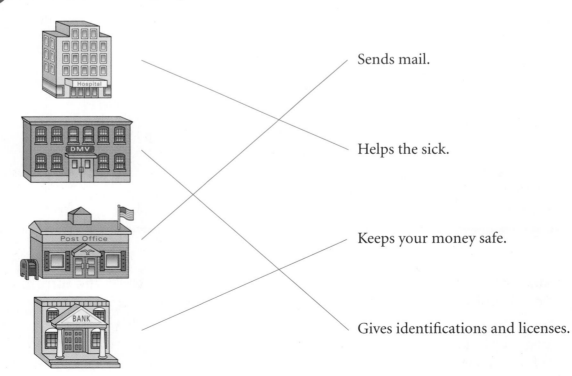

Sends mail.

Helps the sick.

Keeps your money safe.

Gives identifications and licenses.

LESSON PLAN

Objective:
Identify public agencies and services
Key vocabulary:
DMV, bank, post office, fire station, hospital, police station, identification, licenses, keep, sick, mail, service

Warm-up and Review: 10–15 min.

Ask groups to share their directories from the application activity of the previous lesson.

Introduction: 10 min.

Write the following words on the board: *sick people, money, driver's license,* and *letters.* Ask students in their groups to discuss each word quickly. Ask them to name what places in the community they think of when they see these words. Have groups report to the class.

State objective: *Today we are going to learn about different public places in the community.*

Presentation 1: 15–20 min.

Look at the picture with the students.

A What are these places? Talk about the places with your teacher.

Prepare students for focused listening by eliciting from them all the words they associate with each agency in exercise A. List all their responses on the board, arranging them according to agency. In the following practice, they are to listen for these words, which will help them identify the agency. You can also list these places on a cluster diagram if you wish. See Teaching Hints for an explanation of focused listening.

Practice 1: 10–15 min.

B Listen and write the letter under the picture. *(Audio CD Track 31)*

Play the recording. You may need to play it a few times to complete this activity.

C Draw a line from the picture to the service.

Help students understand that a *service* takes place when someone does something for you.

Evaluation 1: 5 min.

Review answers with the students.

STANDARDS CORRELATIONS

CASAS: 2.1.1, 2.5.1, 2.5.2, 2.5.3, 7.2.3, 7.2.6
SCANS: **Interpersonal** Participates as a Member of a Team, Teaches Others New Skills
Information Acquires and Evaluates Information, Interprets and Communicates Information
Technology Applies Technology to Task (optional)
Basic Skills Listening, Speaking
Thinking Skills Creative Thinking, Decision Making, Problem Solving, Seeing Things in the Mind's Eye, Knowing How to Learn, Reasoning

EFF: **Communication** Speak So Others Can Understand, Listen Actively, Observe Critically
Decision Making Solve Problems and Make Decisions
Interpersonal Guide Others, Cooperate with Others
Lifelong Learning Reflect and Evaluate, Learn through Research, Use Information and Communications Technology (optional)

Presentation 2: 10–15 min.

Look at the picture with the class and ask the questions in the box. Ask additional questions about the phone numbers on the notepad. Ask students if they have any special numbers that they keep close to the phone.

Present the dialog. See Teaching Hints for suggestions. Help students see how to substitute information. Then ask them to listen to the dialog. Play the recording.

Practice 2: 10–15 min.

 D Listen to the conversation. Practice the dialog with new information.
(Audio CD Track 32)

For alternative ways to practice dialogs, see Teaching Hints.

Evaluation 2: 5–10 min.

Ask for volunteers to demonstrate in front of the class.

Presentation 3: 10–15 min.

Write *burning* and *badge* on the board. Ask student groups to discuss briefly both words and to identify places in the community with which the words can be linked. Steer them with clues to the *fire* and *police departments*.

Practice 3: 10–15 min.

Ask students in groups to write down an additional problem that might cause them to go to the places listed on the chart in exercise D. Also ask them to write down reasons for calling the fire and police departments.

Ask students to create new dialogs based on the new information they have written down and to practice in pairs.

Evaluation 3: 10–15 min.

Ask volunteers to demonstrate in front of the class.

Application: 10–30 min.

E Make a bar graph of the class. How many students have been to these places in the United States?

Poll the class and put the results on the board. Ask student groups to discuss the results before each student fills in the graph shown in his or her book. Now ask groups to identify two agencies or services (such as the *public library* and *city* or *town hall*) not yet brought up and to make a bar graph along the lines of the one in their books. Groups conduct their own poll by sending representatives to all other groups to obtain the appropriate information.

F Active Task: Find a telephone directory or go to the Yellow Pages on the Internet. Make a list of important numbers for you and put them by the phone.

Refer to the *Activity Bank 1 CD-ROM*, Unit 5 Worksheet 7, for additional activities related to identifying important agencies and their services. *(optional)*

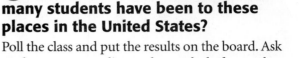

Instructor's Notes for Lesson 5

What are they doing?
Who are they calling?

D **Listen to the conversation. Practice the conversation with new information.**

Emanuela: I need to call the <u>hospital</u>.
Lisa: Why?
Emanuela: <u>My sister is very sick.</u>
Lisa: The number is <u>555-7665</u>.

Place	Problem
hospital	My sister is very sick.
bank	I need to see how much money I have.
DMV	I need a new license.
post office	The mail isn't here.

E **Make a bar graph of the class. How many students have been to these places in the United States?**

(Class works together to answer.)

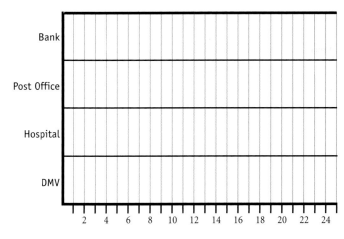

F **Active Task:** Find a telephone directory or go to the Yellow Pages on the Internet. Make a list of important numbers for you and put them by the phone.

GOAL ▶ **Use the telephone**

Gabriela Ramirez
37 Main Street
Landsbury WA 99037

Familia Ramirez
Av. Callao 423
1022 Buenos Aires
Argentina

Who is the package from?
Who is the package to?

A **Read about Gabriela's problem.**

Gabriela needs to go to the post office. She wants to send a package to her family in Buenos Aires, Argentina. She doesn't know what to say at the post office.

B **Talk in a group. What can Gabriela do? Who can help her?**

She can ask *(Answers will vary.)*_____

She can call _____

She can go _____

C **Listen to Gabriela on the phone and answer the questions.**

1. Who does she talk to? _____ *a* _____
   a. her friend David
   b. a machine
   c. David, her brother

2. When does she want to go to the post office? _____ *b* _____
   a. today
   b. tomorrow
   c. Saturday

LESSON PLAN

Objective:
Use the telephone
Key vocabulary:
information, questions, call me back,
answering machine

Warm-up and Review: 10–15 min.

Take a class poll. Ask *Who is nervous when you answer the phone here in the United States? Who likes to call agencies to get information? Who doesn't like to leave messages on answering machines? Who has problems understanding messages on answering machines?*

Students may not at first understand all these questions so ask them with appropriate gestures and explanations. Write the questions on the board and tally the affirmative responses.

Introduction: 1 min.

State objective: *Today we will learn how to use the phone and leave messages.*

Presentation 1: 15–20 min.

Look at the picture on this page with students and ask the questions in the box. Ask any additional questions you consider appropriate.

A Read about Gabriela's problem.

Read the short passage as a class. Ask some comprehension questions to make sure most of the students understand.

B Talk in a group. What can Gabriela do? Who can help her?

Students discuss these questions in groups before answering them in their books.

Prepare students for focused listening by previewing the questions in exercise C before you play the recording. See Teaching Hints.

Practice 1: 15–20 min.

C Listen to Gabriela on the phone and answer the questions. *(Audio CD Track 33)*

Play the recording. You can ask additional questions if you wish. Write the following questions on the board (optional): *What does Gabriela say she needs? When will David get back to her?* You may need to play the recording several times.

Evaluation 1:

Observe the activity.

STANDARDS CORRELATIONS

CASAS: 2.1.7, 2.1.8
SCANS: **Interpersonal** Participates as a Member of a Team, Teaches Others New Skills
Information Acquires and Evaluates Information, Organizes and Maintains Information, Interprets and Communicates Information
Systems Understands Systems, Monitors and Corrects Performance
Basic Skills Reading, Writing, Listening, Speaking

Thinking Skills Creative Thinking, Decision Making, Problem Solving
***EFF:* Communication** Read with Understanding, Convey Ideas in Writing, Speak So Others Can Understand, Listen Actively, Observe Critically
Decision Making Solve Problems and Make Decisions, Plan
Interpersonal Guide Others, Cooperate with Others
Lifelong Learning Take Responsibility for Learning, Reflect and Evaluate

Presentation 2: 5–10 min.

With their books closed, help students understand what makes a good phone message. Write *name, address, phone number, age, marital status,* and *reason for calling* on the board. Ask students to identify which of these elements are good in a phone message.

D Look at the messages. Talk in a group. Circle three good messages.

Write a grid on the board with 6 rows for the 6 examples in this exercise. Ask students to make a similar grid after they have picked 3 good messages.

Name	Reason	Phone
1.		
2.		

Practice 2: 15–20 min.

Ask students to enter the information from exercise D into the grid they created. Tell them to write *none* if information is missing.

Evaluation 2: 5–10 min.

Discuss the 3 good messages with the class.

Presentation 3: 10–15 min.

E There are three important parts of a message. Read the chart with your teacher.

Show students how to use the chart information to prepare them for exercise F. Ask students to draw a separate chart and add 3 more reasons for calling. You might want to explain how to use *because* to show students how to say *I'm calling because . . . .*

Practice 3: 10–15 min.

F Practice leaving a message with two people. Student A writes the information he or she hears.

Be sure that students reverse roles here. If you want to extend this activity, you will find on the

Activity Bank 1 CD-ROM, Unit 5 Worksheet 8 which provides additional reasons for calling *(optional).*

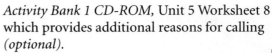

Evaluation 3: 10–15 min.

Ask for volunteers to come to the front to demonstrate leaving messages.

Application: 10–15 min.

Write the following scenarios on the board:
You are at the market and you are late for an appointment at the doctor's office.

You are sick and can't go to school or work.

You or your wife had a baby and you want your family to know.

Ask students in pairs to choose one of the scenarios and to write an appropriate message to leave on an answering machine. Then ask them to practice the message and demonstrate in front of the class. Additional message pad forms are on the *Activity Bank 1 CD-ROM,* Unit 5 Worksheet 9 if you want to give students more message practice *(optional).*

Refer to the *Activity Bank 1 CD-ROM,* Unit 5 Worksheet 10 for additional reading and listening practice with phone messages. The listening is on *AB 1 CD-ROM* Track 10. *(optional)*

Instructor's Notes for Lesson 6

_____

_____

_____

_____

_____

_____

_____

_____

_____

D **Look at the messages. Talk in a group. Circle three good messages.**

1. This is Gabriela. I need help. I want to send a package. Please call me at 543-2344. Thanks.

2. Call me. OK?

3. I am Gabriela. My phone number is 543-2344. Thanks.

4. This is your friend Gabriela from school. Can you help me? Thanks.

5. It is 3 P.M. on Friday. This is your friend Gabriela. My number is 543-2344. Please call me. I have a question for you. Thanks.

6. This is Gabriela. My number is 543-2344. I have a little problem. Can you call me back? Thanks.

E **There are three important parts of a message. Read the chart with your teacher.**

Your name	Reason for calling	Phone
This is Gabriela.	I have a question.	My number is 543-2344.
	I want to talk.	Call me at 543-2344.
	I need some information.	Can you call me back at 543-2344?

F **Practice leaving a message with two people. Student A writes the information he or she hears.**

EXAMPLE:

Student A: Hello, this is Gabriela. I can't come to the phone right now. Please leave a message.

Student B: This is Ramon. I have a question. My number is 543-2344.

(Answers will vary.)

Name: _____

Phone: _____

Reason for calling: _____

_____

Name: _____

Phone: _____

Reason for calling: _____

_____

LESSON 7 — Writing a letter

GOAL ▶ Use simple present and present continuous | **Grammar**

A **Read Gabriela's letter to her family.**

> January 24, 2003
>
> Dear Mom and Dad,
>
>   I need to practice so I'm writing to you in English. I hope you understand. I am happy. I study English every day. I work at the market on First Street. I am a cashier.
>
>   Landsbury is a beautiful place. There are stores and restaurants. I sometimes eat at Bloomfield's Steakhouse in the Mall. The fire station is around the corner from my apartment. The bookstore is next to the fire station. My community is quiet. I am sending you a special map of the town with this letter.
>
>   I love you. Can you write me soon? I miss you.
>
> Love,
>
> Gabriela

B **Ask and answer with a partner.** *(Oral answers may vary. Suggested responses below.)*

1. Where does Gabriela sometimes eat? *She eats at Bloomfield's Steakhouse in the Mall.*

2. When does Gabriela study English? *She studies English every day.*

3. Is Gabriela's community quiet or noisy? *Her community is quiet.*

4. Where does she work? *She works at the market on First Street.*

C **Answer the questions.**

1. Where do you like to eat? _(Answers will vary.)_____

2. When do you study English? _____

3. Is your community quiet or noisy? _____

4. Do you work? If yes, where do you work? _____

LESSON PLAN

Objectives:
Use the present continuous and the simple present, write a letter
Key vocabulary:
market, cashier, quiet, I miss you, noisy, beautiful

Warm-up and Review: 5–10 min.

Ask for more volunteers to read to the class the messages from the previous lesson. As they read, have students who are listening write down the information. There are multiple message forms on Worksheet 9 found in Unit 5 of the *Activity Bank 1 CD-ROM (optional)*.

Introduction: 1 min.

Ask students if they have relatives in other countries. Find out specifically. Ask those who don't if they have friends abroad. Ask students if they write letters to family and friends often, rarely, or never.

State objective: *Today you will learn to use the present continuous and the simple present. You will also write a letter to your family or friend in English.*

Presentation 1: 10–15 min.

Before students open their books, ask if they know which words to use in starting a personal letter. Also ask if they know how to close a letter. Tell students that they are going to read a letter by themselves. Explain that reading a letter containing unfamiliar words is a little like focused listening. Suggest that they read through Gabriela's

letter without stopping and then answer the questions in exercises B and C. They should not use dictionaries.

Practice 1: 10–15 min.

A Read Gabriela's letter to her family.

Ask students to read the letter by themselves in preparation for work with a partner.

B Ask and answer with a partner.

Each partner asks two questions and answers the other two.

C Answer the questions.

Ask students to answer the questions in complete sentences. This task will help them write their letters in the application part of this lesson.

Evaluation 1: 15–20 min.

Review answers in student books, then ask volunteers to write their sentences on the board.

STANDARDS CORRELATIONS

CASAS: 0.2.3
SCANS: **Interpersonal** Participates as a Member of a Team, Teaches Others New Skills, Uses Computers to Process Information (optional)
Technology Applies Technology to Task (optional)
Basic Skills Reading, Writing, Listening, Speaking
Personal Qualities Self-Management

EFF: **Communication** Read with Understanding, Convey Ideas in Writing, Speak So Others Can Understand, Listen Actively, Observe Critically
Interpersonal Guide Others, Cooperate with Others
Lifelong Learning Take Responsibility for Learning, Reflect and Evaluate

Presentation 2: 10–15 min.

D Study the charts with your teacher.

Give students examples of the present continuous. Base your examples on classroom actions so students grasp that the present continuous refers to what is happening at the moment. Contrast this with the simple present, which is used for things we do regularly. Since Gabriela's letter contains two examples of the present continuous, refer to it so students can see the difference in forms clearly. Explain the use of contracted forms of the verb.

Practice 2: 10–15 min.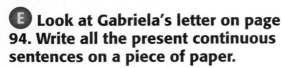

E Look at Gabriela's letter on page 94. Write all the present continuous sentences on a piece of paper.

F Look at Gabriela's letter on page 94. Write all the simple present sentences on a piece of paper.

G What are you doing right now? Write two sentences.

Evaluation 2: 10–15 min.

Review the sentences with the students and ask volunteers to write their responses to exercise G on the board.

Presentation 3: 10–15 min.

Prepare students for dictation by referring back to page 94. Ask them to write the date and *Dear Mom and Dad* on a piece of paper. Advise students that at this level it is very difficult to listen and write at the same time. Explain that in taking dictation, they should listen first and then repeat to themselves what they heard <u>before</u> they begin to write. Allow students to copy this from page 94: *I need to practice so I'm writing to you in English. I hope you understand.* Finally, ask them to close their books.

Practice 3: 10–15 min.

Read the following letter aloud to the students at natural speed. Have students listen without writing anything. Then read the letter again, a sentence at a time after the initial two sentences. Ask students to write down what they hear. Repeat each sentence three times. When you have finished, read the letter one more time from beginning to end at natural speed.

January 24, 2002

Dear Mom and Dad,

I need to practice so I'm writing to you in English. I hope you understand. I am studying right now. I hope I can speak English well soon. My teacher is Mrs. Brooks. She is a very good teacher.

The school is across from a mall. The mall has many stores. I like the ice cream shop. It is next to the restaurant. I eat lunch at the restaurant every day. I hope you are happy.

Love,

Gabriela

Ask students to work on their dictated letters in groups. They should share and edit until they feel they have the letter correct.

Refer to *Stand Out Grammar Challenge 1*, Unit 5, pages 36–37 for more practice. *(optional)*

Evaluation 3: 10–15 min.

Ask volunteers to write the letter one sentence at a time on the board, allowing the other students to peer correct. Ask questions that will prompt students to reflect on the dictation activity itself. For example, *Was it hard or easy? Did other students help you?*

D Study the charts with your teacher.

Present continuous			
Subject	be	Base + ing	
I	am (I'm)	writing	right now.
he, she, it	is (she's)	walking	today.
you, we, they	are (they're)	reading	

100%		50%		0%
always	often	sometimes	rarely	never

Simple present		
Subject	Verb	Example sentence
I	study	I always study English.
he, she, it	works	She never works in a store.
you, we, they	eat	They sometimes eat steak.

E Look at Gabriela's letter on page 94. Write all the present continuous sentences on a piece of paper.

F Look at Gabriela's letter from page 94. Write all the simple present sentences on a piece of paper.

G What are you doing right now? Write two sentences.

1. __(Answers will vary.)_____

2. _____

> **Spelling note:**
> write—writing   sit—sitting
> drive—driving   hit—hitting

Write a letter to a friend.

Date: _____   *(Letters will vary.)*

Dear _____

_____ *I need to practice, so I'm writing to you in English. I hope you understand.* _____

_____

_____

_____

_____

_____

_____

_____

_____

_____

_____

_____

_____

_____

_____

_____

_____

_____

_____

_____

_____

Your friend, _____

_____

Application: 30–40 min.

H Write a letter to a friend.

The letter can be written on the computer. See Teaching Hints for suggestions. Advise students to use Gabriela's letter on page 94 as a guide. Some students may need to finish this activity at home.

Encourage students to search for and identify common errors in their work before handing it in. If necessary, make a list of common errors and ask students to check their work for these errors.

Refer to *Stand Out Grammar Challenge 1,* Unit 5, pages 38–39 for more practice. *(optional)*

Refer to the *Activity Bank 1 CD-ROM,* Unit 5 Worksheet 11 (three pages), for additional practice with the simple present and present continuous. *(optional)*

Instructor's Notes for Lesson 7

REVIEW

Objective:
All previous objectives
Key vocabulary:
all previous Unit 5 vocabulary

Warm up and Review: 10–15 min.

Ask for volunteers to share their letters from the previous application activity.

Introduction: 3–5 min.

State objective: *Today we will review all that we have done in the past unit in preparation for the application project to follow.*

Ask students as a class to try to recall all the goals of this unit without looking at their books. Then remind them of the goals they haven't mentioned.

Unit Goals: Identify places in the community, Read city maps, Give directions, Use prepositions of location, Identify public agencies and services, Use the telephone, Use the present continuous and the simple present.

Presentation 1, Practice 1, and Evaluation 1:

Do the Learner Log on page 100. Notes are adjacent to the page.

Presentation 2: 5–10 min.

Ask students to stand and then give them directions. Ask them to turn right, left, or around while playing "Simon Says."

Show the students how to do both exercises A and B with partners.

Practice 2: 10–15 min.

A Look at the map and ask a partner.

B Give directions to a partner from the car to each location.

Review *Stand Out Grammar Challenge 1*, Unit 5, pages 34–35 for more practice. *(optional)*

Evaluation 2: 5 min.

Examine work in student books.

STANDARDS CORRELATIONS

CASAS: 1.1.3, 1.9.4, 2.2.1, 2.2.5, 2.1.7, 7.1.1, 7.1.4, 7.4.1, 7.4.9, 7.4.10, 7.5.1

SCANS: **Interpersonal** Participates as a Member of a Team, Teaches Others New Skills
Information Acquires and Evaluates Information, Organizes and Maintains Information
Systems Understands Systems

Basic Skills Reading, Arithmetic, Listening, Speaking
Thinking Skills Creative Thinking
Personal Qualities Self-Management
EFF: **Communication** Speak So Others Can Understand
Interpersonal Guide Others, Cooperate with Others
Lifelong Learning Take Responsibility for Learning, Reflect and Evaluate

Review

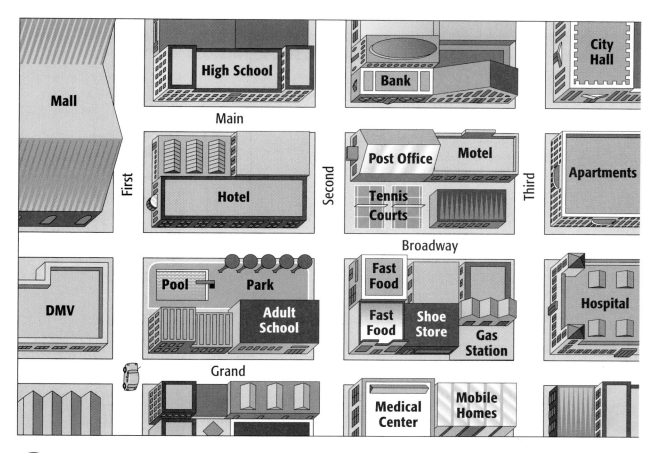

A **Look at the map and ask a partner.**

(Answers may vary for exercises A and B.)

EXAMPLE:

Student A: Where are the tennis courts?

Student B: They are on Broadway, across from the fast-food restaurant.

Ask about these places:

motel	mobile homes	hospital
park	apartments	hotel
public pool	dentist	post office

B **Give directions to a partner from the car to each location.**

EXAMPLE:

Student A: Can you give me directions to the medical center?

Student B: Yes, turn right on Grand. Go one block. It's on the right.

hotel	apartments	City Hall
dentist	hospital	high school
bank	motel	DMV

Review

 C **Listen to the phone conversations. Complete the chart.**

Name	Reason for calling	Phone number
1. Nadia	I have a question.	555-2344
2. Vien	*I want to talk.*	*555-7798*
3. David	*I need information.*	*555-1234*
4. Ricardo	*I need a phone number.*	*555-7343*

D **Write sentences about what you always do, what you often do, what you sometimes do, what you rarely do, and what you never do.**

I always ___*(Answers will vary.)*_____

I often _____

Sometimes I _____

I rarely _____

I never _____

E **With a group, make a list of types of stores in a mall.**

___*(Answers will vary.)*_____   _____   _____

_____   _____   _____

_____   _____   _____

_____   _____   _____

Presentation 3: 5–10 min.

Review focused listening with the students. See Teaching Hints.

Practice 3: 10–15 min.

C Listen to the phone conversations. Complete the chart. *(Audio CD Track 34)*

You may need to play the recording several times.

D Write sentences about what you always do, what you often do, what you sometimes do, what you rarely do, and what you never do.

E With a group, make a list of types of stores in a mall.

Review *Stand Out Grammar Challenge 1,* Unit 5, pages 36–37 for more practice. *(optional)*

Evaluation 3: 10–15 min.

Review the goals achieved in this unit.

Application: 1–2 days

The Team Project Activity on the following page is the application activity to be done on the next day of class.

Post-Assessment: Use the *Stand Out* ExamView® Pro *Test Bank* for Unit 5. *(optional)*

Note: With the ExamView® Pro *Test Bank* CD-ROM you can design a post-assessment that focuses on what students have learned. It is designed for three purposes:

- To help students practice taking a test similar to current standardized tests.
- To help the teacher evaluate how much the students have learned, retained, and acquired.
- To help students see their progress when they compare their scores to the pre-test they took earlier.

Instructor's Notes for Unit 5 Review

_____

_____

_____

_____

_____

_____

_____

_____

_____

_____

_____

_____

_____

_____

_____

_____

_____

_____

_____

_____

_____

_____

_____

_____

_____

_____

_____

Unit 5 Application Activity

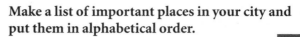

> **TEAM PROJECT: OUR NEW CITY**
> Objective:
> Project designed to apply all the
> objectives of this unit.
> Products:
> A map and brochure

Introduction:

In groups, students will produce a map of an imaginary city and make a brochure. This project can extend over two days.

Stage 1: 5–10 min.

Form a team with four or five students.

Students decide who will lead which steps as described on the student page. Provide well-defined directions on the board for how students should proceed. Explain to them that every task is to be done by each student. Students don't go to the next stage until the previous one is complete.

Stage 2: 5 min.

Choose a name for your city.

Make sure students understand that this is an imaginary city, so they should not use the name of a real city.

Stage 3: 15–20 min.

Make a list of important places in your city and put them in alphabetical order.

Stage 4: 20–30 min.

Make a map.

Supply paper and art materials. Make sure all students work on map production.

Stage 5: 20–30 min.

Make a brochure.

This project segment can be done on a template provided on the *Activity Bank 1 CD-ROM,* Unit 5 Worksheet 12 (two pages). *(optional)*

Stage 6: 15–20 min.

Prepare a presentation for the class.

Consider videotaping these presentations. Students will prepare better for formal presentations if they are videotaped. Another approach is for students to videotape themselves and polish their presentations.

Display maps and brochures in the classroom if possible.

STANDARDS CORRELATIONS

CASAS: 1.1.3, 1.9.4, 2.2.1, 2.2.5, 4.8.1, 4.8.5
SCANS: **Resources** Allocates Time, Allocates Human Resources
Interpersonal Participates as a Member of a Team, Teaches Others New Skills, Exercises Leadership, Works with Cultural Diversity
Information Acquires and Evaluates Information, Organizes and Maintains Information, Interprets and Communicates Information, Uses Computers to Process Information (optional)
Systems Understands Systems, Monitors and Corrects Performance, Improves and Designs Systems
Technology Applies Technology to Task (optional)
Basic Skills Reading, Writing, Listening, Speaking

Thinking Skills Creative Thinking, Decision Making, Problem Solving, Seeing Things in the Mind's Eye, Knowing How to Learn, Reasoning
Personal Qualities Sociability, Self-Management
EFF: **Communication** Read with Understanding, Convey Ideas in Writing, Speak So Others Can Understand, Listen Actively, Observe Critically
Decision Making Make Decisions, Plan
Interpersonal Guide Others, Resolve Conflict and Negotiate, Advocate and Influence, Cooperate with Others
Lifelong Learning Take Responsibility for Learning, Reflect and Evaluate, Learn through Research, Use Information and Communications Technology (optional)

T E A M PROJECT

Our new city

In this project you will make a brochure of a new city and present it to the class.

1. Form a team with four or five students.

   In your team, you need:

Position	Job	Student Name
Student 1 Leader	See that everyone speaks English. See that everyone participates.	
Student 2 City planner	Draw a map of your city with help from the team.	
Student 3 Designer	Make a brochure of your city with help from the team.	
Student 4 Spokesperson	With help from the team, organize a presentation to give to the class.	

2. Choose a name for your city.

3. Make a list of important places in your city and put them in alphabetical order. (See pages 81–82 for help.)

4. Make a map of your city and mark where the important places are. (See pages 84–85 and page 97 for help.)

5. Make a brochure. In the brochure put one paragraph about the city, the names of the team members, and a picture.

6. Prepare a presentation for the class.

PRONUNCIATION

These words all begin with /s/, together with another consonant. Listen and repeat.

study	station	straight	street	sport	special
school	skirt	slow	small	snow	swim

LEARNER LOG

Circle what you learned and write the page number where you learned it.

1. I can identify buildings.
   Yes   Maybe   No   Page _81–82_

2. I can read maps.
   Yes   Maybe   No   Page _83–84_

3. I can follow directions.
   Yes   Maybe   No   Page _85–86_

4. I can give directions.
   Yes   Maybe   No   Page _85–86_

5. I can read a directory.
   Yes   Maybe   No   Page _87–89_

6. I can use prepositions.
   Yes   Maybe   No   Page _87–89_

7. I can write a letter.
   Yes   Maybe   No   Page _94_

8. I can use the simple present and present continuous.
   Yes   Maybe   No   Page _94–96_

Did you answer *No* to any questions? Review the information with a partner.

Rank what you like to do best from 1 to 6. 1 is your favorite activity. Your teacher will help you.

☐ practice listening

☐ practice speaking

☐ practice reading

☐ practice writing

☐ learn new words (vocabulary)

☐ learn grammar

In the next unit I want to practice more

(Answers may vary.) .

Unit 5 Pronunciation and Learner Log

Pronunciation (optional): 10–15 min.
(Audio CD Track 35)

These words all begin with /s/ together with another consonant. Listen and repeat.

Play the recording and pause after each word.

For additional pronunciation practice: (The following words should be used for pronunciation practice, not for vocabulary instruction.) Write the following examples on the board.

stand	steak
strong	stress
special	spend
schedule	scan
slide	slim
smile	smart
snack	snake
sweet	switch

Learner Log

Presentation 1: 10–15 min.

If needed, review the purpose of the Learner Log.

Circle what you learned and write the page number where you learned it. Students research the answers individually. When they've finished, they should share their answers with a partner. These results need not be shared with the class.

Practice 1: 10–15 min.

Rank what you like to do best from 1 to 6. 1 is your favorite activity. Your teacher will help you. Results should be shared with the class in order to demonstrate to students how people learn differently.

Evaluation 1: 10–15 min.

In the next unit I want to practice more _____. Students should fill in the blank with assistance from a partner or from you. They may focus on a skill (e.g., listening), on a vocabulary area (e.g., numbers), on grammar, and so on. Don't limit

them to a single answer. Emphasize that the purpose of completing the sentence is to improve their self-assessment skills.

Instructor's Notes for Unit 5 Team Project, Pronunciation, and Learner Log

_____

_____

_____

_____

_____

_____

_____

_____

_____

_____

_____

_____

_____

_____

_____

_____

_____

_____

_____

_____

_____

LESSON PLAN

Objective:
Identify body parts
Key vocabulary:
nose, mouth, head, tooth, teeth, ears, throat, eyes, arm, foot, feet, back, chest, stomach, leg, hand, hurt, ache, doctor

Pre-Assessment: Use the *Stand Out* ExamView® Pro *Test Bank* for Unit 6. *(optional)*

Warm-up and Review: 5–10 min.

Ask the students if they like going to the doctor. Ask them where they go if they experience a medical problem. Put prompts on the board to help them, such as *the emergency room, the doctor's office,* or *a clinic.* Ask students why they go to a doctor. They may begin to suggest ailments or illnesses. These ailments are generally related to specific body parts. Write the body parts they mention on the board. Then ask students to point to these parts on their own bodies as you say them.

Introduction: 3–5 min.

State objective: *Today you will learn about body parts. In this unit you will learn about health.*

Presentation 1: 10–15 min.

A Use the words from the boxes to label the pictures.

Do this activity with the students and help them with pronunciation. Practice the words with the students by pointing to these areas of your body and having them say the words. Pay special attention to how much the students already know.

Practice 1: 15–20 min.

Ask the students to listen as you read them the following story. Before you start, ask students to point to the parts on their own bodies when they hear them mentioned in the story. To practice, say a few body parts and have them respond. Read the passage at normal speed the first time, then speed up and read it faster and faster.

Karen is a very nice young woman, but she is sick right now. She has a terrible cold. Her nose is stuffy, her eyes are running all the time, and her ears are stopped up so she can't hear. When Karen is sick, she gets very tired. Her legs always hurt, her back is sore, and she also has trouble breathing because her chest becomes congested. Sometimes her head hurts so badly that her stomach aches. Do you ever feel that way?

Read the paragraph a few more times and ask the students to close their books and write down the vocabulary words they hear.

Evaluation 1: 5 min.

Ask a few volunteers to write the vocabulary words on the board. Check their spelling.

Pronunciation:

An optional pronunciation activity is found on the final page of this unit. This pronunciation activity may be introduced during any lesson in this unit, especially if students need practice contrasting the sounds /s/ and /th/. Go to pages 120/120a for Unit 6 Pronunciation.

STANDARDS CORRELATIONS

CASAS: 3.1.1
SCANS: **Interpersonal** Participates as a Member of a Team, Teaches Others New Skills, Exercises Leadership, Works with Cultural Diversity
Information Acquires and Evaluates Information, Interprets and Communicates Information
Basic Skills Reading, Listening, Speaking

Thinking Skills Decision Making
EFF: **Communication** Read with Understanding, Speak So Others Can Understand, Listen Actively, Observe Critically
Decision Making Solve Problems and Make Decisions
Interpersonal Guide Others, Resolve Conflict and Negotiate, Advocate and Influence, Cooperate with Others

Health and Fitness

G O A L S

- Identify body parts
- Identify symptoms and illnesses
- Use *should* for advice

- Read warning labels on medication
- Call 911 in an emergency
- Identify hospital vocabulary
- Use *want* plus infinitive

LESSON **1** **Parts of the body**

GOAL ▷ Identify body parts

Vocabulary

 A **Use the words from the boxes to label the pictures.**

nose
mouth
head
tooth (teeth)
ear(s)
throat
eye(s)

head

ear

eye

nose

tooth

mouth

throat

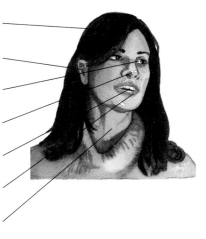

back

chest

arm

hand

stomach

leg

foot

arm(s)	back	chest	leg(s)
stomach	hand(s)	foot (feet)	

> **I have** a headache / a stomachache / a
> toothache / a backache / an earache.
> My feet **hurt**. / My back **hurts**.

B Look at the pictures and complete the sentences.

My ____*feet*____ hurt.   I have a ____*head*____ ache.   My ____*hand*____ hurts.

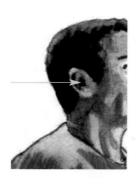
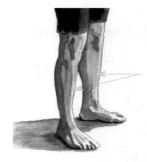

I have a ____*stomach*____ ache.   I have an ____*ear*____ ache.   My ____*legs*____ hurt.

C Listen to these people talking to their doctor. What is the problem? Complete the sentences.

1. *Karen:*   Doctor, my ____*hand*____ hurts.
2. *Roberto:*   Doctor, my ____*leg*____ hurts.
3. *Vien:*   Doctor, I have an ____*ear*____ ache.
4. *Tino:*   Doctor, my ____*foot*____ hurt.
5. *Eric:*   Doctor, I have a ____*stomach*____ ache.

Presentation 2: 15–20 min.

Write the words *hurt* and *ache* on the board. Help students understand the meaning of both words. Go over the box at the top of the page with the students.

B Look at the pictures and complete the sentences.

Do this activity with the students and make sure they understand the difference between *hurt* and *ache.* Write on the board: ***What's the matter?*** and ***What's the problem?*** Pantomime problems like the ones in the pictures. When you act out a problem, encourage students to respond by saying: ***What's the matter?***

Ask students to pair up and briefly practice the pantomime exchange. Now prepare them for focused listening. Remind them to listen carefully for key words. They need not understand every word of the recording. See Teaching Hints.

Practice 2: 10–15 min.

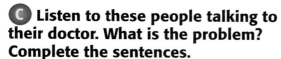

C Listen to these people talking to their doctor. What is the problem? Complete the sentences.
(Audio CD Track 36)

Play the recording several times. Then have students discuss what they heard and compare answers in groups. Play the recording a final time.

Evaluation 2: 5–10 min.

Observe the activity and review the answers. If necessary, play the recording again for clarification.

Presentation 3: 20–30 min.

Write the following sentences on the board and go over them a few times with the class. Then erase the body-part word in each one. Starting at the top, say what remains of each sentence and ask the students to complete it verbally. Re-insert the words on the board as students supply them. Next, ask students to spend about ten minutes memorizing the sentences; then erase them.

People kneel on their knees.
People hear with their ears.
People walk with their legs.
People see with their eyes.
People smell with their nose.
People stand on their feet.
People hold with their hands.
People eat with their mouths.

Practice 3: 30–40 min.

Prepare slips of paper with words from the sentences above. Ask the class to form teams of four or five. They will play a game in which each team is given a number of vocabulary words (at least eight words for each team). The goal is to construct a sentence using each word. A team representative then goes to the board and writes the sentence, without the help of notes. A team earns a point for every correct sentence that it submits. Allow teams to discuss their sentences before they send their representative to the board. The team with the most points wins.

Evaluation 3: 5–10 min.

Observe while refereeing the game. Review answers.

Application: 10–15 min.

Ask students in groups to make a list of the body vocabulary they've learned in this lesson so far. Groups should then rank the body parts according to which are most important to keep healthy and which are least important. Ask groups to report to the class and compare. Everyone in the group must agree. If they don't, further discussion will be necessary.

Refer to the *Activity Bank 1 CD-ROM*, Unit 6 Worksheet 1 (two pages), for additional vocabulary activities related to body parts. *(optional)*

LESSON PLAN

Objective:
Identify symptoms and illnesses
Key vocabulary:
sore throat, runny nose, fever, headache, symptoms, illnesses, cough, cold, flu, sneezing, Fahrenheit, Centigrade, measles, muscles, sick, temperature

---

Warm-up and Review: 5–10 min.

Write *cold* and *flu* on the board. Ask students if they are familiar with these illnesses. Ask individuals how many times a year they catch colds. Ask them why they get colds and what symptoms they get. Write the word *symptoms* on the board, leaving room under it to note student responses. To help them understand the word's meaning and get them started, write *runny nose* under it. You may wish to prompt them by demonstrating a symptom, such as a sneeze.

Introduction: 5–10 min.

State objective: *Today we are going to learn to identify symptoms of illnesses.*

Presentation 1: 10–15 min.

Write *runny nose* on the board if it isn't there already. Ask students what it means. Now ask them to open their books.

(A) Label the picture with the words from the box.

Explain that the words in the box are cold or flu symptoms. Remind students again that focused

listening is a good model for reading difficult passages. They don't have to understand every word to get the idea or message.

(B) What is the matter with Eric? Does he have a cold or the flu? Read the paragraph and find out.

Ask students to read the paragraph to themselves as quickly as possible and not use a dictionary. After they finish, have them close their books.

Draw a chart on the board with two columns:

Cold symptoms	Flu symptoms

Under the word *symptoms,* still on the board from the Warm-up, make sure the following words appear: *high fever, low fever, sore throat, headache, runny nose, dry cough, muscle aches.* Add them on the board if they aren't already there.

Practice 1: 15–20 min.

Ask students in groups to try to complete the Cold/Flu chart on the board. They should draw on their own experiences and from what they've read. Don't allow them to open their books until they complete the chart.

(C) Answer the questions using the information from the paragraph.

Students can answer either in pairs or in their groups.

Evaluation 1: 5–10 min.

Review the answers and compare the charts. Ask students if Eric has a cold or the flu. Make sure students see how much information they derived from a relatively difficult paragraph.

STANDARDS CORRELATIONS

CASAS: 1.1.5, 3.1.1, 7.2.3
SCANS: Interpersonal Participates as a Member of a Team, Teaches Others New Skills
Information Acquires and Evaluates Information, Interprets and Communicates Information
Basic Skills Reading, Listening, Speaking

Thinking Skills Decision Making
EFF: Communication Read with Understanding, Speak So Others Can Understand, Listen Actively, Observe Critically
Decision Making Solve Problems and Make Decisions
Interpersonal Guide Others, Cooperate with Others
Lifelong Learning Reflect and Evaluate

 **LESSON** **Is it a cold or the flu?**

GOAL ▶ **Identify symptoms and illnesses**　　　　　**Vocabulary**

 A **Label the picture with the words from the box.**

| runny nose |
| sore throat |
| fever |
| headache |

fever _____

headache _____

sore throat _____

runny nose _____

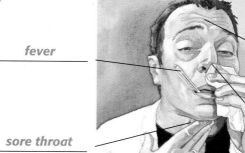

B **What is the matter with Eric? Does he have a cold or the flu? Read the paragraph and find out.**

Colds and the Flu

　　Colds and the flu are similar illnesses and have some of the same symptoms. The symptoms of a cold are a low fever, a sore throat, a headache, and a runny nose. People usually have a cold for one or two weeks. People with the flu feel very tired and sick. They often have a high fever, a dry cough, a headache, and muscle aches. People can have the flu for two to three weeks. Many people get colds or the flu every year and hate them both!

C **Answer the questions using the information from the paragraph.**

EXAMPLE:
People usually have the flu for _____.
○ 1 week   ○ 1–2 weeks   ● 2–3 weeks

1. Colds and the flu are types of _____.
   ○ symptoms   ● illnesses   ○ medicines

2. Headaches and fevers are types of _____.
   ● symptoms   ○ illnesses   ○ medicines

3. When you have a cold, you _____.
   ● have a headache   ○ have muscle aches   ○ feel very tired

4. When you have the flu, you _____.
   ○ have a low fever   ● feel very tired   ○ have a runny nose

D Complete the diagram using the information from page 103.

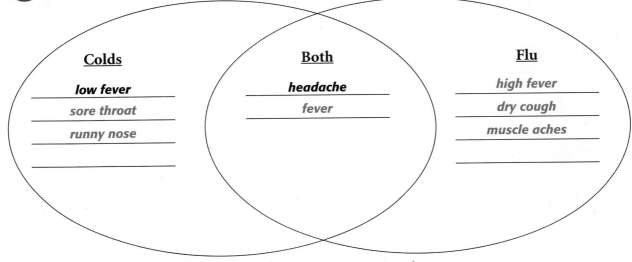

Colds

low fever
sore throat
runny nose
_____

Both

headache
fever
_____

Flu

high fever
dry cough
muscle aches
_____

> I think you have **the** flu.
>
> I think you have **a** cold.

E Listen and complete the conversation.

Doctor: What's the matter?

Miguel: Doctor, I feel very sick. I have a bad cough.

Doctor: Any other symptoms?

Miguel: I have a fever, too.

Doctor: _I think you have the flu._

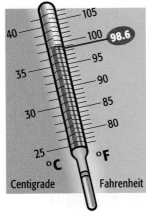

F Practice the conversation above. Use the symptoms from your diagram in exercise D.

A normal temperature is
__98.6__ degrees.

G What other illnesses do you know? What are the symptoms?

Illness	Symptoms
measles	red spots
(Answers will vary.)	

Presentation 2: 15–20 min.

D Complete the diagram using the information from page 103.

As a class, take the information from the Cold/Flu chart students created or from the reading in exercise B and fill in the Venn diagram. Either do this on the board or use a transparency. Review *normal body temperature, high fever,* and *low fever*. Refer to the thermometer illustration on this page.

E Listen and complete the conversation. *(Audio CD Track 37)*

Play the recording and ask students to write the last line of the conversations. Help them hear rhythm and intonation. Present the dialog as described in Teaching Hints. To make the conversation more dynamic, write the following on the board:

1. *Miguel has muscle aches and a headache.*
2. *Tien has a low fever and a runny nose.*
3. *Anya has a runny nose and sore throat.*
4. *Roberto has a sore throat and a headache.*
5. *Tino has a high fever and a dry cough.*

Have each student take on the role of one of the 5 sick persons listed on the board. They are to keep their identity a secret until their partners discover who they are by the symptoms they reveal in their dialog.

Show students how to substitute information. Ask them if they can identify the illness that is present in each of the five people listed on the board.

Practice 2: 15–20 min.

F Practice the conversation above. Use the symptoms from your diagram in exercise D.

Evaluation 2: 5–10 min.

Ask for volunteers to mimic various symptoms for the class.

Presentation 3: 10–15 min.

Review the symptoms a final time with the class. Prepare students for a focused listening activity that involves exchanges between groups. You will find eight different dialogs on the *Activity Bank CD-ROM,* Unit 6 Worksheet 2 (two pages) for Practice 3. Print them out and distribute one dialog to each group.

Practice 3: 30–40 min.

Ask groups to practice their dialogs among themselves. The dialogs come with a chart. See *Activity Bank 1 CD-ROM,* Worksheet 3 for students to complete. This is a simplified jigsaw activity in which students from different groups will mingle, perform the dialog, and then enter the new information on their charts. Go to Teaching Hints for more information on jigsaw activities.

Evaluation 3: 5–10 min.

Review symptoms and illnesses after groups have exchanged all information.

Application: 10–15 min.

G What other illnesses do you know? What are the symptoms?

Ask students to write down the answers on their own.

Refer to the *Activity Bank 1 CD-ROM,* Worksheet 4, for additional cold and flu vocabulary practice. *(optional)*

Instructor's Notes for Lesson 2

_____

_____

_____

_____

_____

_____

_____

_____

LESSON PLAN

Objective:
Use should to give advice.
Key vocabulary:
aspirin, rest, syrup, lozenges, remedies,
stay home, advice, medicine, drugstore,
pharmacy, hiccups, tablets, pills

Warm-up and Review: 5–10 min.

Ask students to share with the class the answers they came up with in the application activity from the previous lesson. Make a list on the board as you review illnesses and symptoms.

Introduction: 1 min.

State the objective: *Today you will learn to use should to give advice about illnesses and symptoms.*

Presentation 1: 5–10 min.

Pantomime having a headache. Encourage students to say *What's the matter?* Say you have a headache. Do the same with several ailments. Write *Symptoms* on the board. Motion again that you have a headache and prompt them to ask *What's the matter?* You respond with *I have a headache. What can I do?* Encourage students to suggest taking aspirin or another pain remedy. List their suggestions on the board under *Advice/Remedies.*

Ask students to open their books and review the new vocabulary in the pictures at the top of this page and in the chart below. Show them how to fill in the chart by completing the first row with them.

Practice 1: 20–25 min.

A What do you usually do when you have these symptoms? Complete the chart.
Ask students in pairs to complete the chart and then compare their answers with another pair.

B What other remedies do you know for these symptoms?
Allow students to discuss this question in groups. Give *stomach* as an example since antacid is not listed on the chart.

Evaluation 1: 5–10 min.

Discuss with the class each group's answers to exercise B. See if other groups agree.

STANDARDS CORRELATIONS

CASAS: 3.1.1, 3.3.1
SCANS: Resources Allocates Materials and Facility Resources
Interpersonal Participates as a Member of a Team, Teaches Others New Skills, Exercises Leadership
Information Acquires and Evaluates Information, Organizes and Maintains Information, Interprets and Communicates Information
Technology Applies Technology to Task (optional)

Basic Skills Listening, Speaking
Thinking Skills Creative Thinking, Decision Making, Problem Solving
EFF: Communication Speak So Others Can Understand, Listen Actively, Observe Critically
Decision Making Solve Problems and Make Decisions
Interpersonal Guide Others, Cooperate with Others
Lifelong Learning Learn through Research, Use Information and Communications Technology (optional)

What should I do?

GOAL ▶ Use *should* for advice

Grammar

aspirin

cough syrup

throat lozenges

 A **What do you usually do when you have these symptoms? Complete the chart.**

Symptoms	Take aspirin.	Rest in bed.	Take cough syrup.	Take throat lozenges.	Go to the doctor.	Other?
fever						
cough						
runny nose						
headache	x					x
sore throat						
stomachache						
backache						
feel tired						

(Answers will vary.)

B **What other remedies do you know for these symptoms?**

1. *(Answers will vary.)* _____

2. _____

3. _____

4. _____

5. _____

Study the charts with your teacher.

Should			
Subject	***should***	**Base**	**Example sentence**
I, you, he, she, it, we, they	should	rest	He should rest.
		stay home	They should stay home.
		go to the doctor	You should go to the doctor.

Negative of *should*			
Subject	***should + not***	**Base**	**Example sentence**
I, you, he, she, it, we, they	should not (shouldn't)	go out	You should not go out.

Wh- questions with *should*				
Question word	***should***	**Subject**	**Base**	**Example sentence**
What	should	I, you, he, she, it, we, they	do	What should I do?

D **Ask and answer with five students. Use the symptoms from exercise A.**

EXAMPLE:
Student A: I have a headache. What should I do?
Student B: You should take some aspirin.
Student A: Thanks. That's a good idea!

Presentation 2: 10–15 min.

Study the charts with your teacher.

Help students understand that *should* **is used when a suggestion is made.** Pantomime a headache again and go through the same dialog you did in Presentation 1, this time adding *should:*

Students: *What's the matter?*
Teaching: *I have a headache. What should I do?*
Students: *You should take some aspirin.*

Go over common symptoms with the class once again.

Practice 2: 15–20 min.

D Ask and answer with five students. Use the symptoms from exercise A.

Ask a few pairs using different symptoms to perform the conversation in front of the class.

Evaluation 2: 5 min.

Ask two volunteers to demonstrate the symptom/remedy exchange for the class.

 Refer to *Stand Out Grammar Challenge 1,* Unit 6, page 43 for more practice. *(optional)*

Presentation 3: 20–25 min.

Question the students again to make sure they understand how to use *should*. Ask students to close their books and, in pairs or individually, to write out one of the previous symptom/remedy dialogs. Write 4 of the symptoms across the board and ask volunteers to write out the dialog below each one.

Practice 3: 15–20 min.

 E Read the problem and give advice. Write one thing they *should* do and one thing they *shouldn't* do. Add two more problems of your own.

Evaluation 3: 10–15

Visit individual students as they work on **exercise E.** Share responses as a class. Have students write new problems and advice from items 9 and 10 on the board.

Application: 20–30 min.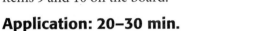

Ask the students where they can buy medicine. Hopefully, they will reply *drugstore* or *pharmacy.* After naming a few symptoms, ask them what they would do if they couldn't get the medicine to treat these symptoms. Then write the following on the board:

Home Remedy
Name: Joe Smith
Country: United States
Symptom or illness: Hiccups
Ingredients: Water
Instructions: Drink a glass of water as fast as you can.

 A worksheet with a Home Remedy template is also available on the *Activity Bank CD-ROM,* Unit 6 Worksheet 5 (two pages), if you wish to print it out.

Ask students to talk about any home remedies they remember using in their native country to treat colds, flu, hiccups, or other common ailments. If you wish, have students write a short paragraph about those home remedies.

F Active Task: Find more information about colds and flu remedies at home or on the Internet. Bring the information to school to share with the class.

Refer to *Stand Out Grammar Challenge 1,* Unit 6, pages 43–45 for more practice. *(optional)*

Refer to the *Activity Bank 1 CD-ROM,* Unit 6 Worksheet 6 for additional activities using *should*. *(optional)*

Instructor's Notes for Lesson 3

_____

_____

_____

_____

_____

_____

_____

_____

_____

_____

_____

_____

_____

_____

_____

_____

_____

Read the problem and give advice. Write one thing they *should* do and one thing they *shouldn't* do. Add two more problems of your own.

1. Roberto has a cold.

   He should take some cold medicine. He shouldn't drink cold drinks.

2. Phuong and Nam have the flu.

   They   *(Answers may vary.)* _____

3. Michael has a sore throat.

   He _____

4. Ayumi has a high fever.

   She _____

5. Piedra has a backache.

   She _____

6. Oscar feels very tired.

   He _____

7. Tien is coughing a lot.

   She _____

8. Omar has a stomachache.

   He _____

9. _____

   _____

10. _____

    _____

  Active Task: Find more information about cold and flu remedies at home or on the Internet. Bring the information to school to share with the class.

| GOAL ▶ | Read warning labels on medication | *Life Skill* |

What is Karen talking about?
What is the doctor writing?

A Read about Karen.

The doctor is giving Karen a prescription for some medicine. Karen is talking about the prescription with the doctor. The doctor is giving her instructions. The medicine is safe, but Karen needs to be careful.

B Listen to the conversation between Karen and the doctor. What kind of instructions does the doctor give? Write the correct letter below each picture.

A

D

C

B

LESSON PLAN

Objective:
Read warning labels on medication
Key vocabulary:
safe, dangerous, prescription, warning, drugs, same, different, reach, medicine cabinet

Warm-up and Review: 10–15 min.

Ask for volunteers to share their home remedies or those found on the Internet.

Introduction: 3–5 min.

Write the words *safe* and *dangerous* on the board. Ask the students if it is safe to take thirty aspirin in a day. Help them understand the difference between the two key words.

State objective: *Today you will learn to read labels on medication.*

Presentation 1: 15–20 min.

Write *prescription* on the board and ask the students where they can get prescriptions. Ask them to open their books and look at the picture. Ask the questions in the box and any others you think appropriate.

A Read about Karen.

Read the paragraph as a class and ask a few basic comprehension questions.

Look at the pictures in exercise B along with the students. Alert them that they will be doing a focused listening activity in which they will choose one of the pictures. Ask students to identify any words they recognize while listening. For example, they may hear *children* or *child* in association with the first picture. Help them understand the connection between the pictures and the words they will hear. See Teaching Hints, for help with focused listening.

You may wish to pre-teach some relevant words e.g. *reach, medicine cabinet.* For example, students might be curious about the word *reach.*

Practice 1: 10–15 min.

B Listen to the conversation between Karen and the doctor. What kind of instructions does the doctor give? Write the correct letter below each picture.
(Audio CD Track 38)

Play the recording several times. Ask students to listen and see if they can identify which picture goes with which instruction from the doctor.

Evaluation 1: 5 min.

Review the activity.

STANDARDS CORRELATIONS

CASAS: 3.3.1, 3.3.2, 3.4.1
SCANS: Interpersonal Teaches Others New Skills
Information Acquires and Evaluates Information, Interprets and Communicates Information

Basic Skills Reading, Listening, Speaking
EFF: Communication Read with Understanding, Speak So Others Can Understand, Listen Actively
Interpersonal Guide Others, Cooperate with Others

Presentation 2: 15–20 min.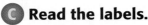

Write the word *Warning* on the board. Give examples of different warnings and help the class understand what it means.

C Read the labels.

Read each label with the students. Make sure they understand the information contained on the labels. Clarify any vocabulary questions students may ask. Ask them to circle the word *Warning* on each label in their books. Ask students to find and circle other items that appear on each label.

Write *same* and *different* on the board. Make sure they understand what both words mean.

Practice 2: 10–15 min.

D Answer the questions.

Help students with the first one by explaining that they can answer with the label items they just circled. They can work on this activity in pairs.

Evaluation 2: 10–15 min.

Ask volunteers to write their answers on the board.

Presentation 3: 5–10 min.

You will find more labels to interpret on Worksheet 7 in Unit 6 of the *Activity Bank 1 CD-ROM*. Help students understand the directions. Review and briefly quiz the students on the new vocabulary.

Practice 3: 20–30 min.

Ask the students in pairs or individually to do the exercise on Worksheet 7 from Unit 6 on the *Activity Bank 1 CD-ROM*.

Evaluation 3: 10–15 min.

Review the completed worksheet with students.

Application: 15–20 min.

Ask students on their own to make a dialog between a doctor and patient in which the doctor prescribes one of the medicines in exercise C.

Remind them of how to use *should* and *shouldn't*. Write the following dialog on the board as a guide.

Doctor: You are very sick. Here is a prescription for some medicine.
Karen: Thank you, doctor. How much should I take?
Doctor: You should take 2 tablets every 4 hours and please keep it away from your children.
Karen: Can I drink alcohol?
Doctor: No. You shouldn't drink alcohol with this medicine.

If time permits, allow a few students to demonstrate their dialogs for the class.

Refer to the *Activity Bank 1 CD-ROM*, Unit 6 Worksheet 8, for additional activities with *should* and reading labels. *(optional)*

Instructor's Notes for Lesson 4

Read the labels.

a.

Warning:

Do not drink alcohol with this drug. Keep this drug and all drugs out of reach of children.

Follow directions carefully.

b.
Warning:

Follow directions carefully.
●
Keep this drug and all drugs out of reach of children.
●
Do not take if pregnant.

c.
Warning:

Not for children under 12. Keep this drug and all drugs out of reach of chidren.

Follow directions carefully.

d.
Warning:

Keep this drug and all drugs out of reach of children.

Follow directions carefully.

Don't take for more than 10 days.

 Answer the questions.

1. Look at the labels. Write what is the same on all the labels.

   Warning:
   _____

   Follow directions carefully.
   _____

   Keep this drug and all drugs out of the reach of children.
   _____

2. Write what is different on label a.

   Do not drink alcohol with this drug.
   _____

   _____

3. Write what is different on label b.

   Do not take if pregnant.
   _____

   _____

4. Write what is different on label c.

   Not for children under 12.
   _____

   _____

5. Write what is different on label d.

   Don't take for more than 10 days.
   _____

   _____

LESSON **5** Emergencies

GOAL ▶ **Call 911 in an emergency**

A **Talk about the pictures with your teacher.**

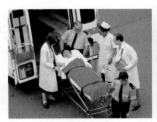

medical emergency

fire emergency

police emergency

> Remember! You should only dial 911 when there is a fire or a medical or police emergency.

B **Talk about the problems with your teacher. Learn the new words and complete the chart in a group.**

Problem	Emergencies			Not an emergency
	Fire	**Medical**	**Police**	
Someone has a heart attack.		x		
Someone has the flu.				x
A house is on fire.	x			
Your car is stolen.			x	
Someone has a cold.				x
Someone is hurt in a car accident.		x		
You need transportation.				x
You see a robbery.			x	

C **Listen to these four conversations and circle the emergency.**

Who calls 911?	Type of emergency		
Ex. Rodrigo	robbery	car accident	(fire)
1. Anya	(heart attack)	fire	robbery
2. Felipe	(car accident)	fire	robbery
3. Brian	fire	(robbery)	heart attack

LESSON PLAN
Objective:
Call 911 in an emergency
Key vocabulary:
robbery, heart attack, fire, accident, transportation, stolen, emergency, dial

Warm-up and Review: 5–10 min.

Write *911* on the board and ask students to tell you when you should call this phone number. Make a list of their responses on the board.

Introduction: 1 min.

Explain to the class that sometimes it isn't necessary to call 911. If you brought them to class, use sample medicine containers to show that a pharmacy or drugstore can help when the situation is not an emergency.

State objective: *Today you are going to learn about making emergency calls.*

Presentation 1: 20–30 min.

A Talk about the pictures with your teacher.

Write any new vocabulary on the board and review the words with the class.

B Talk about the problems with your teacher. Learn the new words and complete the chart in a group.

Make sure students know how to do this activity before instructing them to complete the chart. This is still part of presentation so you shouldn't give them too much time to finish this activity. The purpose is to prepare them for the focused listening

that is to follow. Remind the students of the principles of focused listening. See Teaching Hints.

Practice 1: 10–15 min.

C Listen to these four conversations and circle the emergency.
(Audio CD Track 39)

Play the recording several times to get the students used to listening for the specific information.

Note: Practice 3 on page 111a will use the same recording but ask for additional information.

Evaluation 1: 5–10 min.

Review answers and evaluate student progress.

Presentation 2: 10–15 min.

Look at the picture with the students. Ask them the questions in the box and any additional ones you think are appropriate.

D Listen and practice the conversation.
(Audio CD Track 40)

Play the recording. Help students with rhythm and intonation. Ask them to practice the dialog a few times in pairs.

E Answer the questions about the conversation.

After walking the students through this activity, ask them to underline the *who, what,* and *where* in the dialog itself.

Practice 2: 10–15 min.

F With a partner, make a new conversation with one of the ideas.

Direct students to use the chart as a guide. Students may also substitute their own ideas and addresses from their town or city.

Evaluation 2: 5–10 min.

Ask volunteers to demonstrate making a 911 call.

Presentation 3: 5–10 min.

Review with students exercise C on the previous page. Ask them to identify the correct type of emergency. Inform students that they are going to do another focused listening exercise. They will hear the conversations again but this time they will need to complete a table with *who, what,* and *where* questions.

Practice 3: 20–30 min.

Play the recording from exercise D again. Have students listen for the key information with books closed. Ask them to write down the key information. This will not be an easy exercise, especially since students may not know how to spell names and addresses correctly.

After you have played the recording a few times, review clarification skills with students and ask that they use them in getting and giving spelling

help with each other. Before answers are finalized, students meet in groups to compare answers.

Evaluation 3: 5 min.

Observe the group activity. Have volunteers write answers on the board.

Application: 15–20 min.

Ask students to practice calling 911 with a partner. Have them demonstrate making the call to each other without looking at books or worksheets. Set the scene by saying *Your house is on fire.* After dialing 911 and reaching the fire department, a partner will need to specify *who, what,* and *where.*

Refer to the *Activity Bank 1 CD-ROM,* Unit 6 Worksheet 9, (two pages) for additional activities dealing with emergencies. *(optional)*

AB

```
Instructor's Notes for Lesson 5
_____
_____
_____
_____
_____
_____
_____
_____
_____
_____
_____
_____
_____
```

What is the problem?
What is Victor doing?

 D **Listen and practice the conversation.**

Operator: 911. What is your emergency?
Victor: There's a car accident.
Operator: Where is the accident?
Victor: It's on Fourth and Bush in Santa Ana.
Operator: Is anyone hurt?

Victor: Yes.
Operator: What's your name?
Victor: It's Victor Karaskov.
Operator: OK, Victor, the police and
ambulance are on the way.

E **Answer the questions about the conversation.**

1. **Who** is calling in the emergency? *Victor Karaskov is calling.*

2. **What** is the emergency? *There's a car accident.*

3. **Where** is the emergency? *It's on Fourth and Bush in Santa Ana.*

F **With a partner, make a new conversation with one of the ideas.**

Who	What	Where
Antonio	My father is having a heart attack.	Broadway and Nutwood.
Karen	There is a car accident.	First and Grand.
Tran	A house is on fire.	234 Jones Ave.

LESSON 6 Emergency room

GOAL ▶ Identify hospital vocabulary

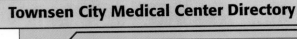

Townsen City Medical Center Directory

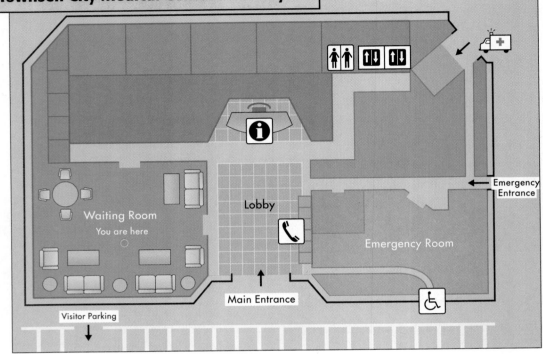

Waiting Room
You are here

Lobby

Emergency Room

Emergency
Entrance

Main Entrance

 Visitor Parking

b

a

c

 d

e

f

A Write the letter next to the correct symbol.

a. wheelchair entrance   c. elevators   e. pay phones

b. restrooms   d. Information   f. ambulance entrance

B Ask questions about places on the directory.

EXAMPLES:
Student A: Excuse me, where is Information?
Student B: It's over here. (Student B points to the map.)

Student B: Excuse me, where are the elevators?
Student A: They are over there. (Student A points to the map.)

LESSON PLAN

Objective:
Identify hospital vocabulary
Key vocabulary:
directory, symbol, wheelchair, entrance,
elevator, pay phone, ambulance, waiting
room, lobby

Warm-up and Review: 5–10 min.

Ask the students for the location of the hospital nearest to where they live. As a review, ask students in pairs to write out directions to the respective hospitals. Then call for volunteers to write their directions on the board. As they do so, ask them what buildings or landmarks are next to, behind, and around the corner from that particular hospital.

Introduction: 1 min.

State objective: *Today we will learn about hospital vocabulary.*

Presentation 1: 15–20 min.

(A) Write the letter next to the correct symbol.

Do this as a class. Look at the floor plan of the hospital emergency room and discuss new vocabulary with students. Test their comprehension right away. Then ask where specific hospital areas or features are located. Ask students to point to the sites on the directory in their books while saying *It's over here* or *They're over there.*

Review with the class the plural and singular use of the verb *be* in the present tense.

Practice 1: 10–15 min.

(B) Ask questions about places on the directory.

Ask students to practice in pairs. Make sure they understand how to use *over there* when a particular site is far away and *over here* for sites close by.

To make this practice more challenging, have students add to their answers *next to, around the corner,* and *between,* as appropriate.

Evaluation 1: 5–10 min.

Observe the pair activity. Ask volunteers to perform the dialog if they are using prepositions in their responses.

Presentation 2: 10–15 min.

Review the vocabulary for giving directions from Unit 5. Specifically, review the use of *turn right, turn left,* and *go straight ahead.* Now add *Go down the hall.* Reinforce student use of these phrases by having them give you directions to various spots in the classroom. Follow their directions.

C Practice giving directions with a partner. You are in the waiting room.

Present this dialog as one that will help students master the new vocabulary. See Teaching Hints. Coach students in rhythm and intonation. Prepare them for exercise D by showing them again how to substitute information.

Practice 2: 10–15 min.

D Ask about these places and make new conversations using the directory.

For alternate ways to practice dialogs, see Teaching Hints.

Evaluation 2: 10–15 min.

Ask for volunteers to demonstrate their new conversations.

Presentation 3: 15–20 min.

To further reinforce the vocabulary, prepare students for dictation by having them say all the new words they learned in this lesson. As you list the words on the board, ask the class to help you arrange them in alphabetical order.

Practice 3: 10–15 min.

Give students the following dictation. Remind them that they will have trouble writing and listening at the same time and that they should first listen, then repeat what they hear to themselves before they write.

Mario is very sick. He drives to the emergency room at the hospital. A nurse has a wheelchair for him. She takes him to the elevators. They are between the restrooms and the pay phones. Mario is sick, but the doctors can help.

Evaluation 3: 15–20 min.

Ask volunteers to write one dictated sentence at a time on the board. Allow students to peer correct.

Application: 30–40 min.

E Make groups of four students. Prepare a short skit using words from this unit. Each person in your group will play these roles.

Help students get started by setting the stage: a local hospital on a weekday morning. It will be difficult for some, so try to put weaker students in the same groups as stronger students. Review the suggestions below the instruction line.

Ask groups to enact their scenes for the class.

F Active Task: Visit the main lobby of a hospital. Is there a floor directory? Write down three words you want to understand better.

Refer to the *Activity Bank 1 CD-ROM,* Unit 6 Worksheet 10 (two pages) for additional practice with hospital vocabulary and focused listening. The listening is found on *AB1 CD-ROM* Track 11. (*optional*)

Instructor's Notes for Lesson 6

_____

_____

_____

_____

_____

_____

_____

C **Practice giving directions with a partner. You are in the waiting room.**

Student A: Excuse me, where are the elevators?
Student B: They are close to the restrooms.
Student A: Which way are they?
Student B: Go down the hall and turn left.

D **Ask about these places and make new conversations using the directory.**

the restrooms   the pay phones   the main entrance

the wheelchair entrance   Information   the main lobby

E **Make groups of four students. Prepare a short skit using words from this unit. Each person in your group will play one of these roles.**

Student A: You work in Information.
Student B: You are very sick.
Student C: You are a family member.
Student D: You are a nurse.

Some things you can say:	Some things the nurse can ask:
My son is very sick.	What's the matter?
We need a doctor.	What is your health insurance?
Where is the . . . ?	Are you pregnant?
I'm calling his wife.	Are you taking any medication?
We need a wheelchair.	Are you allergic to any medication?

F **Active Task:** Visit the main lobby of a hospital. Is there a floor directory? Write down three words you want to understand better.

GOAL ▶ Use *want* plus infinitive | *Grammar*

 A **Read the information about exercise.**

Why is exercise important?

Exercise

We need to exercise for many reasons. First, exercise is good for our hearts. Exercise builds muscles and makes us flexible. It is also good for our weight. Finally, when we exercise, we feel good. Exercise is very important for everybody.

B **Match the sentences and the pictures.**

__d__ Exercise builds muscles.   __b__ Exercise makes us flexible.

__c__ Exercise is good for our weight.   __a__ Exercise helps us feel good.

a.

b.

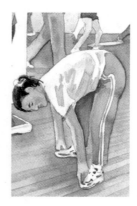

c.

d.

LESSON PLAN

Objective:
Use want plus infinitive
Key vocabulary:
weights, exercise, muscles, flexible, feel, swimming, running, vacuuming, gardening, housework, healthy, unhealthy

Warm-up and Review: 10–15 min.

Ask groups that didn't have the chance to present the skits in the last lesson's application to do so now.

Introduction: 5–10 min.

Ask students if exercise is healthy. Write the word *healthy* on the board, followed by *unhealthy.* Increase understanding of these words by putting examples under each one. Ask for student input. If no one offers *exercise,* write it on the board under *healthy.*

State objective: *Today we are going to learn about exercise and we are going to set health goals for ourselves.*

Presentation 1: 20–30 min.

Look at the pictures with the students at the top of the page and discuss what people are doing. Ask the question in the box.

A Read the information about exercise.

Read the paragraph with the students and ask them to underline any words they don't know and try to work out the meaning.

B Match the sentences and the pictures.

Do this as a class and continue reviewing the vocabulary with the students.

STANDARDS CORRELATIONS

CASAS: 3.5.9
SCANS: Interpersonal Participates as a Member of a Team, Teaches Others New Skills, Exercises Leadership, Works with Cultural Diversity
Information Acquires and Evaluates Information, Organizes and Maintains Information, Interprets and Communicates Information
Technology Applies Technology to Task (optional)
Basic Skills Reading, Listening, Speaking

Thinking Skills Decision Making, Seeing Things in the Mind's Eye, Knowing How to Learn, Reasoning
EFF: Communication Read with Understanding, Speak So Others Can Understand, Listen Actively, Observe Critically
Decision Making Solve Problems and Make Decisions, Plan
Interpersonal Guide Others, Cooperate with Others
Lifelong Learning Reflect and Evaluate, Learn through Research, Use Information and Communications Technology (optional)

C Talk about the pictures and read about exercise.

Read this passage with the class and ask comprehension questions to make sure students understand. Have students look at the four pictures and identify the activities. Discuss with students if they are good forms of exercise or not.

Practice 1: 10–15 min.

D Talk to three students and fill in the chart.

Briefly explain the dialog exchange in exercise D.

E Write two or three exercise goals. How much do you want to exercise every week?

Remind students what *goals* are and why it is important to set them.

Evaluation 1: 5–10 min.

Poll the class to see how much exercise students do weekly.

Refer to *Stand Out Grammar Challenge 1,* Unit 6, page 45 for more practice. *(optional)*

C **Talk about the pictures and read about exercise.**

Exercise is important, but how much? Doctors say that 30 minutes a day is good. You can exercise at different times during the day. For example, try 10 minutes in the morning, 10 minutes at lunchtime, and 10 minutes at night. Running, swimming, housework, and yard work are all good exercise.

D **Talk to three students and fill in the chart.**

EXAMPLE:
Student A: How much do you exercise every week?
Student B: I exercise about 1 hour every week.

Name	0 minutes	Up to 1 hour	1–2 hours	2–3 hours	More than 3 hours
Ex. Karen			x		

(Answers will vary.)

E **Write two or three exercise goals. How much do you want to exercise every week?**

What exercise do you want to do?	When do you want to do this exercise?	How long do you want to do this exercise?
Ex. swim	8 A.M. on Saturday	40 minutes

(Answers will vary.)

F **Study the chart with your teacher.**

Subject	Verb	Infinitive (*to* + base)		Example sentence
I, you, we, they	want	to	exercise	I want to run.
he, she, it	wants		walk	We want to exercise.
			run	They want to walk.
			ride	He wants to ride a bike.
			do	She wants to go to the gym.
			go	

G **Write sentences about your goals from exercise E.**

EXAMPLE:
I want to run 20 minutes every day.

1. *(Answers will vary.)* _____

2. _____

3. _____

H **Ask three students about their exercise goals and write. Ask: What exercise do you want to do?**

EXAMPLE:
Karen wants to swim 40 minutes every day.

1. *(Answers will vary.)* _____

2. _____

3. _____

4. _____

5. _____

6. _____

  Active Task: Find a health guide in the library or on the Internet and find your ideal weight. Use the information to make a plan for healthy eating and exercise.

Presentation 2: 10–15 min.

F Study the chart with your teacher.

Instruct the class on the use of the infinitive as well as on the third-person singular *s*.

Practice 2: 15–20 min.

G Write sentences about your goals from exercise E.

H Ask three students about their exercise goals and write. Ask: What exercise do you want to do?

Students write two sentences for each person.

Evaluation 2: 10–15 min.

Ask volunteers to write their sentences on the board.

 ### Refer to *Stand Out Grammar Challenge 1,* Unit 6, page 45 for more practice. *(optional)*

Presentation 3: 10–15 min.

Ask the students to help you make a list of all the types of exercise that come to mind. The list might include *walking, running, swimming, playing sports, lifting weights, bicycling, cleaning house,* and *doing yard work.*

Practice 3: 15–20 min.

Ask students in groups of four or five to make bar graphs. Each group will make graphs showing the types of exercise students engage in. A representative from each group will find out the exercise preferences of all other groups by visiting them and posing questions. A worksheet for this activity is available on the *Activity Bank 1 CD-ROM,* Unit 6 Worksheet 11 *(optional)*. The vertical axis of the graph will indicate number of students, and the horizontal will indicate different types of exercise. One bar on this axis should indicate the number of students that get no exercise at all.

Evaluation 3: 10–15 min.

Examine the different bar graphs and compare them.

Application: 10–15 min.

Ask students in pairs to complete a Venn diagram activity. Draw two intersecting circles on the board:

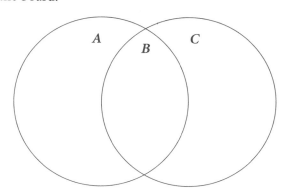

A: *Exercise goals I have*
C: *Exercise goals my partner has*
B: *Exercise goals we BOTH have*

Ask student pairs to complete the Venn diagram by writing two complete sentences in each circle. Then ask volunteers to present their work to the class. Blank Venn diagram templates may be found on the *Activity Bank 1 CD- ROM*, Unit 6 Worksheet 12 *(optional)*.

I Active Task: Find a health guide in the library or on the Internet and find your ideal weight. Use the information to make a plan for healthy eating and exercise.

Refer to the *Activity Bank 1 CD-ROM* Unit 6 Worksheet 13 (2 pages), for more practice with exercise goals and infinitives after *want*. *(optional)*

Instructor's Notes for Lesson 7

_____

_____

_____

_____

_____

_____

> ### LESSON PLAN
>
> Objective:
> All previous objectives
> Key vocabulary:
> All previous Unit 6 vocabulary

Warm-up and Review: 5–10 min.

Ask for more students to share their sentences from the last lesson's application.

Introduction: 3–5 min.

State objective: *Today we will review all that we have done in the past unit in preparation for the application project to follow.* Ask students as a class to try to recall all the goals of this unit without looking at their books. Then remind them of the goals they haven't mentioned.

Unit Goals: Identify body parts, Identify symptoms and illnesses, Use *should* for advice, Read warning labels on medication, Call 911 in an emergency, Understand hospital vocabulary, Use want plus infinitive.

Presentation 1, Practice 1, and Evaluation 1:

Do the Learner Log on page 120. Notes are adjacent to the page.

Presentation 2: 5–10 min.

Point to parts of the body and briefly quiz students. Pantomime problems that affect different parts of the body and elicit *What's the matter?* You will respond with *My _____ hurts.*

Practice 2: 10–15 min.

A Look at the picture. Write the words.

Students may check their answers by looking back at page 101.

B Match the symptoms and the remedy.

C Practice the conversation with a partner. Make similar conversations using the words from exercise B.

Evaluation 2: 5 min.

Review the work in student books together.

STANDARDS CORRELATIONS

CASAS: 2.1.2, 2.5.1, 3.1.1, 3.3.1, 3.3.2, 3.4.1, 7.1.1, 7.1.4, 7.4.1, 7.4.9, 7.4.10, 7.5.1
SCANS: Information Acquires and Evaluates Information, Organizes and Maintains Information
Basic Skills Reading, Writing
EFF: Communication Read with Understanding, Convey Ideas in Writing

Interpersonal Guide Others, Resolve Conflict and Negotiate, Advocate and Influence, Cooperate with Others
Lifelong Learning Take Responsibility for Learning, Reflect and Evaluate, Learn through Research, Use Information and Communications Technology

Review

A **Look at the picture. Write the words.**

head

neck

arm

hand

leg

foot

eye

nose

teeth

throat

chest

stomach

B **Match the symptoms and the remedy.**

_d_ 1. fever   a. lozenges

_c_ 2. backache   b. syrup

_a_ 3. sore throat   c. rest

_b_ 4. cough   d. aspirin

C **Practice the conversation with a partner. Make similar conversations using the words from exercise B.**

EXAMPLE:

Student A: What's the matter?

Student B: I have a _____. / My _____ hurt(s).

Student A: You should _____.

Student B: Thanks. That's a good idea.
(Answers will vary.)

Review

D **You often find these warnings on medicine labels. Fill in the missing words.**

alcohol	reach	children	pregnant

1. Not for _____*children*_____ under 12.
2. Keep this drug out of the _____*reach*_____ of children.
3. Do not take if you are _____*pregnant*_____ .
4. Do not drink _____*alcohol*_____ with this drug.

E **Read the conversation and put the sentences in the correct order.**

___2___ *Victor:* There's a car accident.

___1___ *Operator:* 911. What is your emergency?

___6___ *Victor:* Yes.

___4___ *Victor:* It's on Fourth and Bush in Santa Ana.

___5___ *Operator:* Is anyone hurt?

___7___ *Operator:* OK. The police and ambulance are on the way.

___3___ *Operator:* Where is the accident?

F **Write six words you can see in a hospital.** *(Answers may include the following.)*

ambulance	waiting room	elevator
information	emergency room	restrooms

G **What kind of exercise do you do every day? How often?**

1. *(Answers will vary.)* _____

2. _____

Presentation 3: 5–10 min.

Briefly go over each activity on this page and ask the students to do them in pairs.

Practice 3: 30–45 min.

D **You often find these warnings on medicine labels. Fill in the missing words.**

E **Read the conversation and put the sentences in the correct order.**

F **Write six words you can see in a hospital.**

G **What kind of exercise do you do every day? How often?**

Evaluation 3: 10–15 min.

Discuss students' work as a class.

Application: 1–2 days

The team project on the following page is the application activity to be done on the next day of class.

Post-Assessment: Use the *Stand Out* ExamView® Pro *Test Bank* for Unit 6. *(optional)*

Note: With the ExamView® Pro *Test Bank* you can design a post-assessment that focuses on what students have learned. It is designed for three purposes:
· To help students practice taking a test similar to current standardized tests.
· To help the teacher evaluate how much the students have learned, retained, and acquired.
· To help students see their progress when they compare their scores to the pre-test they took earlier.

Instructor's Notes for Unit 6 Review

Unit 6 Application Activity

> **TEAM PROJECT: AN EMERGENCY**
> Objective:
> Project designed to apply all the
> objectives of this unit.
> Product:
> A medical skit

Introduction:

Student teams produce a skit in a hospital setting and perform it for the class. This project can extend over two days.

Stage 1: 5–10 min.

Form a team with four or five students.

Students decide who will lead which steps as described on the student page. Provide well-defined directions on the board for how students should proceed. Explain to them that every task is to be done by each student. Students don't go to the next stage until the previous one is complete.

Stage 2: 10–15 min.

Choose an accident or illness.

Worksheet 14 from Unit 6 of the *Activity Bank 1 CD-ROM* shows students how to develop the skit. You may instead decide to ask teams to write skits on their computers and have the class read each skit aloud *(optional)*.

Stage 3: 20–25 min.

Write a 911 call.

Stage 4: 15–20 min.

Write a conversation with the hospital admitting person and/or the doctor.

Stage 5: 10–15 min.

Write instructions and a warning for the medicine the doctor gives.

Stage 6: 40–50 min.

Practice the skit and present it to the class.

Consider videotaping these presentations. Students will prepare better for formal presentations if they are videotaped. Another approach is for students to videotape themselves and polish their presentations.

STANDARDS CORRELATIONS

CASAS: 3.1.1, 3.3.1, 3.5.9, 4.8.1, 4.8.5
SCANS: **Resources** Allocates Time, Allocates Money, Allocates Material and Facility Resources, Allocates Human Resources
Interpersonal Participates as a Member of a Team, Teaches Others New Skills, Serves Clients/ Customers, Exercises Leadership, Works with Cultural Diversity
Information Acquires and Evaluates Information, Organizes and Maintains Information, Interprets and Communicates Information, Uses Computers to Process Information (optional)
Systems Understands Systems, Monitors and Corrects Performance, Improves and Designs Systems
Technology Applies Technology to Task (optional)

Basic Skills Reading, Writing, Listening, Speaking
Thinking Skills Creative Thinking, Decision Making, Problem Solving, Knowing How to Learn, Reasoning
Personal Qualities Responsibility, Self-Esteem, Sociability, Self-Management
EFF: **Communication** Read with Understanding, Convey Ideas in Writing, Speak So Others Can Understand, Listen Actively, Observe Critically
Decision Making Solve Problems and Make Decisions, Plan
Interpersonal Guide Others, Resolve Conflict and Negotiate, Advocate and Influence, Cooperate with Others
Lifelong Learning Take Responsibility for Learning, Reflect and Evaluate, Learn through Research (optional), Use Information and Communications Technology (optional)

T E A M
P R O J E C T

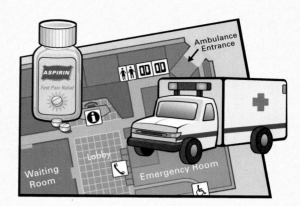

An emergency

In this project you will make a role play or a skit. Your group will perform the skit for the class. Members of your group will play the roles of: a patient, a family member, a 911 operator, an admitting person, a doctor.

1. Form a team with four or five students.

   In your team, you need:

Position	Job	Student Name
Student 1 Leader	See that everyone speaks English. See that everyone participates.	
Student 2 Secretary	Write out the skit and make parts for everyone with help from the team.	
Student 3 Director	Direct the skit.	
Student 4 Spokesperson	Introduce the skit.	

2. Choose an accident or illness. Write down the symptoms. Who is the patient in your group? What is his or her name in the skit? (See pages 103–106.)

3. Write a 911 call. Who is the operator? Who is the patient? Who is calling? Do you need to drive, or is an ambulance coming? (See page 111.)

4. Write a conversation with the doctor. Who is the doctor in your group? (See page 104.)

5. Write instructions and a warning for the medicine the doctor gives. (See pages 106–109.)

6. Practice the skit and present it to the class.

PRONUNCIATION

Listen to the sounds /s/ and /th/. Can you hear the difference? Listen and repeat.

think	sink	thick	sick	thigh	sigh	thumb	sum
mouse	mouth	moss	moth	mass	math	pass	path

a sore throat   a healthy sport   a thin slice   three spoons

LEARNER LOG

Circle what you learned and write the page number where you learned it.

1. I can identify body parts.
   Yes   Maybe   No   Page *101–102*

2. I can identify symptoms.
   Yes   Maybe   No   Page *103–104*

3. I can use *should* to give advice.
   Yes   Maybe   No   Page *105–107*

4. I can understand medicine labels.
   Yes   Maybe   No   Page *108–109*

5. I can call 911.
   Yes   Maybe   No   Page *110–111*

6. I can follow directions in a hospital.
   Yes   Maybe   No   Page *112–113*

7. I can use *want to*.
   Yes   Maybe   No   Page *114–116*

8. I can make exercise goals.
   Yes   Maybe   No   Page *116*

Did you answer *No* to any questions? Review the information with a partner.

Rank what you like to do best from 1 to 6. 1 is your favorite activity. Your teacher will help you.

☐ practice listening

☐ practice speaking

☐ practice reading

☐ practice writing

☐ learn new words (vocabulary)

☐ learn grammar

In the next unit I want to practice more

(Answers will vary.)

_____ .

Unit 6 Pronunciation and Learner Log

Pronunciation *(optional)*: **10–15 min.**

Listen to the sounds /s/ and /th/. Can you hear the difference? Listen and repeat. *(Audio CD Track 41)*

Play the recording and pause after each word.

For additional pronunciation practice: (The following words should be used for pronunciation practice, not for vocabulary instruction.) Write these pairs of words on the board. Read as a class and then have students read one word from each pair to a partner. The partners must spell the word they think they've heard.

(initial sound)

thin	*sin*
thought	*sought*
thank	*sank*

(final sound)

faith	*face*
Beth	*Bess*
myth	*miss*

Learner Log

Presentation 1: 10–15 min.

If needed, review the purpose of the Learner Log.

Circle what you learned and write the page number where you learned it. Students research the answers individually. When they've finished, they should share their answers with a partner. These results need not be shared with the class.

Practice 1: 10–15 min.

Rank what you like to do best from 1 to 6. 1 is your favorite activity. Your teacher will help you. Results should be shared with the class in order to demonstrate to students how people learn differently.

Evaluation 1: 10–15 min.

In the next unit I want to practice more **_____.** Students should fill in the blank with assistance from a partner or from you. They

may focus on a skill (e.g., listening), on a vocabulary area (e.g., numbers), on grammar, and so on. Don't limit them to a single answer. Emphasize that the purpose of completing the sentence is to improve their self-assessment skills.

> Instructor's Notes for Unit 6 Team Project, Pronunciation, and Learner Log
>
> _____
> _____
> _____
> _____
> _____
> _____
> _____
> _____
> _____
> _____
> _____
> _____
> _____
> _____
> _____
> _____
> _____
> _____
> _____
> _____
> _____

LESSON PLAN

Objective:
Identify job titles
Key vocabulary:
server, artist, cashier, office worker,
lawyer, homemaker, mechanic, teacher,
teller, restaurant, garage, courthouse,
studio, job

Pre-Assessment: Use the *Stand Out* ExamView® Pro *Test Bank* for Unit 7. *(optional)*

Warm-up and Review: 15–20 min.

Write on the board *What do you do?* Ask various students this question. At first, students may describe what they are doing at the moment.

Then ask a few other students to name their jobs or occupations. Explain that the question often means "*What is your job?*"

Make a list of students' jobs on the board . Make sure they know that being a student or a homemaker is also a job. Help students with pronunciation.

Introduction: 1 min.

State objective: *Today you are going to learn about job titles and what many people do every day.*

Presentation 1: 10–15 min.

Before students open their books, act out the five jobs shown on this page. Ask students to identify the jobs. For job titles that are more difficult to act out, give students a few additional verbal hints. For example, for *mechanic,* tell them that *this person works with cars.* Write their responses on the board even if they are not exactly accurate.

Go over the words you've written on the board several times, correcting inaccuracies as you go.

Practice 1: 15–20 min.

Ask students to open their books and point to the job titles you acted out. Do the presentation again.

(A) Write the job under the picture.

Ask students to write the words and then check them as a class.

(B) In pairs, ask questions about each person.

You may want to mention that students can use *He's/She's* instead of *He/She is* and to highlight the difference between the contraction of *is* and possessive *'s.*

Ask students to individually rank the jobs in exercise A ranging from those they most prefer to those they least prefer. Then, in groups, have them compare their answers.

Evaluation 1: 5–10 min.

Ask volunteers to report on their rankings and discuss them as a class.

Pronunciation:

An optional pronunciation activity is found on the final page of this unit. This pronunciation activity may be introduced during any lesson in this unit, especially if students need practice contrasting the sounds of long **e** and short **i.** Go to pages 140/140a for Unit 7 Pronunciation.

STANDARDS CORRELATIONS

CASAS: 4.1.8, 4.8.1
SCANS: Interpersonal Participates as a Member of a Team, Teaches Others New Skills
Information Acquires and Evaluates Information, Organizes and Maintains information, Interprets and Communicates Information

Basic Skills Writing, Listening, Speaking, Decision Making
EFF: Communication Read with Understanding, Convey Ideas in Writing, Speak So Others Can Understand, Listen Actively
Decision Making Solve Problems and Make Decisions
Interpersonal Guide Others, Cooperate with Others

UNIT 7

Working on It

GOALS

- Identify job titles
- Understand job vocabulary
- Use the simple past
- Prepare for a job interview
- Identify tools and skills for work
- Understand safety signs and warnings
- Use adjectives and adverbs

LESSON 1   What's your job?

GOAL ▶ Identify job titles

Vocabulary

A Write the job under the picture.

| teller | nurse | office worker | server | mechanic |

Alan

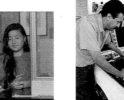

server

Michelle

office worker

Isabel

teller

Tony

mechanic

Huong

nurse

B In pairs, ask questions about each person.

EXAMPLE:
Student A: What is Tony's job?
Student B: He is a mechanic.

C **Where do these people work? Complete the sentences using the words from the box. Then add one sentence of your own.**

restaurant	school	hospital	supermarket
office	bank	studio	garage

a nurse
an artist

EXAMPLE:
A nurse works in a hospital.

1. A mechanic *works in a garage* .

2. An office worker *works in an office* .

3. A teller *works in a bank* .

4. A server *works in a restaurant* .

5. A cashier *works in a supermarket* .

6. An artist *works in a studio* .

7. A teacher *works in a school* .

8. *(Answers will vary.)* .

D **Talk to four students.**   *(Answers will vary.)*

Name	What is your job?	Where do you work?
Ex. *Huong*	*nurse*	*hospital*
1.		
2.		
3.		
4.		

E **Make sentences about each student in exercise D.**

EXAMPLE:
Huong is a nurse. She works in a hospital.

1. *(Answers will vary.)* .

2. _____ .

3. _____ .

4. _____ .

Presentation 2: 10–15 min.

Ask students again what they do and also where they work. Help them by saying that you are a teacher and work at a school. Write the questions *What do you do?* and *Where do you work?* on the board. Ask for students' answers and write them on the board in complete sentences. For example, *Huong's a nurse. She works in a hospital.*

Ask students to open their books and look at the example.

Practice 2: 15–20 min.

C Where do these people work? Complete the sentences using the words from the box. Then add one sentence of your own.

Encourage students to use their own ideas for the final sentence. Walk around the classroom to read their work, correcting as necessary.

Evaluation 2: 5–10 min.

Ask volunteers to write their sentences on the board.

Presentation 3: 5–10 min.

Draw a cluster diagram on the board. Make a central circle and inside it write *Places people work.* Connect three to five secondary circles to the central circle. Write the names of common employers in these outer circles. For example, you might write *restaurant, hospital,* and *school.*

Now ask students to name the kinds of jobs that are associated with a school. Write the information in yet smaller circles around the one labeled *schools.*

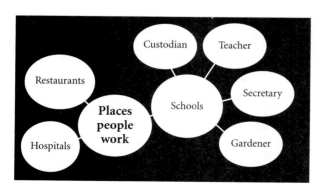

Practice 3: 15–20 min.

Ask student groups to either think of other places where people work or use the ones you've written on the board. Groups should then make a list of jobs associated with those places.

Evaluation 3: 10 min.

Ask each group to report their list of jobs to the class without revealing the identity of the employers. The class will try and guess those identities.

Application: 15–20 min.

D Talk to four students.

Have students walk around the classroom to question those not seated nearby.

E Make sentences about each student in exercise D.

Refer to the *Activity Bank 1 CD-ROM*, Unit 7 Worksheet 1, for additional vocabulary and listening activities about job titles. The listening is on *AB1 CD-ROM* Track 12. (*optional*)

Instructor's Notes for Lesson 1

> ### LESSON PLAN
>
> *Objective:*
> *Interpret general workplace vocabulary*
> *Key vocabulary:*
> *part-time, full-time, apply, benefits,*
> *application, experience, sick leave,*
> *insurance, vacation*

Warm-up and Review: 15–20 min.

Ask the students who did the application from the previous lesson to present another student to the class. Students should stand up and say something similar to *This is Huong. She is a nurse.*

Introduction: 5–10 min.

Ask the class where students can find out about jobs. Make a list of their responses on the board. Ask them if they know about help wanted ads in the newspaper and if it is difficult to understand them.

State objective: *Today we will learn how to understand job vocabulary used in newspaper classified ads.*

Presentation 1: 10–15 min.

Write the word *benefits* **on the board** and ask the students what they think it means. Ask for examples. Write *vacation, sick leave,* and *health insurance* on the board and make sure students understand the meaning of each word.

Have students open their books and look at the classified ad. Ask them to find the job title, the pay, and the phone number.

Review the entire vocabulary box in exercise A with the class.

A Write the words with the abbreviations above.

Do this activity as a class.

Prepare the class for focused listening. See Teaching Hints for help with focused listening.

Practice 1: 10–15 min.

B Listen to the conversations. Which benefits are they talking about? Fill in the circle next to the correct answer.
(Audio CD Track 42)

Play the recording a few times if necessary.

Ask the students what they think is a reasonable amount of vacation per year. Ask them what they think is a reasonable amount of sick leave per year.

Evaluation 1: 10–15 min.

Review student comprehension of job-related benefits. Ask if students know about other benefits in their jobs (e.g. money for education). Explain any new vocabulary.

STANDARDS CORRELATIONS

CASAS: 4.1.3, 4.1.6, 4.1.8
SCANS: Interpersonal Participates as a Member of a Team, Teaches Others New Skills, Exercises Leadership
Information Acquires and Evaluates Information, Organizes and Maintains Information, Interprets and Communicates Information, Uses Computers to Process Information (optional)
Systems Understands Systems
Technology Applies Technology to Task (optional)
Basic Skills Reading, Writing, Listening, Speaking

Thinking Skills Creative Thinking, Decision Making, Problem Solving
EFF: Communication Read with Understanding, Convey Ideas in Writing, Speak So Others Can Understand, Listen Actively, Observe Critically
Decision Making Solve Problems and Make Decisions
Interpersonal Guide Others, Cooperate with Others
Lifelong Learning Use Information and Communications Technology (optional)

LESSON 2 Job hunting

GOAL ▶ **Understand job vocabulary**

Vocabulary

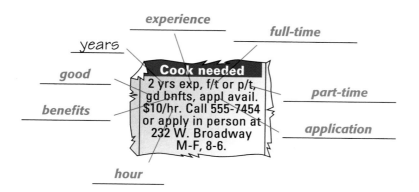

experience
years
full-time
good
benefits
part-time
application
hour

> **Cook needed**
> 2 yrs exp, f/t or p/t,
> gd bnfts, appl avail.
> $10/hr. Call 555-7454
> or apply in person at
> 232 W. Broadway
> M-F, 8-6.

 A **Write the words with the abbreviations above.**

~~years~~	experience	application	part-time
hour	good	full-time	benefits

 B **Listen to the conversations. Which benefits are they talking about? Fill in the circle next to the correct answer.**

1. Listen to Roberto and his boss. Circle the benefit.
   ● vacation　　○ sick leave　　○ insurance

2. Listen to Anya and her supervisor. Circle the benefit.
   ○ vacation　　○ sick leave　　● insurance

3. Listen to Steve and his manager. Circle the benefit.
   ○ vacation　　● sick leave　　○ insurance

What are benefits?

sick leave — you get paid if you are sick

insurance — you can get health insurance through your job

vacation — you get paid for a number of vacation days each year

---

Read the advertisements.

1.
    Nurse
    f/t, gd bnfts,
    2 yrs/exp necessary,
    $22/hr.
    call 555-3456

2.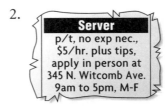
    Server
    p/t, no exp nec.,
    $5/hr. plus tips,
    apply in person at
    345 N. Witcomb Ave.
    9am to 5pm, M-F

3.
    ★ **Driver** ★
    f/t or p/t, work 7 days,
    bnfts., $18/hr,
    no exp, will train,
    current driver's license,
    speak Eng. and Span.
    Call Emily at 555-5432

4.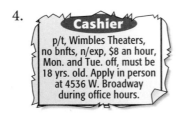
    Cashier
    p/t, Wimbles Theaters,
    no bnfts, n/exp, $8 an hour,
    Mon. and Tue. off, must be
    18 yrs. old. Apply in person
    at 4536 W. Broadway
    during office hours.

5.
    Mechanic
    Mike's Garage,
    f/t, night shift,
    $12, bnfts, no exp,
    will train.
    Call 555-7469

D **Complete the chart about the advertisements.**

Position	Experience?	F/T or P/T	Benefits?	Pay
1. *nurse*	2 years	*full-time*	Yes	*$22/hr*
2. server	*no*	*part-time*	*No*	*$5/hr plus tips*
3. *driver*	*no*	full-time and part-time	*Yes*	*$18/hr*
4. *cashier*	*no*	*part-time*	No	*$8/hr*
5. *mechanic*	*no*	*full-time*	Yes	$12/hr

E **Work in pairs. Ask and answer the questions about your job.**

1. What do you do? *(Answers will vary.)* _____

2. How many years of experience do you have? _____

3. Do you work full-time or part-time? _____

4. Do you have benefits? _____

 F **Active Task:** Look in a newspaper or on the Internet and find a job you want. Tell the class.

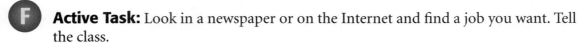

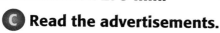

Presentation 2: 5 min.

C Read the advertisements.

Go over each ad. Ask students comprehension questions to confirm that they understand. Ask focused listening questions like *Which job pays $12 an hour?* and *Which jobs are full-time positions?* Use all the new vocabulary in your questions. Show students how to complete the chart in exercise D.

Practice 2: 10–15 min.

D Complete the chart about the advertisements.

Ask students to work in pairs.

Evaluation 2: 5–10 min.

Review the completed charts with students.

Presentation 3: 10–15 min.

Review the new vocabulary. Write all the words on the board. Ask students to make abbreviations for each of the words. There are no precise abbreviations for classified ads. As long as the ads convey the intended meaning, they are acceptable.

Practice 3: 15–20 min.

Ask students in groups to make their own classified ads about a job held by someone in their group. Make sure they understand that they should use abbreviations. The ads can be put on the computer in a template for a newspaper page, available on the *Activity Bank 1 CD-ROM,* Unit 7 Worksheet 2 *(optional).*

Evaluation 3: 10–15 min.

Ask groups to report by reading their classified ads to the class. Make sure they pronounce whole words represented by the abbreviations.

Application: 15–20 min.

E Work in pairs. Ask and answer the questions about your job.

F Active Task: Look in a newspaper or on the Internet and find a job you want. Tell the class.

Refer to the *Activity Bank 1 CD-ROM,* Unit 7 Worksheet 3 for additional practice with job vocabulary and classified ads. *(optional)*

Instructor's Notes for Lesson 2

LESSON PLAN

Objectives:
Discuss job history,
Scan for information, Use the
simple past
Key vocabulary:
mail carrier, start, count, fix, deliver,
busboy, salesperson, sell, serve, cook,
prepare, move

Warm-up and Review: 10–15 min.

For shorter classes, review parts of an
advertisement and ask students in groups to
make a classified ad advertising a job opening.
For longer classes that did this activity in the
previous lesson, ask the students to write another
classified ad. These ads should be related to a job
held by a student in the group.

Introduction: 5–10 min.

Ask students what jobs they had (if any) before
coming to the United States.

State objective: *Today you will learn to talk
about jobs in the past using the simple
past tense.*

Presentation 1: 20–30 min.

Ask students to look at the picture at the top of
the page and answer the questions in the box.
Add any other questions you consider
appropriate.

A Read about Francisco.

Read the story as a class. Make sure the students
understand by asking comprehension questions.

Practice 1: 10–15 min.

B Answer the questions.

C Fill in the job history for Francisco.

Allow students in pairs or groups to try to figure
out how to complete the chart. Give them enough
time to struggle through this activity before you
step in to help.

Refer to *Stand Out Grammar Challenge 1*, Unit 7, page 49 for more practice. *(optional)*

Evaluation 1: 5–10 min.

Review the completed charts.

LESSON 3 — What was your job before?

GOAL ▶ Use the simple past   **Grammar**

What is Francisco's job?
Does he work inside or outside?

A **Read about Francisco.**

My name is Francisco. I'm from Guatemala. Now I work in the United States. I'm a mail carrier. I deliver mail to about 200 houses every day. I started my job in July of 1999. Before I moved to the United States, I was a cook. I cooked hamburgers and French fries in a fast-food restaurant.

B **Answer the questions.**

1. Where is Francisco from? *Francisco is from Guatemala.*

2. What is his job now? *He is a mail carrier.*

3. What does he do in his job? *He delivers mail to about 200 houses every day.*

4. When did he start his job? *He started his job in July of 1999.*

5. What was his job in Guatemala? *He was a cook.*

6. Where did he work in Guatemala? *He worked in a fast-food restaurant.*

C **Fill in the job history for Francisco.**

Position	Company	From	To	Duties
Mail Carrier	U.S. Government	*07-1999*	*present*	*Delivered mail*
Cook	*Fast-food restaurant*	*03-1995*	*07-1999*	*Cooked hamburgers and french fries*
Bus boy	La Cantina	03-1992	03-1995	Cleaned tables

Study the chart with your teacher.

Simple past: Regular verbs			
Subject	**Base + *ed***		**Example sentence**
I	cleaned	tables	I cleaned tables.
you	cooked	hamburgers	You cooked hamburgers.
he	prepared	breakfast	He prepared breakfast.
she	delivered	packages	She delivered packages.
it	counted	the money	It counted the money.
we	helped	other workers	We helped other workers.
they	moved	to the United States	They moved to the United States.

Simple past: *be*			
Subject	***be***		**Example sentence**
I, he, she, it	was	a mail carrier	I was a mail carrier.
we, you, they	were	happy	You were happy.

E   **Write sentences about these workers.**

EXAMPLE:
Anya was an office worker.
(type) She **_typed_** letters.

1. Ernesto was a delivery person.

   (deliver) He _____*delivered*_____ packages.

2. David was a cashier.

   (count) He _____*counted*_____ money.

3. Anita was a nurse.

   (help) She _____*helped*_____ sick people.

4. Eva and Anya were teachers.

   (work) They _____*worked*_____ in a school.

Presentation 2: 20–30 min.

D Study the chart with your teacher.

Practice the grammar structure with the students. Help them see that the *ed* form is the regular form of the verb. At this point, students are probably not ready for an explanation of pronunciation of the past tense ending.

 Refer to *Stand Out Grammar Challenge 1,* Unit 7, page 50 for more practice. *(optional)*

E Write sentences about these workers.

As an extension of the chart, do this exercise with the students.

(Presentation 2 is continued on page 127a.)

Presentation 2 (continued):

Prepare students for exercise F by practicing the dialog together. See Teaching Hints for suggestions on presenting dialogs. Show students how to substitute the information below.

Practice 2: 10–15 min.   2⁺

F Practice the conversation with your partner. Then make new conversations using the information below.

You may want to review the past tense of all these verbs before and after doing the exercise.

 Refer to *Stand Out Grammar Challenge 1*, Unit 7, pages 51–52 for more practice. *(optional)*

Evaluation 2: 10–15 min.   2⁺

Ask for volunteers to demonstrate the dialog in front of the class.

Presentation 3: 10–15 min.   3

 Prepare the students to do Worksheet 4 from Unit 7 in the Activity Bank 1 CD-ROM for Practice 3. The worksheet asks students to take information from a job history and write sentences in the simple past tense.

Practice 3: 20–25 min.   3

Ask students to pair up and complete the worksheet.

Evaluation 3: 5–10 min.   3

Review student worksheets.

Application: 20–30 min.   1.5⁺

Preview the questions in exercise G. Show the class how to do this activity by demonstrating the questions with a few students.

G Talk to four students. Ask them questions and fill in the chart.

 Refer to the *Activity Bank 1 CD-ROM*, Unit 7 Worksheet 5, for additional activities related to using the simple past tense. *(optional)*

Instructor's Notes for Lesson 3

Practice the conversation with your partner. Then make new conversations using the information below.

EXAMPLE:
Miyuki: What was your last job?
Anya: I was an office worker.
Miyuki: What did you do as an office worker?
Anya: I typed letters.
Miyuki: What do you do now?
Anya: I'm a student. I study English.

BEFORE	NOW
1. cashier / count money	homemaker/look after my family
2. teacher / help students	writer / write books
3. mechanic / fix cars	driver / drive a taxi
4. mail carrier / deliver letters	salesperson / sell computers
5. cook / cook hamburgers	server / serve food
6. busboy / clean tables	actor / make movies

G **Talk to four students. Ask them questions and fill in the chart.**

(Answers will vary.)

Name	What was your last job?	What did you do as a _____?
Ex. Francisco	I was a cook.	I cooked hamburgers.

GOAL ▶ **Prepare for a job interview** | **Life Skill** |

 Look at the pictures. What is good in a job interview and what is not good?

chewing gum

smoking

good posture

bright clothing

firm handshake   eye contact

 Use the words above to complete the chart and add your own ideas.

Good in a job interview	Not good in a job interview
good posture	*chewing gum*
firm handshake	*smoking*
eye contact	*bright clothing*
(Other answers will vary.)	*(Other answers will vary.)*

> **LESSON PLAN**
> Objective:
> Prepare for a job interview
> Key vocabulary:
> interview, chewing gum, handshake,
> eye contact, smoking, posture,
> on file, appointment

Warm-up and Review: 10–15 min. (1.5⁺)

Turn to a student and shake his or her hand.
Remind the class of how to shake hands the American way by curling the fingers around the other person's hand firmly. Write on the board *I'm looking for a job. Do you have any openings?* Shake hands with a few other students and say that statement and question. Call on volunteers to do the same. Then have all students walk around the room and practice the exchange for a few minutes. You can also add to the board typical responses to the question, such as *Yes, here's an application.*

Introduction: 5 min. (1.5⁺)

State objective: *Today you will learn about how to prepare for a job interview.*

Presentation 1: 15–20 min. (1.5⁺)

Look at the pictures at the top of the page and help students with new vocabulary. Avoid talking about what makes a good or bad interview at this point. The students will determine this in the practice.

Do some focused listening by talking about each item. Ask the students to identify what you are

talking about. For example, you might say, *I'm going in for an interview today and I really need some help. I'm so hungry. Maybe I'll chew some gum so my stomach won't growl.*

Practice 1: 15–20 min. (1.5⁺)

A Look at the pictures. What is good in a job interview and what is not good?
Ask the students in pairs to discuss the question and fill in the chart.

B Use the words above to complete the chart and add your own ideas.
Ask the students to continue but now to work in groups. After allowing sufficient time, ask groups to send a representative to another group to seek other ideas to bring back.

Evaluation 1: 5–10 min. (1.5⁺)

Draw the chart on the board and ask group representatives to enter their information. If students disagree, for example, about whether bright clothing is good for an interview or not, then discuss how different cultures view these things differently.

STANDARDS CORRELATIONS

CASAS: 4.1.5, 4.1.7
SCANS: **Interpersonal** Participates as a Member of a Team, Teaches Others New Skills
Information Acquires and Evaluates Information, Organizes and Maintains Information, Interprets and Communicates Information
Systems Understands Systems, Monitors and Corrects Performance, Improves and Designs Systems
Basic Skills Reading, Writing, Listening, Speaking

Thinking Skills Creative Thinking, Decision Making, Problem Solving
EFF: **Communication** Read with Understanding, Convey Ideas in Writing, Speak So Others Can Understand, Listen Actively, Observe Critically
Decision Making Solve Problems and Make Decisions
Interpersonal Guide Others, Resolve Conflict and Negotiate, Advocate and Influence, Cooperate with Others
Lifelong Learning Reflect and Evaluate

Presentation 2: 10–15 min.

Write *Do you have any openings?* **on the board.** Help students understand the question. Then write *We will keep your application on file.* Ask students if they know what this sentence means. Then have them open their books and look at the picture. Ask the questions in the box and add any others you consider appropriate.

Practice 2: 15–20 min.

 **Read the conversations below. What is the next line in each conversation? Write the sentences from the box with the correct conversations. Then listen and check your answers.** *(Audio CD Track 43)*

Ask students to practice the conversation in pairs and to try to determine what a correct response might be. Write their ideas on the board. Do not give the correct answers or play the recording at this point.

Evaluation 2: 5 min.
(Audio CD Track 43)

Play the recording again so that students can check their answers.

Presentation 3: 5–10 min.
(Audio CD Track 43)

Ask students to listen to the recordings again and see if they can tell what is important. For example, the word *please* is used regularly.

Practice 3: 15–20 min.

 Ask students to do *Activity Bank 1 CD-ROM, Unit 7 Worksheet 6* for this lesson. Students are to study lines from an interview, then compose their own interview.

Evaluation 3: 10–15 min.

Have volunteer pairs perform their own interview dialog. Ask the class if the questions and answers were clear.

Application: 20–30 min.

Ask the students in pairs to write and perform new dialogs using all the information in this unit. Ask half of the class to prepare dialogs that show good examples and the other half to show bad interviews.

Instructor's Notes for Lesson 4

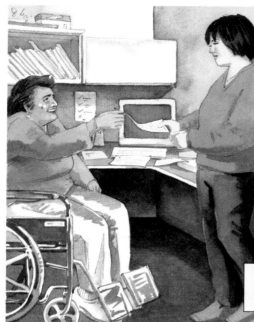

Where is Miyuki?
What is she doing?

C **Read the conversations below. What is the next line in each conversation? Write the sentences from the box with the correct conversations. Then listen and check your answers.**

Thanks. I'll wait here.	No, but I'm good at math and I learn quickly.
Can I make an appointment, please?	OK, can I have an application please?

1. *Miyuki:* Excuse me. I'm interested in a job. Do you have any openings?
   Manager: Not right now, but we can keep your name on file.

   Miyuki: *OK, can I have an application please?* _____

2. *Miyuki:* Here is my application. Can I see the manager?
   Worker: Not just now, she's busy.

   Miyuki: *Can I make an appointment, please?* _____

3. *Manager:* Are you interested in a job as a clerk?
   Miyuki: Yes, that's right.
   Manager: Do you have any experience?

   Miyuki: *No, but I'm good at math and I learn quickly.* _____

4. *Miyuki:* I want to make an appointment to see the manager.
   Worker: Just a moment, I'll see if she's free.

   Miyuki: *Thanks. I'll wait here.* _____

GOAL ▶ **Identify tools and skills for work**   **Vocabulary**

A **Talk about the tools with your teacher.**

computer   saw and   wrench   broom   phone   copy
               hammer   and mop   machine

B **Write one or two tools for each job.** *(Answers may vary. Suggestions below.)*

Job	Tool	Skill
carpenter	*saw and hammer*	*makes furniture*
computer programmer	*computer*	*writes programs*
construction worker	*saw and hammer*	*builds houses*
custodian	*broom and mop*	*cleans offices*
delivery person	*truck, phone, map*	*delivers packages*
driver	*truck or car, phone*	*drives a truck*
mechanic	*wrench*	*fixes cars*
office worker	*phone, copy machine*	*types letters*
student	*computer, pencil*	*listens carefully*
teacher	*computer, board*	*helps students*

C **Look at the skills below. Complete the chart above with the skills from the box.**

drives a truck	builds houses	delivers packages	writes programs
makes furniture	helps students	types letters	cleans offices
fixes cars	listens carefully		

LESSON PLAN

Objective:
Identify common tools and skills
required for one's job
Key vocabulary:
carpenter, computer programmer,
construction worker, custodian, delivery
person, driver, mechanic, office worker,
hammer, saw, wrench, broom, mop, tools

Warm-up and Review: 15–20 min.

Ask volunteers to perform their dialogs from the previous lesson.

Introduction: 1 min.

Write the word *tools* on the board and ask students if they know what it means. Write a few examples under the word to help students understand. You might also say *A hammer is a tool used by a carpenter* as you make a hammering motion to help them understand.

State objective: *Today you will learn about tools at work.*

Presentation 1: 15–20 min.

A Talk about the tools with your teacher.

Quiz the students on the vocabulary. Pantomime the use of some tools and ask the students to guess what they are. Invite other students to do similar pantomimes in front of the class.

Practice 1: 10–15 min.

B Write one or two tools for each job.

Ask students to work in groups and write the tools in the chart.

C Look at the skills below. Complete the chart above with the skills from the box.

Evaluation 1: 10–15 min.

Review completed student charts.

STANDARDS CORRELATIONS

CASAS: 4.1.2, 4.1.8, 4.5.1
SCANS: **Interpersonal** Participates as a Member of a Team, Teaches Others New Skills, Serves Clients/Customers
Information Acquires and Evaluates Information, Organizes and Maintains Information, Interprets and Communicates Information
Systems Understands Systems, Monitors and Corrects Performance
Technology Applies Technology to Task (optional)

Basic Skills Reading, Writing, Listening, Speaking
Thinking Skills Decision Making, Problem Solving
EFF: **Communication** Read with Understanding, Speak So Others Can Understand, Listen Actively, Observe Critically
Decision Making Solve Problems and Make Decisions, Plan
Interpersonal Guide Others, Cooperate with Others
Lifelong Learning Take Responsibility for Learning, Reflect and Evaluate, Use Information and Communications Technology (optional)

Presentation 2: 10–15 min.

D Study the job history part of Ricardo's application.

Ask comprehension questions about the dates. Help students see that in a job history section they should always enter their most recent job first. Ask what positions Ricardo has had and what companies he has worked for.

Review *can* with the students by referring to the adjacent box.

 Refer to *Stand Out Grammar Challenge 1*, Unit 7, page 54 for more practice. *(optional)*

Practice 2: 10–15 min.

E What is Ricardo's experience? What can he do? Write sentences.

After the students have written this, ask them in groups to identify the tools that Ricardo might use in each job.

Evaluation 2: 5–10 min.

Review students' work and write the tools the students came up with on the board.

Presentation 3: 15–20 min.

Write the following dialog on the board:
Applicant: *Excuse me. I'm a carpenter. Do you have any openings?*
Business Owner: *Yes. We need a carpenter. Do you have your own tools?*
Applicant: *Yes. I have a hammer and a saw.*
Business Owner: *That's great. Can you start tomorrow?*
Applicant: *Sure, I can.*

Prepare students to form new dialogs following this model by asking them to refer to exercise B on the previous page. See Teaching Hints for help with presenting dialogs.

Practice 3: 10–15 min.

Ask the students to practice the dialog in pairs and substitute the information from exercise B page 130. See Teaching Hints for alternate ways to practice dialogs.

Evaluation 3: 10–15 min.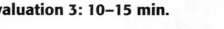

Ask volunteers to demonstrate the dialog in front of the class.

Application: 10–15 min.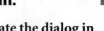

F What can you do? What tools can you use? Make a list.

G Active Task: Get a job application from a local business or from the Internet. What information does it ask for? Tell the class.

 Refer to the *Activity Bank 1 CD-ROM*, Unit 7 Worksheet 7 (two pages), for additional activities related to tools, office machines and use of the modal *can*. *(optional)*

Instructor's Notes for Lesson 5
_____
_____
_____
_____
_____
_____
_____
_____
_____
_____
_____
_____
_____

D   **Study the job history part of Ricardo's application.**

can = ability
I can work.
You can sweep.
He can type.
She can drive.
We can help.
They can build.

Position	Company	From	To	Duties
Manager	The Happy Lunch Deli	9-18-99	present	managed 22 employees
Cashier	The Happy Lunch Deli	3-15-92	9-17-99	worked the cash register
Mechanic	Self-employed	7-2-83	3-14-86	fixed cars
Delivery Person	Mindanao Reporter	8-11-81	6-27-83	delivered newspapers

E   **What is Ricardo's experience? What can he do? Write sentences.**

1. *Ricardo can manage 22 employees.*
2. *He can* *work a cash register.*
3. *He can fix cars.*
4. *He can deliver newspapers.*

F   **What can you do? What tools can you use? Make a list.**

Skills _____   Tools _____

I can *(Answers will vary.)* _____   *(Answers will vary.)* _____

_____   _____

_____   _____

 G   **Active Task:** Get a job application from a local business or from the Internet. What information does it ask for? Tell the class.

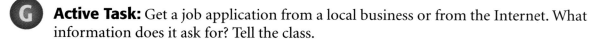

6 Keep out!

GOAL ▶ Understand safety signs and warnings   **Life Skill**

1.

2.

3.

4.

5.

6.

A **Study the signs with your teacher. Write the warning words.**

1. **Caution**

2. *Danger*

3. *Fire Hazard*

4. *Danger*

5. *Notice*

6. *Warning*

 B **Listen to the description of a factory. Write the correct number next to each warning.**

_4_ You must keep your hands away from this machine.

_6_ You must watch your step when this area is wet.

_3_ You must not smoke here.

_1_ You must wear a hard hat.

_5_ You must keep this area clear.

_2_ You must not enter.

LESSON PLAN

Objectives:
Read safety signs and warnings, Use *must* Key vocabulary:
be careful, protection, caution, hazard, keep hands clear, danger, warning, notice

Warm-up and Review: 10–15 min.

Ask students to talk to a partner about what work they can do and what abilities and experience they have. They wrote this information for exercise F in the previous lesson. Then ask volunteers to report to the class about their partner's skills and abilities.

Introduction: 1 min.

Write *Be careful!* **on the board and help students understand what it means.** Ask if they have ever seen a sign that reads *Warning.* Inform students that such a sign is a signal to be careful. Remind them of warning labels on medications.

State objective: *Today you will learn about warning signs at your job.*

Presentation 1: 15–20 min.

A Study the signs with your teacher. Write the warning words.

There is a lot of vocabulary in these signs. The most important words for this lesson are the ones they write in the exercise. Ask students to think of names of places where they might see these signs.

Prepare the class for focused listening. See Teaching Hints for help with focused listening. Students will be listening for information that matches the sentences in exercise B.

Practice 1: 10–15 min.

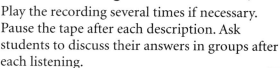 **B Listen to the description of a factory. Write the correct number next to each warning.** *(Audio CD Track 44)*

Play the recording several times if necessary. Pause the tape after each description. Ask students to discuss their answers in groups after each listening.

Evaluation 1: 5 min.

(Audio CD Track 44)

Review the answers and play the recording again.

STANDARDS CORRELATIONS

CASAS: 4.3.1
SCANS: **Resources** Allocates Materials and Facility Resources
Interpersonal Participates as a Member of a Team, Teaches Others New Skills, Exercises Leadership
Information Acquires and Evaluates Information, Organizes and Maintains Information, Interprets and Communicates Information
Systems Understands Systems, Monitors and Corrects Performance, Improves and Designs Systems
Basic Skills Reading, Listening, Speaking

Thinking Skills Creative Thinking, Decision Making, Problem Solving, Knowing How to Learn, Reasoning
EFF: **Communication** Read with Understanding, Speak So Others Can Understand, Listen Actively, Observe Critically
Decision Making Solve Problems and Make Decisions, Plan
Interpersonal Guide Others, Resolve Conflict and Negotiate, Advocate and Influence, Cooperate with Others
Lifelong Learning Take Responsibility for Learning, Reflect and Evaluate, Learn through Research, Use Information and Communications Technology

Presentation 2: 10–15 min. `1.5+`

C Study the chart with your teacher.

Practice and explain the new structure with the students.

Refer to *Stand Out Grammar Challenge 1,* Unit 7, page 55 for more practice. *(optional)*

Practice 2: 10–15 min. `2+`

D Where can you see these warning signs, and what do they mean? Write one sentence for each sign using *must* or *must not.*

Demonstrate some examples for exercise D verbally. Then have students write the sentences using *must* and *must not.*

Evaluation 2: 5–10 min. `2+`

Ask groups to report to the class.

Presentation 3: 10 min. `3`

Use Worksheet 8 from Unit 7 of the *Activity Bank 1 CD-ROM.* Help the students understand that they will read signs and discuss where to place them on the floor plan of the factory. Review vocabulary first.

Practice 3: 20–25 min. `3`

Ask students to complete Worksheet 8 from the *AB1 CD-ROM* in groups.

Evaluation 3: 10–15 min. `3`

Review the worksheet with the class.

Application: 20–30 min. `1.5+`

E Look in the classroom and in your school. What warnings can you say to another student?

Ask students to do this activity either in pairs or in groups.

Refer to the *Activity Bank 1 CD-ROM,* Unit 7 Worksheet 9, for additional practice reading safety signs and using the modal *must.* *(optional)*

Instructor's Notes for Lesson 6

C **Study the chart with your teacher.**

must				
Subject	*must*	**Base**		**Example sentence**
I, you, he, she, it, we, they	must	wear	head and eye protection	We must wear head and eye protection.
	must not	smoke	in this area	You must not smoke in this area.

D **Where can you see these warning signs, and what do they mean? Write one sentence for each sign using *must* or *must not*.**

EXAMPLES:
Danger No Entry ***You must not enter.***
Head protection required ***You must wear a hard hat.***

1. Keep out   *You must not enter.*
2. No parking   *You must not park.*
3. Foot protection required   *You must wear foot protection.*
4. Go slow   *You must go slow.*
5. Hot surface   *You must not touch the surface.*
6. Moving vehicles   *You must watch out for moving vehicles.*

E **Look in the classroom and in your school. What warnings can you say to another student?**

1. ***Be careful. You must***
2. ***You must not***
3.
4.
   (Answers will vary.)

 **LESSON 7**

She's a very careful driver.

GOAL ▶ **Use adjectives and adverbs**   **Grammar**

 A   **Look at Fernando's evaluation. What is good? What is a problem?**

Evaluation Form

Date: May 4, 2003
Company: Paul's Radio and CD
Name: Fernando Gaspar
Position: Sales Clerk
Supervisor: Leticia Garcia

Punctuality:

(Needs improvement)   Good   Superior

Appearance (professional dress and grooming):

Needs improvement   Good   (Superior)

Communication Skills:

Needs improvement   (Good)   Superior

Product knowledge:

Needs improvement   (Good)   Superior

Comments:

Fernando is a good employee. I worked with him for eight hours today. He talked
with the customers well. He was 10 minutes late to work. This is a problem. He
says he has problems with his car. Fernando is a good salesperson and has a
very good knowledge of the product.

Signed:

Leticia Garcia

 B   **Look at the evaluation. Answer the questions.**

1. Where does Fernando work? _He works at Pauls's Radio and CD._

2. What is his supervisor's name? _His supervisor's name is Leticia Garcia._

3. What does Fernando do well? _He talks with the customers well._

4. What does he do very well? _He has very good knowledge of the product._

5. What does he need to improve? _He needs to improve his punctuality._

LESSON PLAN

Objectives:
Use adjectives and adverbs; Read and interpret a job evaluation
Key vocabulary:
evaluation, improve(ment), superior, product knowledge, punctuality, appearance, supervisor

Warm-up and Review: 10–15 min.

Ask students in groups to make a warning sign about something in the classroom. For example, if you have computers in the room, you may want groups to make a sign that keeps people from turning off computers incorrectly. Ask groups to come up with other useful signs to display in the classroom.

Introduction: 5–10 min.

Ask the students what they think makes a good worker. Write their ideas on the board. Help them with specific words. Write new vocabulary words next to the ideas students suggest. For example, write *punctuality* next to *Comes to work on time.*

State objective: *Today we will learn to read evaluation forms and use adjectives and adverbs to talk about good and bad work habits.*

Presentation 1: 10–15 min.

A Look at Fernando's evaluation. What is good? What is a problem?

Ask comprehension questions and help students understand the basic vocabulary.

Read the Comments paragraph about his performance with the students. Make sure they understand all the new words.

Practice 1: 10–15 min.

B Look at the evaluation. Answer the questions.

Ask students to work in pairs.

Evaluation 1: 5 min.

Review student answers.

STANDARDS CORRELATIONS

CASAS: 4.4.1, 4.4.4
SCANS: **Interpersonal** Participates as a Member of a Team, Teaches Others New Skills, Exercises Leadership
Information Acquires and Evaluates Information, Interprets and Communicates Information
Systems Understands Systems, Monitors and Corrects Performance
Interpersonal Guide Others, Cooperate with Others

Basic Skills Reading, Listening, Speaking
Thinking Skills Creative Thinking, Decision Making, Problem Solving
EFF: **Communication** Read with Understanding, Speak So Others Can Understand, Listen Actively, Observe Critically
Decision Making Make Decisions
Lifelong Learning Reflect and Evaluate

Presentation 2: 10–15 min.

C Study the chart and read the examples with your teacher.

Look back to the evaluation form on the previous page to make additional examples. Ask students questions to obtain responses that include adjectives and adverbs.

Refer to *Stand Out Grammar Challenge 1,* Unit 7, page 56 for more practice. *(optional)*

Practice 2: 15–20 min.

D Read the sentences and underline the correct word.

Go over the example with the students and then ask them to work in pairs. After they finish, they should check with other students to see if their answers are the same. See if students can make up their own sentences following the same pattern.

E Ask your partner. Use the words below.

Demonstrate this activity with a volunteer and allow him or her to practice it. Then ask the volunteer to walk around and converse with four other students.

Evaluation 2: 5 min.

Observe student exchanges. Try to make sure students use the correct words. Have volunteer pairs read a dialog to the class.

Study the chart and read the examples with your teacher.

Adjective	Example sentence	Adverb	Example sentence
good	I am a good speaker.	well	I speak well.
bad		badly	
slow	He is a slow driver.	slowly	He drives slowly.
quick		quickly	
loud		loudly	
quiet		quietly	
careful	They are careful workers.	carefully	They work carefully.

 Read the sentences and underline the correct word.

> An *adjective* goes before a noun.
> An *adverb* goes after a verb.

EXAMPLE:
He speaks English good/<u>well</u>.

1. She wears nice clothes to work. She always dresses good/<u>well</u>.

2. He speaks quiet/<u>quietly</u>, and I can't hear.

3. Anya can type very quick/<u>quickly</u>.

4. Rigoberto is a <u>careful</u>/carefully driver.

5. I don't have any experience, but I can learn quick/<u>quickly</u>.

6. Anya is a teacher, but she doesn't speak very loud/<u>loudly</u>.

7. A cashier counts money very careful/<u>carefully</u>.

8. Fernando is a <u>good</u>/well salesperson.

 Ask your partner. Use the words below.

EXAMPLE:
Student A: Do you drive slowly?
Student B: Yes, I do. / No, I don't. I drive quickly.

1. drive/carefully   3. speak/loudly

2. cook/well   4. type/quickly

Evaluation Form

Date: May 2, 2003
Company: Paul's Radio and CD
Name: John Perkins
Position: Sales Clerk
Supervisor: Leticia Garcia

Punctuality:

Needs improvement   (Good)   Superior

Appearance (professional dress and grooming):

(Needs improvement)   Good   Superior

Communication Skills:

Needs improvement   Good   (Superior)

Product knowledge:

(Needs improvement)   Good   Superior

Comments:

I worked with John for 4 hours. He is new. He needs to learn more about the product. He does not dress well and he needs to comb his hair. He says he was tired today. I think he has three jobs. This is a problem. John communicates well with the customers.

Signed:

Leticia Garcia

 Read John's evaluation and answer the questions in a group. *(Suggested responses below.)*

1. What does John do well? *He communicates well with the customers.*

2. What does he do badly? *He does not dress well. He needs to learn more about the product.*

3. Who is the better employee, Fernando or John? Why? *(Answers will vary.)*

 Talk to your partner. In your opinion, what makes a good employee? And what makes a good supervisor?

Presentation 3: 10–15 min.

Review the evaluation on this page as you did for page 134. Make sure that students understand all the new vocabulary.

Practice 3: 15–20 min.

Read John's evaluation and answer the questions in a group.

Ask groups of three or four to choose a leader. The leader's job is to make sure every group member asks and answers every question.

Evaluation 3: 5–10 min.

Observe the activity. Ask a member of each group to report on their group answers.

Application: 10–15 min.

G Talk to your partner. In your opinion, what makes a good employee? And what makes a good supervisor?

Make sure the students know that an employee is a worker. Ask them to talk together and make a list of their answers.

 Refer to the *Activity Bank 1 CD-ROM*, Unit 7 Worksheet 10 (two pages), for additional practice using adjectives and adverbs. *(optional)*

Instructor's Notes for Lesson 7

REVIEW
Objective:
All previous objectives
Key vocabulary:
All previous Unit 7 vocabulary

Warm-up and Review: 10–15 min.

Write *Good Employee* on the board, as well as *Good Interview.* Ask students in groups to make a list of what good employees do and another list of what people do in a good interview. Ask group representatives to write the information on the board.

Introduction: 3–5 min.

State objective: *Today we will review all that we have done in the past unit in preparation for the application project to follow.*

Ask students as a class to try to recall all the goals of this unit without looking at their books. Then remind them of the goals they haven't mentioned.

Unit Goals: Identify job titles, Understand job vocabulary, Use the simple past, Prepare for a job interview, Identify tools and skills for work, Understand safety signs and warnings, Use adjectives and adverbs.

Presentation 1, Practice 1, and Evaluation 1:

Do the Learner Log on page 120. Notes are adjacent to the page.

Presentation 2: 10–15 min.

Ask the students with their books closed to give you names of jobs they do. Write them on the board. Ask the students what tools and skills or experience they need to do the jobs listed on the board.

Practice 2: 15–20 min.

A **Write the name of the job below each picture.**

B **Read the ads and complete the chart.**

C **What tools and skills do you need for these jobs?**

Evaluation 2: 10 min.

Review student work as a class. Put charts for exercises B and C on the board or on an overhead transparency.

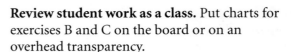

STANDARDS CORRELATIONS

CASAS: 4.1.3, 4.1.5, 4.3.1, 4.5.1, 7.1.1, 7.1.4, 7.4.1, 7.4.9, 7.4.10, 7.5.1
SCANS: **Interpersonal** Participates as a Member of a Team, Teaches Others New Skills
Information Acquires and Evaluates Information, Organizes and Maintains Information, Interprets and Communicates Information
Basic Skills Reading, Writing, Listening, Speaking
Thinking Skills Creative Thinking, Decision Making, Problem Solving

Personal Qualities Responsibility, Self-Esteem, Self-Management
EFF: **Communication** Read with Understanding, Convey Ideas in Writing, Speak So Others Can Understand, Listen Actively, Observe Critically
Decision Making Solve Problems and Make Decisions, Plan
Interpersonal Guide Others, Resolve Conflict and Negotiate, Cooperate with Others
Lifelong Learning Take Responsibility for Learning, Reflect and Evaluate

Review

A Write the name of the job below each picture.

nurse

office worker

teller

B Read the ads and complete the chart.

1.
Office assistant
f/t, gd bnfts,
4 yrs/exp necessary,
$17/hr.
call **555-2298**

2.
Restaurant Manager
p/t, restaurant exp nec,
$14/hr.,
apply in person at
2222 E. Fourth St.
8am to 12pm, M-F

3.
Delivery Person
p/t, work 7 days, no bnfts.,
$8/hr, no exp, will train,
current driver's license,
speak Eng. and Span.
Call at 555-5477

4.
Carpenter
f/t, good bnfts, n/exp,
$22 an hour, must be
18 yrs. old. Apply in person
at 3333 W. Broadway
during office hours.

5.
Mechanic,
Mike's Garage,
f/t, night shift,
$12, bnfts, no exp,
will train.
Call 555-7469

Position	Experience?	F/T or P/T	Benefits?	Pay
1. Office assistant	4 years	f/t	yes	$17/hr
2. Restaurant manager	yes	p/t	no	$14/hr
3. Delivery person	no	p/t	no	$8/hr
4. Carpenter	no	f/t	yes	$22/hr
5. mechanic	no	f/t	yes	$12/hr

C What tools and skills do you need for these jobs?

Job	Tools	Skill(s)
office worker		*(Answers will vary.)*
cook		
mechanic		
student		
teacher		

D What should you do in a job interview? What should you not do? Add sentences to this list. *(Answers may vary. Suggestions below.)*

Should

You should be on time.

You should have good posture.

You should have a firm handshake and eye contact.

Should not

You should not chew gum.

You should not smoke.

You should not wear bright colors.

E Fill in the missing words with verbs from the box. Choose the present or past tense.

be	move	have	chop	be
deliver	help	live	work	like

Francisco ____*worked*____ in Guatemala before he ____*moved*____ to California. In Guatemala, he ____*was*____ a cook in a small fast-food restaurant. He ____*chopped*____ vegetables, and ____*helped*____ in the kitchen. He ____*worked*____ fourteen hours every day and he ____*had*____ no free time. Now he ____*is*____ a mail carrier in California. He ____*delivers*____ letters and packages. He ____*likes*____ his new job very much.

F Underline the correct adverb or adjective for each sentence.

1. David is a <u>careful</u>/carefully driver. You can feel safe in his car.

2. Anya types quick/<u>quickly</u>—almost 70 words per minute.

3. Eva speaks loud/<u>loudly</u> because she has a lot of students in her class.

4. Antonio practices English every day, and he speaks English very good/<u>well</u>.

G What do these warnings mean? Write one sentence for each warning. Use *must* or *must not*.

1. No smoking *You must not smoke.*

2. Go slow *You must go slow.*

3. No parking *You must not park here.*

4. Head protection required *You must use head protection.*

Presentation 3: 5–10 min.

Review the grammar charts in the various lessons of this unit. Remind the students how to use the word *should* from the previous lesson.

 Use *Grammar Challenge 1,* pages 50–56 for Unit 7 review practice. *(optional)*

Practice 3: 30–45 min.

All the activities in Practice 3 can be done in pairs, then discussed with the class.

D What should you do in a job interview? What should you not do? Add sentences to this list.

E Fill in the missing words with verbs from the box. Choose the present or past tense.

F Underline the correct adverb or adjective for each sentence.

G What do these warnings mean? Write one sentence for each warning. Use *must* or *must not.*

Evaluation 3: 10–15 min.

Review students' work.

Application: 1–2 days

The Team Project activity on the following page is the application activity to be done on the next day.

 Post-Assessment: Use the *Stand Out* ExamView® Pro *Test Bank* for Unit 7. *(optional)*

With the ExamView® Pro *Test Bank* you can design an assessment that focuses on what students have learned. It is designed for three purposes:

- To help students practice taking a test similar to current standardized tests.
- To help the teacher evaluate how much the students have learned, retained, and acquired.
- To help students see their progress when they compare their scores to the pre-test they took earlier.

Instructor's Notes for Unit 7 Review

_____

_____

_____

_____

_____

_____

_____

_____

_____

_____

_____

_____

_____

_____

_____

_____

_____

_____

_____

_____

_____

_____

_____

Unit 7 Application Activity

TEAM PROJECT: A NEW JOB

Objective:
Project designed to apply all the objectives of this unit.
Product:
A job-hunting advice pamphlet

 Introduction:

In teams, students will develop a pamphlet explaining to others how to get and keep a job. They will be guided by a series of worksheets available on the *Activity Bank 1 CD-ROM*. There is also a template available to install on the computer if you wish to have students develop a more professional product. This project can extend over two days.

Stage 1: 10 min.

Form a team with four or five students.

Let students decide who will lead which steps described on the student page. Provide well-defined directions on the board to show how students should proceed. Explain that every student does every task. Students don't go to the next stage until the previous one is complete.

 ## Stage 2: 10–15 min.

Make a list of points to cover in the pamphlet about what a good employee needs to do.

See Worksheet 11, page 2, from Unit 7 on the *Activity Bank 1 CD-ROM*. The cover of the pamphlet is Worksheet 11, page 1 (p. 125).

Stage 3: 15–20 min.

Write a classified ad. Direct the students to decide on a job and write the ad for it on Worksheet 11, page 2. (See p. 124 for assistance.)

Stage 4: 10–15 min.

Complete the job history in an application. Have students use Worksheet 11, page 3 to fill out a sample application (pp. 125, 131).

Stage 5: 10–15 min.

Write what you should and shouldn't do in an interview. Have students use Worksheet 11, page 4 (pp. 128–129).

Stage 6: 20–30 min.

Make a list of special tools and skills needed for five different jobs including the job in the classified ad.

See Worksheet 11, page 4 on the *Activity Bank 1 CD-ROM*. (optional)

Stage 7: 20–30 min.

Make a presentation to the class. Have students use the template available on Worksheet 12 to rewrite or retype their previous Worksheets. Staple or photocopy into a final pamphlet. Share with the class. Consider sharing information with other classes either through the pamphlets or the presentations.

Consider videotaping these presentations. The students will prepare better for formal presentations if they are videotaped. Another approach would be for the students to videotape each other's presentations.

STANDARDS CORRELATIONS

CASAS: 4.8.1, 4.8.2, 4.8.5
SCANS: **Resources** Allocates Time, Allocates Material and Facility Resources, Allocates Human Resources
Interpersonal Participates as a Member of a Team, Teaches Others New Skills, Exercises Leadership, Works with Cultural Diversity
Information Acquires and Evaluates Information, Organizes and Maintains Information, Interprets and Communicates Information, Uses Computers to Process Information
Systems Understands Systems, Monitors and Corrects Performance, Improves and Designs Systems
Technology Applies Technology to Task (optional)
Basic Skills Reading, Writing, Arithmetic, Listening, Speaking

Thinking Skills Creative Thinking, Decision Making, Problem Solving, Seeing Things in the Mind's Eye, Knowing How to Learn, Reasoning
Personal Qualities Responsibility, Self-Esteem, Sociability, Self-Management, Integrity/Honesty
EFF: **Communication** Read with Understanding, Convey Ideas in Writing, Speak So Others Can Understand, Listen Actively, Observe Critically
Decision Making Solve Problems and Make Decisions, Plan
Interpersonal Guide Others, Resolve Conflict and Negotiate, Advocate and Influence, Cooperate with Others
Lifelong Learning Take Responsibility for Learning, Reflect and Evaluate

T E A M
P R O J E C T

A new job

In this project you will write a pamphlet to show people how to get and keep a job.

1. Form a team with four or five students.

   In your team, you need:

Position	Job	Student Name
Student 1 Leader	See that everyone speaks English. See that everyone participates.	
Student 2 Artist	Organize the pamphlet with help from the team.	
Student 3 Writer	Write the ideas with help from the team.	
Student 4 Spokesperson	With help from the team, organize a presentation to give to the class.	

2. Write the first section of your pamphlet. What does a good employee need to do? Make a list of points, e.g., *A good employee dresses well.*

3. The next section is about looking for a job. Write an example classified ad for a position. Put it in your pamphlet.

4. Fill out an application carefully. Write an example of a job history.

5. What do you do in an interview? Write what you should and shouldn't do in an interview.

6. You should learn about the skills and equipment needed for your job. Make a list of special skills and tools needed for five different jobs.

7. Make a presentation to the class.

PRONUNCIATION

Listen to the vowel sound in these words. Underline the words with a long /e/ sound. Circle the words with a short /i/ sound. Then listen again and repeat.

speak   need   (quick)   teacher   (build)   (little)

(listen)   feel   clean   (fix)   (fill)   please

LEARNER LOG

Circle what you learned and write the page number where you learned it.

1. I can identify jobs.
   Yes   Maybe   No   Page _121–122_

2. I can read classified ads.
   Yes   Maybe   No   Page _123–124_

3. I can use the regular simple past.
   Yes   Maybe   No   Page _125–127_

4. I can prepare for an interview.
   Yes   Maybe   No   Page _128–129_

5. I can identify tools and skills at work.
   Yes   Maybe   No   Page _130–131_

6. I can understand warning signs at work.
   Yes   Maybe   No   Page _132–133_

7. I can read a work evaluation.
   Yes   Maybe   No   Page _134, 137_

8. I can use adjectives and adverbs.
   Yes   Maybe   No   Page _135_

Did you answer *No* to any questions? Review the information with a partner.

Rank what you like to do best from 1 to 6. 1 is your favorite activity. Your teacher will help you.

☐ practice listening

☐ practice speaking

☐ practice reading

☐ practice writing

☐ learn new words (vocabulary)

☐ learn grammar

In the next unit I want to practice more

_____*(Answers will vary.)*_____.

Unit 7 Pronunciation and Learner Log

Pronunciation *(optional)*: **10–15 min.**

Listen to the vowel sound in these words. Underline the words with a long /e/ sound. Circle the words with a short /i / sound. Then listen again and repeat. *(Audio CD Track 45)*

Play the recording and pause after each word.

For additional pronunciation practice: (The following words should be used for pronunciation practice, not for vocabulary instruction.)

/e/	/i/
heat	*hit*
leave	*live*
meal	*mill*
peat	*pit*
peel	*pill*
wheel	*will*

Learner Log

Presentation 1: 10–15 min.

If needed, review the purpose of the Learner Log.

Circle what you learned and write the page number where you learned it. Students research the answers individually. When they've finished, they should share their answers with a partner. These results need not be shared with the class.

Practice 1: 10–15 min.

Rank what you like to do best from 1 to 6. 1 is your favorite activity. Your teacher will help you. Results should be shared with the class in order to demonstrate to students how people learn differently.

Evaluation 1: 10–15 min.

In the next unit I want to practice more _____. Students should fill in the blank with assistance from a partner or from you. They may focus on a skill (e.g., listening), on a vocabulary area (e.g., numbers), on grammar, and so on. Don't limit them to a single answer. Emphasize that the purpose of completing the sentence is to improve their self-assessment skills.

Instructor's Notes for Unit 7 Team Project, Pronunciation, and Learner Log

LESSON PLAN

Objective:
Discuss ways to study English
Key vocabulary:
review, textbook, journal, notebook, study

Pre-Assessment: Use the *Stand Out ExamView® Pro Test Bank* for Unit 8. (*optional*)

Warm-up and Review: 10–15 min. `1.5+`

Write the word *study* on the board. Ask students what they should study if they want to learn English. Help them get started by writing *vocabulary* on the board. They may need additional help, so lead them through different aspects of classroom study, like *grammar, vocabulary,* and *life skills.*

Introduction: 3–5 min. `1.5+`

State objective: *Today you will learn how to study when you are not in school.*

Presentation 1: 10–15 min. `1.5+`

Ask students to look at the picture of Nubar. Ask the questions in the box and add any other questions you consider appropriate.

A Read about Nubar.

Read the paragraph as a class. Ask comprehension questions to make sure students understand that Nubar's school is not in session but he wants to continue learning English anyway.

Write on the board *Things Nubar can do to study outside of class.* Write *Study the textbook* under it. Show students how to turn this into a sentence by writing *He can study his textbook.* Then explain how to do exercise B.

Practice 1: 10–15 min. `1.5+`

B What are things Nubar can do to study? Make a list with a group on a separate piece of paper. Then go to other groups and add to your list.

Make sure students work in their groups for about 5–10 minutes before group representatives visit other groups to obtain information.

Evaluation 1: 5–10 min. `1.5+`

Ask groups to report their ideas to the class. Add your own ideas to the list.

Pronunciation:

An optional pronunciation activity is found on the final page of this unit. This pronunciation activity may be introduced during any lesson in this unit, especially if students need practice with the sounds of **ir** as in *first* and **ar** as in *farm.* Go to pages 160/160a for Unit 8 Pronunciation.

STANDARDS CORRELATIONS

CASAS: 6.7.2, 7.1.1, 7.3.1, 7.3.2, 7.4.1
SCANS: **Interpersonal** Participates as a Member of a Team, Teaches Others New Skills, Exercises Leadership
Information Acquires and Evaluates Information, Organizes and Maintains Information, Interprets and Communicates Information, Uses Computers to Process Information (optional)
Systems Understands Systems, Monitors and Corrects Performance, Improves and Designs Systems
Technology Applies Technology to Task (optional)
Basic Skills Reading, Writing, Listening, Speaking

Thinking Skills Creative Thinking, Decision Making, Problem Solving, Seeing Things in the Mind's Eye, Knowing How to Learn, Reasoning
Personal Qualities Responsibility
EFF: **Communication** Read with Understanding, Convey Ideas in Writing, Speak So Others Can Understand, Listen Actively, Observe Critically
Decision Making Solve Problems and Make Decisions, Plan
Interpersonal Guide Others, Cooperate with Others
Lifelong Learning Take Responsibility for Learning, Reflect and Evaluate, Learn through Research, Use Information and Communications Technology (optional)

UNIT 8
People and Learning

GOALS

- Talk about ways to study English
- Improve your study skills
- Use *going to* for future plans
- Use *will* to talk about the future
- Make choices about your future
- Ask and answer yes/no questions
- Evaluate your study skills

LESSON 1 Learning outside the classroom

GOAL ▶ Talk about ways to study English   *Life Skill*

What is Nubar doing?
Why?

A Read about Nubar.

Nubar is an ESL student at Franklin Adult School. The school is closed for two months. Nubar wants to study. He wants to prepare for the start of the new school year. He is studying his textbook from class. He likes to review the vocabulary and the grammar.

B What are things Nubar can do to study? Make a list with a group on a separate piece of paper. Then go to other groups and add to your list.
(Answers may vary.)

C **Read about ways to practice English.**

Many people come to the United States and don't speak English. They want to learn so they can get a better job. Some students practice at work. Others practice with their families. They also keep a journal or a vocabulary notebook. Sometimes they watch TV or listen to the radio to practice listening. It's fun to find new ways of practicing English outside of class!

D **Write six things you can do to practice English outside of class.**

1. *Practice at work.*
2. *Practice with my family.*
3. *Keep a journal.*
4. *Keep a vocabulary notebook.*
5. *Watch TV.*
6. *Listen to the radio.*

E **How do you study now? Make a list and talk to a partner.**

(Answers will vary.)

What do I do?	What does my partner do?

 F **Active Task:** Find out about books in your library or Internet sites that can help you study English. Tell the class.

Presentation 2: 10–15 min.

Ask students where they can practice and study English. Accept all answers. Answers might include *at work, at home, in the market,* etc. Tell the students that they are about to read a paragraph that is a little difficult. Help them understand that reading difficult passages can be made easier by using the same strategies they have used for focused listening techniques. They don't need to understand every word to get the main idea.

Practice 2: 10–15 min.

C Read about ways to practice English.
Ask students to read the passage by themselves, then do exercise D in pairs. They should not use dictionaries.

D Write six things you can do to practice English outside of class.

Evaluation 2: 10–15 min.

Ask for volunteers to write different answers on the board and then review them.

Presentation 3: 5–10 min.

Remind students how to make a bar graph. Put a sample on the board. Explain that in this activity they will research what other students think about studying English and make graphs.

Practice 3: 15–20 min.

Ask students in groups to investigate what other students think by sending representatives to different groups. Each group can have a different assignment. Some assignments might include:

• What ways do students study outside of class now?
• Where do students study when not in class?
• How many hours a week do students study outside of class?
• From exercise D, what are the easiest things to do?
• From exercise D, what are the most difficult things to do?

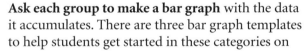 **Ask each group to make a bar graph** with the data it accumulates. There are three bar graph templates to help students get started in these categories on

the *Activity Bank 1 CD-ROM,* Unit 8 Worksheet 1. Bar graphs can also be designed on the computer. See Teaching Hints for ideas on using bar graphs.

Evaluation 3: 10–15 min.

Have groups display their bar graphs. Discuss.

Application: 10–15 min.

E How do you study now? Make a list and talk to a partner.
Ask students to fill in the chart and report to the class.

F Active Task: Find out about books in your library or Internet sites that can help you study English. Tell the class.

 Refer to the *Activity Bank 1 CD-ROM,* Unit 8 Worksheet 2 (two pages), for additional practice about studying outside of class. *(optional)*

Instructor's Notes for Lesson 1

LESSON PLAN

Objective:
Identify and improve study skills
Key vocabulary:
checkout, counter, semester,
notebook, organized, section

Warm-up and Review: 10–15 min.

Ask students who didn't share with the class
during the application activity in the previous
lesson to do so now.

Introduction: 1 min.

State objective: *Today you are going to learn a
few ways to keep organized and study.*

Presentation 1: 10–15 min.

Talk about the pictures with your teacher.

Ask questions about each picture and then ask
students to do exercise B.

What do you learn in English class? Write the words with the picture.

C As a class, write other things you learn in class.

Write the chart headings in exercise D on the
board. Make sure students understand them.
Share with the class something you personally do
well. Point out and name a student who speaks
very well in class.

Practice 1: 10–15 min.

D Complete the chart.

After the students have 5 or 10 minutes to write
down the information, do a corners activity.
Designate the corners of the room as *reading,
writing, speaking,* and *listening.* Then ask the
students to go to the corner that represents what
they do best.

Evaluation 1: 5–10 min.

Observe the activity. Discuss what students
discovered from the activity. For example: Is there
a consensus on what people do well or do students
have different skills?

STANDARDS CORRELATIONS

CASAS: 7.1.4, 7.4.1, 7.4.3
SCANS: **Interpersonal** Participates as a Member of a
Team, Teaches Others New Skills
Information Acquires and Evaluates Information,
Organizes and Maintains Information, Interprets and
Communicates Information
Systems Understands Systems, Monitors and Corrects
Performance, Improves and Designs Systems
Basic Skills Reading, Writing, Listening, Speaking
Thinking Skills Creative Thinking, Decision Making,
Knowing How to Learn, Reasoning

Personal Qualities Responsibility, Self-Management
EFF: **Communication** Read with Understanding, Convey
Ideas in Writing, Speak So Others Can Understand, Listen
Actively, Observe Critically
Decision Making Solve Problems and Make
Decisions, Plan
Interpersonal Guide Others, Cooperate with Others
Lifelong Learning Take Responsibility for Learning, Reflect
and Evaluate, Learn through Research

LESSON 2 Helping yourself learn

| GOAL ▶ | Improve your study skills | | *Life Skill* |

A Talk about the pictures with your teacher.

listening

speaking

writing

APT FOR RENT
2 bed, 1 bath apt,
818 Sundry Ave. #19.
$750, furn a/c
all utls pd 1 mth dep.
call 555-7744

life skills

be	
Subject	
I	
Verb	
am	
Example sentence	
I am from Mexico.	

grammar

reading

teamwork

vocabulary

B What do you learn in English class? Write the words with the pictures.

grammar	reading	writing	life skills
speaking	vocabulary	listening	teamwork

C As a class, write other things you learn in class.

(Answers will vary.) _____ _____

_____ _____

D Complete the chart. *(Answers will vary.)*

Things I do well	Things I need help with

E Make a notebook with sections to study at home. What are the sections in your notebook?

vocabulary _____ _____ _____

(Answers will vary.) _____ _____ _____

_____ _____ _____

F Read the journal notes below.

> Date: September 5
>
> _____
>
> New words: checkout, counter, cough
>
> Skill: I practiced in the supermarket: "Where is the medicine?"
>
> Book: I reviewed pages 10-15 in the textbook from last semester.
>
> Listening: TV - I watched channel 20 for 10 minutes at 7 AM.
>
> Writing: I wrote in my journal.

G Make your own journal notes. What did you do today to practice English?

_____

(Answers will vary.) _____

_____

_____

_____

_____

_____

_____

_____

_____

_____

Presentation 2: 10–15 min.

Show students a notebook before they look at this page. Tell them that notebooks and journals are good ways to organize their work.

E Make a notebook with sections to study at home. What are the sections in your notebook?

Encourage students to make their own notebooks. If they can't buy dividers, suggest they make dividers out of file folders. Discuss notebook sections with the students by referring to ideas on the previous page.

Write the word *Journal* on the board. Help students see that a journal will help them keep track of what and how much they learn. Refer them to the learner logs at the end of every unit. Help students see that a journal is especially useful if entries are made daily.

F Read the journal notes below.

Make students understand that journal entries need not be lengthy and that often just a few words will help speed their learning.

Practice 2: 15–20 min.

Make a chart on the board:

Name	New Words	Book Pages	Listening Practice

Ask students to get information about what three other students did or learned on this particular day. Write the following questions on the board:
What new words did you learn?
What book pages did you study?
How did you practice listening?

Evaluation 2: 10–15 min.

Ask volunteers to report on what one other student did or learned today.

Presentation 3: 15–20 min.

Write three columns on the board with the headings *Vocabulary, Grammar,* and *Life skills.* Ask students to go back to Unit 1 in the book. Tell them that their goal is to identify the different sections of each lesson in the unit. Have them first find only the grammar sections. Show them how to enter the grammar objectives in the proper column. Also have them jot down the page numbers. Assign different columns to different groups or pairs.

Practice 3: 20–30 min.

Ask students to complete the column they are working on by going through the book and writing down the information.

Evaluation 3: 10–15 min.

If time permits, have volunteers write the column information on the board. Then ask students to transfer the information to their notebooks for future study.

Application: 15–20 min.

G Make your own journal notes. What did you do today to practice English?

Refer to the *Activity Bank 1 CD-ROM, Unit 8 Worksheet 3,* for a journal template. *(optional)*

Instructor's Notes for Lesson 2
_____
_____
_____
_____
_____
_____
_____

LESSON PLAN

Objective:
Use *going to* to talk about future plans

Key vocabulary:
goals, flashcards, diary

Warm-up and Review: 10–15 min. 1.5⁺

Write the word *goals* **on the board.** Ask students what they think it means. Write some typical student goals below the word, such as *learn English.* Make a list of other student goals. Then ask the students how they think they can best achieve them. Ask them what they can do to improve their English.

Introduction: 5–10 min. 1.5⁺

State objective: *Today you will learn how to use going to to describe future plans and set study goals.*

Presentation 1: 5–10 min. 1.5⁺

Tell the students that they are going to read a diary entry. Explain that a journal and a diary are almost the same. Each is a record of what happens to a person or what he or she sees, thinks, or feels. A diary, however, is generally a more private and personal record. Ask students to pay attention to the goals Nubar sets in his diary entry.

Practice 1: 10–15 min. 1.5⁺

A **Read Nubar's diary and answer the questions about his goals.**

B What are your plans?

Evaluation 1: 10–15 min. 1.5⁺

Ask for volunteers to share their answers with the class or in small groups. Observe the activity.

Refer to *Stand Out Grammar Challenge 1,* Unit 8, page 57 for more practice. *(optional)*

STANDARDS CORRELATIONS

CASAS: 2.3.1, 6.6.6, 7.1.1, 7.1.4, 7.4.1
SCANS: Resources Allocates Time
Information Acquires and Evaluates Information, Organizes and Maintains Information, Interprets and Communicates Information
Basic Skills Reading, Writing, Arithmetic, Listening, Speaking
Thinking Skills Decision Making, Problem Solving

Personal Qualities Responsibility, Self-Management
EFF: Communication Read with Understanding, Convey Ideas in Writing, Speak So Others Can Understand, Listen Actively, Observe Critically
Decision Making Solve Problems and Make Decisions, Plan
Lifelong Learning Take Responsibility for Learning, Reflect and Evaluate

GOAL ▶ Use *going to* for future plans

Grammar

Date: September 5

       I want to make some goals. I need to prepare for school next semester. I'm going to study four pages in the textbook every weeknight for thirty minutes. I'm going to study in my kitchen at home.

A **Read Nubar's diary and answer the questions about his goals.**

1. When is Nubar going to study?

Every weeknight.

2. What is he going to study?

Four pages in the textbook.

3. Where is he going to study?

In his kitchen.

4. How long is he going to study each day?

Thirty minutes.

B **What are your plans?**

1. When are you going to study?

(Answers will vary.)

2. What are you going to study?

3. Where are you going to study?

4. How long are you going to study each day?

C **Study the chart with your teacher.**

going to			
Subject	**be + going to**	**Base**	**Example sentence**
I	am going to (I'm going to)	learn listen	I am going to learn English.
you, we, they	are going to (you're / we're / they're going to)	practice read speak	We are going to listen.
he, she, it	is going to (she's / he's / it's going to)	study write	She is going to write.

D **Look at each clock. Then listen to Nubar speak about his plans. Pretend you are Nubar. Write what you are going to do next to the clocks.**

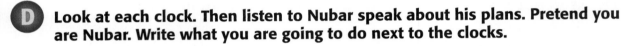

listen to the radio   read the newspaper   review my vocabulary notebook

study my textbook   write in my journal

From [clock] to [clock]   *I am going to listen to the radio.*

From [clock] to [clock]   *I am going to read the newspaper.*

From [clock] to [clock]   *I am going to study.*

From [clock] to [clock]   *I am going to review my vocabulary notebook. Then I am*

going to write in my journal.

E **Tell a friend about Nubar's plans.**

EXAMPLE: He is going to listen to the radio from 6:30 to 6:45 A.M.

Presentation 2: 10–15 min.

C Study the chart with your teacher.

Practice the new sentence structure with the students. Go back to the previous page so they can see how it is used in Nubar's diary entry.

Prepare the class for focused listening. See Teaching Hints for help with focused listening. Look at each clock and review the time of day. Go over the words in the box and make sure students know what to listen for.

Note: Shorter classes can look at the listening script for exercise D for homework.

 Refer to *Stand Out Grammar Challenge 1*, Unit 8, pages 57–58 for more practice. *(optional)*

Practice 2: 15–20 min.

 D Look at each clock. Then listen to Nubar speak about his plans. Pretend you are Nubar. Write what you are going to do next to the clocks. *(Audio CD Track 46)*

Play the recording several times. Remind students to simply listen at first.

E Tell a friend about Nubar's plans.

After explaining this activity, you may want to add the amount of time. For example, *He is going to listen to the radio from 6:30 to 6:45. That's 15 minutes.*

Evaluation 2: 10–15 min.

Ask volunteers to write their answers to exercise E on the board.

Presentation 3: 10–15 min.   **1.5⁺**

F **Write sentences about Nubar's plans.**

Review Nubar's diary entry on page 145 again. Tell the students that they will write a similar entry but using their own information. Exercise G will help them to collect ideas for their journal entry.

G **Write your plans.**

Practice 3: 15–20 min.   **3**

Ask students to write a paragraph about their **future study plans.** Remind students to indent.

Evaluation 3: 10–15 min.   **3**

Invite a few volunteers to read their paragraphs.

Application: 20–30 min.   **1.5⁺**

H **Ask about the plans of 4 students in the class and complete the chart.**

Review the questions with students first.

 Refer to the *Activity Bank 1 CD-ROM*, Unit 8 Worksheet 4 (two pages), for additional activities related to using *going to*. (optional)

Instructor's Notes for Lesson 3

F **Write sentences about Nubar's plans.**   *(Answers may vary slightly.)*

1. *He is going to listen to the radio from 6:30 to 6:45 A.M.*
2. *He is going to read the newspaper from 7:00 to 7:30 A.M.*
3. *He is going to study four pages in his textbook from 8:00 to 8:45 P.M.*
4. *He is going to review his vocabulary notebook and then write in his journal from 9:00 to 9:15 P.M.*

G **Write your plans.**

1. *I am going to listen to the radio from _____ to _____ .*
2. *(Answers will vary.)*
3. _____
4. _____
5. _____
6. _____

H **Ask about the plans of four students in the class and complete the chart.**

Ask: When are you going to listen to the radio?

When are you going to practice speaking?

When are you going to read the newspaper?

When are you going to study your textbook?

(Answers will vary.)

Student name	Listen	Speak	Read	Study

GOAL ▶ Use *will* to talk about the future   *Grammar*

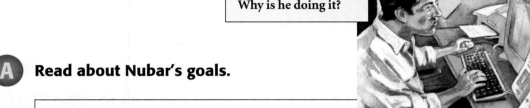

What is Nubar doing?
Why is he doing it?

A Read about Nubar's goals.

Date: June 12

    I have many goals for the future. Some of my goals will take a long time, but I'm going to work hard. I will study every day and get my GED. After that, I want to start college in about three years. I also want to get married and have children sometime in the future. I need a good job too, so I can help my family. I am going to be a computer technician one day.

GED = General Educational Development, the same level as a high school diploma

B Nubar wants to do many things. Write his goals in the table.

Family goals	Educational goals	Work goals
get married	*get a GED*	*get a good job*
have children	*start college*	*be a computer technician*

C You can use *will* to talk about future plans. Study the chart with your teacher.

will			
Subject	**Future**	**Base**	**Example sentence**
I, you, he, she, it, we, they	will	study	I will study every day.
		work	She will work hard.
		get married	They will get married.

LESSON PLAN

Objective:
Use will *to talk about future goals*
Key vocabulary:
GED, diploma, get, finish, college,
university

Warm-up and Review: 10–15 min.

Write the word *goals* **on the board in a central circle to start a cluster diagram.** Make three lines that stem from a central circle and lead to three smaller circles. Then ask students to talk about different kinds of goals in their groups. Ask groups to report after a few minutes. Make a list of what they wrote. If they have trouble, lead them to the primary goals discussed in this unit. Write *Educational goals, Family goals,* and *Work goals* inside the smaller circles.

Introduction: 3–5 min.

Explain that people need to decide what is important to them before they set any kind of goal.

State objective: *Today we will use "will" to talk about future goals.*

Presentation 1: 10–15 min.

Ask students to cover the paragraph in exercise A and look only at the picture at the top of the page. (Alternatively, you can make a transparency with the paragraph covered.) Ask the students the questions in the box and any other questions you consider appropriate. Point to the cluster diagram still on the board. Explain that they will be looking

for three goals in each category as they read the entry. Put three lines next to each goal noted in the cluster.

Practice 1: 10–15 min.

A Read about Nubar's goals.

Ask the students to read the entry. They can read individually or together in groups.

B Nubar wants to do many things. Write his goals in the table.

Evaluation 1: 5–10 min.

Ask different individuals to come to the board and finish the cluster diagram.

Presentation 2: 15–20 min.

C You can use *will* to talk about future plans in these different ways. Study the chart with your teacher.

Refer to the chart on page 146 while reviewing this chart with the students. Make sure they understand the new usage.

Note: The differences between using *going to, will,* and *want to* are not discussed in this book because this discussion is more appropriate at a higher level. Nevertheless, students should get an idea of how the forms work and understand that there are several ways to express the future in English. Help the students see how to say the goals in exercise B in complete sentences.

(Presentation 2 continues on the next page.)

STANDARDS CORRELATIONS

CASAS: 7.1.1, 7.1.4, 7.2.3
SCANS: **Information** Acquires and Evaluates Information, Organizes and Maintains Information, Interprets and Communicates Information, Uses Computers to Process Information (optional)
Technology Applies Technology to Task (optional)
Basic Skills Reading, Writing, Listening, Speaking
Thinking Skills Decision Making, Problem Solving, Seeing Things in the Mind's Eye

Personal Qualities Responsibility, Self-Management
EFF: **Communication** Read with Understanding, Convey Ideas in Writing, Speak So Others Can Understand, Listen Actively
Decision Making Solve Problems and Make Decisions, Plan
Lifelong Learning Take Responsibility for Learning, Reflect and Evaluate

Presentation 2 (continued):

D Study these verbs and time expressions with your teacher. Make sentences about the future.

Continue practice with future forms and prepare students for doing exercise E.

Practice 2: 15–20 min.

E Talk to students in the class about their future plans. Ask, *What will you do in the future?* Use the words from the chart above to write sentences about students in your class.

Write the question on the board and show students how to conduct this activity.

 Refer to *Stand Out Grammar Challenge 1*, Unit 8, page 59 for more practice. *(optional)*

Evaluation 2: 5–10 min.

Review the information that the students gathered by writing it on the board. It is possible that some didn't find a match for each future plan mentioned. These plans will be discussed more fully in Presentation 3.

Study these verbs and time expressions with your teacher. Make sentences about the future.

Verbs			
to buy	to finish	to help	to move
to eat	to get	to learn	to start
to exercise	to have	to take	to study

Time expressions			
in two years	in five years	in ten years	in a few years
next week	next month	next year	sometime

 Talk to students in the class about their future plans. Ask, *What will you do in the future?* Use the words from the chart above to write sentences about students in your class.

Examples:
Nubar *will* start college next year.
Roberto *is going to* finish college in three years.
Gabriela *wants to* buy a house next year.

(Answers will vary.)

Student name	Future plan		When?
		his/her GED	
		college	
		a new job	
		a computer	
		how to use a computer	
		married	
		another city/country	

F **Write your goals and when you want to do them.**

EXAMPLES:
I am going to study next September.
I will take my GED next year.
I want to start college in three years.

(Answers will vary.)

_____

_____

_____

G **Write a paragraph for your journal. Write about your family, educational, and work goals. Look at Nubar's journal on page 148 for some ideas.**

I have many goals for the future.

(Answers will vary.)

_____

_____

_____

_____

_____

_____

H **Active Task:** Start a journal. Write your goals on the first page.

Presentation 3: 15–20 min.

Discuss the future plans listed in exercise E on the previous page. Make sure the students understand the goals. Ask for additional ones to add to the list.

Practice 3: 30–40 min.

 Write your goals and when you want to do them.

Encourage students to focus on educational, work, and family goals. Make sure that they list at least three goals.

Write the following dialogs on the board. Ask students to find out a partner's goals and then answer questions about their own goals.
Student 1: *What are some of your future goals?*
Student 2: *I want to _____ and _____ .*

Ask the students to perform this second exchange with 4 other students:
Student 1: *Who did you talk to?*
Student 2: *I talked to _____.*
Student 1: *What are his/her goals?*
Student 2: *She/he is going to _____, _____, and _____.*

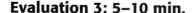 **Refer to *Stand Out Grammar Challenge 1*, Unit 8, pages 60–61 for more practice.** *(optional)*

Evaluation 3: 5–10 min.

Observe student exchanges. Ask for a few pairs to demonstrate the dialogs.

Application: 15–20 min.

Remind students how to form a paragraph. Tell them that, like a good story, a good paragraph has a beginning, middle, and end.

Write a paragraph for your journal. Write about your family, educational, and work goals. Look at Nubar's journal on page 148 for some ideas.

This activity may take more than the time remaining in the class. Assign it for homework if necessary to encourage students to give it plenty of thought.

Active Task: Start a journal. Write your goals on the first page.

Refer to the *Activity Bank 1 CD-ROM*, Unit 8 Worksheet 5, for additional speaking, reading, and listening activities about future plans. The listening is on *AB1 CD-ROM* Track 13. *(optional)*

Instructor's Notes for Lesson 4

_____
_____
_____
_____
_____
_____
_____
_____
_____
_____
_____
_____
_____
_____
_____
_____
_____
_____
_____
_____
_____
_____

LESSON PLAN

Objective:
Make choices about future plans
Key vocabulary:
wants to be, degree, skills, high school,
university, Bachelor's degree,
Associate's degree

Warm-up and Review: 15–20 min.

Ask volunteers to share what they have written about their goals from the previous lesson.

Introduction: 1 min.

Ask students where they can go to get information. Get them started by writing the words *Internet* and *library* on the board. Add whatever suggestions they make to this list.

State objective: *Today you will learn how to make good choices about your future.*

Presentation 1: 10–15 min.

A Read the information about these students. Listen to their conversations with a counselor. What advice does the counselor give each student? Check the choices for each student.
(Audio CD Track 47)

Look at the photos with the class and read what each of the six students wants to do. Ask if their goals relate to work, family, or education. Talk briefly about the schools beneath each goal. You don't need to mention length of schooling at this point, since that will be covered in Practice 2. Prepare students for focused listening. See

Teaching Hints for help with focused listening. Ask students to pay close attention to the kinds of schools they hear in the conversations.

Practice 1: 10–15 min.

What advice does the counselor give each student? Listen to the recording and have students compare answers in pairs.

Evaluation 1: 5 min.

Review the answers with the students.

Presentation 2: 10–15 min.

Ask students to close their books and, in groups, discuss each kind of school. Let them try to figure out how many years it usually takes to complete each one.

Discuss their answers as a class. Then tell students that they are going to read a difficult paragraph. Remind them to apply the focused listening strategies to their reading. That is, they don't need to know every word to get the main idea.

Practice 2: 10–15 min.

B Read about schools in the United States.

C Talk in pairs about schools in the United States. How many years do students go to each type of school?

Ask student groups to review the answers they came up with in their earlier group discussion on length of schooling.

Evaluation 2: 10–15 min.

See how many groups came up with the correct lengths of schooling on the first try.

STANDARDS CORRELATIONS

CASAS: 7.1.1, 7.2.6
SCANS: **Interpersonal** Participates as a Member of a Team, Teaches Others New Skills, Serves Clients/Customers, Exercises Leadership
Information Acquires and Evaluates Information, Organizes and Maintains Information, Interprets and Communicates Information
Technology Applies Technology to Task (optional)
Basic Skills Reading, Listening, Speaking

Thinking Skills Creative Thinking
Personal Qualities Responsibility, Self-Management
EFF: **Communication** Read with Understanding, Speak So Others Can Understand, Listen Actively
Decision Making Plan
Interpersonal Guide Others, Cooperate with Others
Lifelong Learning Take Responsibility for Learning, Reflect and Evaluate, Learn through Research, Use Information and Communications Technology (optional)

GOAL ▶ Make choices about your future

Life Skill

 A **Read the information about these students. Listen to their conversations with a counselor. What advice does the counselor give each student? Check the choices for each student.**

1.

Ahmed

☑ high school diploma/GED
☑ two-year college
❑ university
☑ trade school

2.

Minh

❑ high school diploma/GED
☑ two-year college
☑ university
❑ trade school

3.

Mario

☑ high school diploma/GED
❑ two-year college
❑ university
❑ trade school

4.

Akiko

❑ high school diploma/GED
❑ two-year college
☑ university
❑ trade school

5.

Alan

❑ high school diploma/GED
❑ two-year college
❑ university
☑ trade school

6.

Marie

❑ high school diploma/GED
❑ two-year college
☑ university
❑ trade school

 B **Read about schools in the United States.**

In the United States, students go to school for about twelve years and then get a high school diploma, or adults can go to an adult program to get a GED. After high school some students go to a two-year college where they prepare for a university or get an Associate's Degree. Other people go from high school to a university for four years or more. After four years, students can get a Bachelor's Degree. Some students go to trade school for one to four years after high school to learn about specific job skills.

 C **Talk in pairs about schools in the United States. How many years do students go to each type of school?**

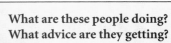

What are these people doing?
What advice are they getting?

D **Where can you get advice to make good choices? Talk in a group.**

For your health: *(Answers will vary.)* _____

_____

For your education: _____

_____

For your career: _____

_____

E **Did you get advice from anyone this past year? Tell the group.**

I talked to   *(Answers will vary.)* _____

_____

_____

F **Active Task:** What books or Internet sites can help you with your educational choices? Tell the class.

Presentation 3: 10–15 min.

Look at the photos with the class. Ask the questions in the box and add any others you consider appropriate. Try to get students to come up with words such as *encyclopedia, counselor, advisor, training.*

Practice 3: 10–15 min.

D Where can you get advice to make good choices? Talk in a group.

Make sure students understand what *health* and *career* mean.

Ask groups to send representatives to other groups to get additional ideas.

Evaluation 3: 5–10 min.

Discuss the group reports as a class and write all the ideas on the board.

Application: 30–45 min.

E Did you get advice from anyone this past year? Tell the group.

F Active Task: What books or Internet sites can help you with your educational choices? Tell the class.

 Refer to the *Activity Bank 1 CD-ROM,* Unit 8 Worksheet 6 (two pages), for additional activities about future plans and timelines.

Instructor's Notes for Lesson 5

LESSON PLAN

Objective:
Ask and answer yes/no questions
Key vocabulary:
handle money, work alone, technology, personal inventory, counselor

Warm-up and Review: 10–15 min.

Ask students to define *goals* again and to give you examples of their own goals. List these on the board. Add *counselor* on the board and ask students if any of them have ever talked with a school counselor. Ask students what questions counselors might ask them. Write some of these questions on the board.

Introduction: 1 min.

State objective: *Today you will learn to answer and ask "yes/no" questions.*

Presentation 1: 10–15 min.

Write *Personal Inventory* on the board. Explain to the class that counselors often ask the people they advise to make a personal inventory. When it is finished, counselors can learn what the people like to do and what skills they have. Answer a few of the questions as a class in exercise A so students understand how to do the rest.

Practice 1: 10–15 min.

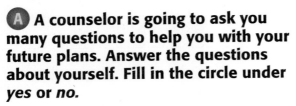

A **A counselor is going to ask you many questions to help you with your future plans. Answer the questions about yourself. Fill in the circle under *yes* or *no*.**

B Write sentences below for six of your *yes* answers in exercise A.

Review with students the short and longer answers by referring to the questions. Work with the students so they are able to do the activity on their own.

Evaluation 1: 10–15 min.

Ask volunteers to write some of their answers to exercise B on the board.

STANDARDS CORRELATIONS

CASAS: 7.1.1, 7.5.1
SCANS: Interpersonal Teaches Others New Skills
Information Acquires and Evaluates Information, Organizes and Maintains Information
Systems Understands Systems, Monitors and Corrects Performance
Basic Skills Reading, Listening, Speaking,

Personal Qualities Responsibility, Self-Management
EFF: Communication Speak So Others Can Understand, Listen Actively, Observe Critically
Decision Making Plan
Interpersonal Guide Others
Lifelong Learning Take Responsibility for Learning, Reflect and Evaluate

GOAL ▶ **Ask and answer *yes/no* questions** | *Grammar*

A **A counselor is going to ask you many questions to help you with your future plans. Answer the questions about yourself. Fill in the circle under *yes* or *no*.**

Personal Inventory *(Answers will vary.)*

Yes	No	
○	○	Do you have a high school diploma or GED?
○	○	Do you have good study skills?
○	○	Do you have experience?
○	○	Do you like technology (computers, machines)?
○	○	Do you like to do the same thing every day?
○	○	Do you like to handle money?
○	○	Do you like to read?
○	○	Do you like to study and to learn new things?
○	○	Do you like to listen?
○	○	Do you like to talk on the phone?
○	○	Do you like to travel?
○	○	Do you like to work with other people?
○	○	Do you like to work at night?
○	○	Do you like to work in the daytime?
○	○	Do you like to work with your hands?
○	○	Do you like your job?
○	○	Do you work now?
○	○	Do you have goals for the future?

B **Write sentences on a separate sheet of paper for six of your *yes* answers in exercise A.**

EXAMPLE:

Yes, I do. I like technology.

(Answers will vary.)

Study the charts with your teacher.

Yes/No questions				
do	**Subject**	**Base**	**Infinitive**	
Do	I	like	to study?	
	you	want	to travel?	
	we	need	to work with your hands?	
	they		to talk?	
Does	he		to work alone?	
	she		to handle money?	
	it		to talk on the phone?	
do	**Subject**	**Base**	**Noun / Adverb**	
Do	I	like	technology?	
	you	want		
	we	need		
	they			
Does	he	work	right now?	
	she	have	a high school diploma or GED?	
	it		good study skills?	

D **Ask a partner questions with the words below and fill in the chart.**

EXAMPLE:
Student A: Do you like technology? *Student B:* No, I don't. / Yes, I do.

Partner's name: _____

Question	Yes	No
_____ technology?		
_____ work alone?		
_____ phone?		
_____ experience?		
_____ goals?		

(Answers will vary.)

E **Find a new partner and ask about his or her last partner.**

EXAMPLE:
Student A: Does Cecelia like technology?
Student B: Yes, she does. / No, she doesn't.

Presentation 2: 10–15 min.

C Study the charts with your teacher.

Walk the class through the new constructions. Asking questions is a very complicated issue that will be addressed much more in depth in more advanced levels. However, even now students should feel comfortable framing basic questions by using verbs other than the *be* verb.

Refer to *Stand Out Grammar Challenge 1,* Unit 8, page 64 for more practice. *(optional)*

Show students how to do exercise D by practicing with one or two of them in front of the class.

Practice 2: 10–15 min.

D Ask a partner questions with the words below and fill in the chart.

Remind students to use the verbs *like, want,* and *need* in this exercise. This activity can be extended to more exchanges by using the grid available on the *Activity Bank 1 CD-ROM,* Unit 8 Worksheet 7.

Evaluation 2: 5–10 min.

Ask a few students who they talked to. Ask about their partners.

Presentation 3: 10–15 min.

Use Worksheet 8 (two pages) from Unit 8 of the *Activity Bank 1 CD-ROM* for Practice 3. Show the students what to do with the worksheets.

Practice 3: 15–20 min.

Ask students to do the "Personal Inventory" worksheet. Partners will ask each other questions and fill out the partner inventory.

Evaluation 3:

Observe the activity.

Application: 20–30 min.

E Find a new partner and ask about his or her last partner.

Ask students to walk around the room and tell the new partner about the former one.

Instructor's Notes for Lesson 6

LESSON PLAN

Objective:
Evaluate personal study skills
Key vocabulary:
study skills, percent, total, score,
questionnaire, honesty

Warm-up and Review: 5–10 min.

Ask students what makes a good student. Write student responses on the board.

Introduction: 1 min.

Ask students to rate themselves. Are they *OK, good,* or *super* students? Have them write their answers on a piece of paper and put the papers aside for now.

State objective: *Today we will evaluate our learning skills and how to become super students.*

Presentation 1: 10–15 min.

Refresh students on percentages by making a pie chart on the board. Divide it in half and label each side *50%.* Then divide one side again and label each new slice *25%.*

Explain to students that it is important to look at themselves honestly if they want to become better students. Write the word *honesty* on the board and make sure the students understand its meaning.

Make a bar graph on the board and ask students to calculate how many hours they studied outside of class over the semester.

Let the vertical axis represent the number of students and the horizontal axis represent the number of hours per week. Make one bar for 10 hours or more, another for 5–10 hours, and a third for less than 5 hours. Poll the students and fill in the chart as a class.

Practice 1: 20–25 min.

A **Answer the questions about this course. Fill in the circle for each answer.**

Evaluation 1: 10–15 min.

Discuss the different scores with the students and check their books to make sure everyone tallied correctly. Have students check what they wrote on the paper during the introduction.

STANDARDS CORRELATIONS

CASAS: 7.1.4, 7.4.1
SCANS: **Resources** Allocates Time
Information Acquires and Evaluates Information, Organizes and Maintains Information, Interprets and Communicates Information
Basic Skills Reading, Writing, Arithmetic, Listening, Speaking
Thinking Skills Decision Making, Problem Solving, Seeing Things in the Mind's Eye, Knowing How to Learn

Personal Qualities Responsibility, Self-Management, Integrity/Honesty
EFF: **Communication** Read with Understanding, Convey Ideas in Writing, Speak So Others Can Understand, Listen Actively, Observe Critically
Decision Making Use Math to Solve Problems and Communicate, Solve Problems and Make Decisions, Plan
Lifelong Learning Take Responsibility for Learning, Reflect and Evaluate

LESSON 7 — How are your study habits?

GOAL ▶ **Evaluate your study skills**

Academic Skill

 A **Answer the questions about this course. Fill in the circle for each answer.**
(Answers will vary.)

Study Habits Questionnaire

1. How often did you come to class?
   ○ a. most of the time   ○ b. more than 50%   ○ c. less than 50%

2. Did you come to class on time?
   ○ a. most of the time   ○ b. more than 50%   ○ c. less than 50%

3. How much did you study at home each week?
   ○ a. more than 10 hours   ○ b. 5-10 hours a week   ○ c. less than 5 hours

4. Did you speak English in class and participate?
   ○ a. most of the time   ○ b. more than 50%   ○ c. less than 50%

5. Did you teach and help other students in class?
   ○ a. a lot   ○ b. a little   ○ c. never

6. Did you listen to the radio in English?
   ○ a. a lot   ○ b. a little   ○ c. never

7. Did you watch TV in English?
   ○ a. a lot   ○ b. a little   ○ c. never

8. Did you ask the teacher or other students questions
   when you didn't understand?
   ○ a. a lot   ○ b. a little   ○ c. never

How many *a* answers, *b* answers, and *c* answers do you have?

# of *a* answers	# of *b* answers	# of *c* answers

Do the math below.

# of *a* answers x 3 = _____
# of *b* answers x 2 = _____
# of *c* answers x 1 = _____
Total = _____

Score: 20-24 Super – You have
　　　great study habits!
Score: 16-19 Good – You have
　　　good study habits.
Score: Under 16 – You need to change
　　　your study habits!

B Study the charts with your teacher.

Regular verbs	
Base	**Simple past**
study	studied
participate	participated
help	helped
listen	listened
watch	watched
ask	asked

Irregular verbs	
Base	**Simple past**
come	came
see	saw
write	wrote
speak	spoke
read	read
teach	taught

C Write sentences about what you did in this course.

(Answers will vary.)

_____

_____

_____

_____

_____

D Review the charts about the future on pages 146 and 148 and make goals for next semester.

EXAMPLE:

I'm going to come to school every day.

(Answers will vary.)

_____

_____

_____

_____

_____

_____

E **Active Task:** Write the goals in your journal.

Presentation 2: 10–15 min.

 B Study the charts with your teacher.

Go over the verbs with the class repeatedly. You may also wish to help a bit with pronunciation. This is a review of the simple past, which was studied earlier. The focus of this lesson is not on grammar, but students will need to master these words to finish the lesson.

 Refer to *Stand Out Grammar Challenge 1*, Unit 8, page 62 for more practice. *(optional)*

Practice 2: 15–20 min.

 C Write sentences about what you did in this course.

Write an example on the board based on the study habits questionnaire students filled out on the previous page.

Evaluation 2: 10–15 min.

Ask volunteers to write their sentences on the board.

Presentation 3: 10–15 min.

Review the future by asking students to turn to page 148 and study the chart in exercise C again. Then refer to the questionnaire once more and ask students to think about what they will do next year.

Practice 3: 15–20 min.

D Review the charts about the future on pages 146 and 148 and make goals for next semester.

 Refer to *Stand Out Grammar Challenge 1*, Unit 8, page 61 for more practice. *(optional)*

Evaluation 3: 10–15 min.

Ask volunteers to write their goals on the board.

Application: 20–30 min.

Ask students to form a paragraph by using some of the sentences they wrote in the previous two activities.

E Active Task: Write the goals in your journal.

Refer to the *Activity Bank 1 CD-ROM*, Unit 8 Worksheet 9 (two pages), for additional practice on questions. *(optional)*

Instructor's Notes for Lesson 7

_____

_____

_____

_____

_____

_____

_____

_____

_____

_____

_____

_____

_____

_____

_____

_____

_____

_____

REVIEW

Objectives:
All previous objectives
Key vocabulary:
All previous Unit 8 vocabulary

Warm up and Review: 5–10 min.

Ask volunteers to read the paragraphs they wrote in the previous lesson application.

Introduction: 3–5 min.

State objective: *Today we will review all that we have done in the past unit in preparation for the application project to follow.*

Ask students as a class to try to recall all the goals of this unit without looking at their books. Then remind them of the goals they haven't mentioned.

Unit Goals: Talk about ways to study English, Improve your study skills, Use "going to" for the future, Use "will" to talk about the future, Make choices about your future, Ask and answer "yes/no" questions, Evaluate your study skills.

Presentation 1, Practice 1, and Evaluation 1:

Do the Learner Log on page 160. Notes are adjacent to the page.

Presentation 2: 5–10 min.

Ask students if any of them have children in school. Write on the board the types of schools those children attend. Then have students help you complete a list of types of schools.

Ask students if there are places besides home where they can study. Briefly talk about those places.

Practice 2: 10–15 min.

A **Fill in the missing words in the paragraph below.**

B **What are four ways to practice English outside of class?**
This activity can be done in pairs or groups.

C **What are three things you can do to improve your study skills?**
This activity can be done in pairs or groups.

Evaluation 2: 5–10 min.

Ask volunteers to write sentences from exercises B and C on the board.

STANDARDS CORRELATIONS

CASAS: 7.1.1, 7.1.3, 7.1.4, 7.4.1, 7.4.9, 7.5.10, 7.5.1
SCANS: Interpersonal Participates as a Member of a Team, Teaches Others New Skills
Information Acquires and Evaluates Information, Organizes and Maintains Information
Basic Skills Writing, Speaking
Thinking Skills Decision Making, Problem Solving, Knowing How to Learn, Reasoning

Personal Qualities Responsibility, Self-Management
EFF: Communication Convey Ideas in Writing, Speak So Others Can Understand
Decision Making Solve Problems and Make Decisions, Plan
Interpersonal Guide Others, Cooperate with Others
Lifelong Learning Take Responsibility for Learning, Reflect and Evaluate

Review

A Fill in the missing words in the paragraph below.

Degree	college	trade	diploma	twelve	four	GED

   In the United States, students go to school for about _____*twelve*_____ years and then get a high school _____*diploma*_____, or adults can go to an adult program to get a _____*degree*_____. After high school some students go to a two-year _____*college*_____ where they prepare for university or get an Associate's _____*degree*_____. Other people go from high school to a university for _____*four*_____ years or more. Some students go to _____*trade*_____ school to learn about specific job skills.

B What are four ways to practice English outside of class?

EXAMPLE: *I can read the newspaper.*   *(Answers may include the following.)*

1. *I can listen to the radio.*
2. *I can watch TV.*
3. *I can practice with my friends.*
4. *I can practice with my family.*

C What are three things you can do to improve your study skills?

1. *(Answers will vary.)*
2. _____
3. _____

D Make sentences with the words below about yourself in the future. Use *going to, want to,* or *will.*

learn   *I'm going to learn* _____

eat   *I will* _____

exercise   *(Answers will vary.)* _____

visit   _____

finish   _____

get   _____

help   _____

find   _____

start   _____

study   _____

E What are six things you did in this course to help you study English? Use the verbs from the box.

participate	help	speak	ask	read	listen

EXAMPLE:
I came to class every day.

1. *(Answers will vary.)* _____

2. _____

3. _____

4. _____

5. _____

6. _____

Presentation 3: 5–10 min.

Review the verb chart on page 148. Quiz them so they remember the correct use for *will*.

Practice 3: 30–45 min.

D Make sentences with the words below about yourself in the future. Use *going to, want to,* or *will*.

E What are six things you did in this course to help you to study English? Use the verbs from the box.

Evaluation 3: 10–15 min.

Ask a few volunteers to write their sentences on the board.

 Refer to *Activity Bank 1 CD-ROM,* Unit 8 Worksheet 10 (three pages) for additional practice with bar graphs about class study habits. *(optional)*

Application: 1–2 days

The Team Project Activity on the following page is the application activity to be done on the next day of class.

 Post-Assessment: Use the *Stand Out* ExamView® Pro *Test Bank* for Unit 8. *(optional)*

With the ExamView®Pro *Test Bank* you can design an assessment that focuses on what students have learned. It is designed for three purposes:

- To help students practice taking a test similar to current standardized tests.

- To help the teacher evaluate how much the students have learned, retained, and acquired.

- To help students see their progress when they compare their scores to the pre-test they took earlier.

Instructor's Notes for Unit 8 Review

Unit 8 Application Activity

> **TEAM PROJECT: MY GOALS**
>
> Objective:
> Project designed to apply all the objectives of this unit.
> Product:
> A calendar, two paragraphs, and a goal chart

Introduction:

Students will plan a personal study schedule and create a calendar to keep track of it. Students will also write two paragraphs pertaining to their studying goals. This project can extend over two days.

Although this activity is not by definition a "team project," it is the sum of the work completed with teams. Students may rely on each other to assist while they complete individual work. Like the atmosphere in a positive workplace, individuals can rely on each other for assistance and peer review.

Stages 1 and 2: 15–20 min.

Complete a calendar for this and next month.

Ask the students to develop their calendars. They may use Worksheet 11 (two pages) from Unit 8 on the *Activity Bank 1 CD-ROM* if they wish. *(optional)*
Have students compare calendars with a group.

Stage 3: 30–45 min.

Write a paragraph about your plans.

Use Worksheet 12 (two pages) from Unit 8 on the *Activity Bank 1 CD-ROM* for formal goal

statements if you like. The second page is also a template available for putting these statements on the computer. *(optional)*

Stage 4: 30–45 min.

Write another paragraph about your goals for good study habits.

Worksheet 13 (two pages) from Unit 8 on the *Activity Bank 1 CD-ROM* for formal goal statements can be used here if you like. Page 2 of Worksheet 13 is a template available to put these statements on the computer. *(optional)*

Stages 5 and 6: 20–30 min.

Read your paragraph to a partner.

Ask partners to peer edit each other's work. There is a peer edit checklist on the *Activity Bank 1 CD-ROM*, Unit 8 Worksheet 14 (two pages). *(optional)*

Stage 7: 15–20 min.

Design a goal chart for your home.

Have students work as a team to organize their goal ideas into chart form. Provide large paper or have students work on the computer. Then students work individually to make their own charts.

Stage 8: 15–20 min.

Present your calendar and read your paragraphs to the class. Display the goal charts.

Encourage students to bring the goal chart home and put their calendars in a place they'll check regularly such as near the goal chart or in a notebook.

Videotape the presentations if students would like to review their presentations privately or as a class.

STANDARDS CORRELATIONS

CASAS: 7.1.1, 7.1.2, 7.1.3, 7.1.4, 7.4.1
SCANS: Resources Allocates Time
Information Organizes and Maintains Information, Interprets and Communicates Information, Uses Computers to Process Information (optional)
Systems Understands Systems, Monitors and Improves Performance
Technology Applies Technology to Task (optional)
Basic Skills Reading, Writing, Listening, Speaking

Thinking Skills Creative Thinking, Decision Making, Problem Solving, Knowing How to Learn, Reasoning
Personal Qualities Responsibility, Self-Management
EFF: Communication Read with Understanding, Convey Ideas in Writing, Speak So Others Can Understand, Listen Actively, Observe Critically
Decision Making Solve Problems and Make Decisions, Plan
Lifelong Learning Take Responsibility for Learning, Reflect and Evaluate

TEAM PROJECT

My Goals

In this project you will plan your study time on a calendar. You will also write out your goals and plans in two paragraphs. You will present your calendar and your paragraphs to the class.

1. Complete a calendar for this and next month.

   Write what days and what times you are going to:

   > study in the textbook
   > listen to the radio
   > read the newspaper
   > watch TV
   > practice flashcards
   > write in your journal

2. Discuss your plans with your team.

3. Write a paragraph about your plans on the calendar on another piece of paper. Start your paragraph like this:

   I have many goals. I'm going to study English outside of class.

   First, . . .

4. Write another paragraph about your goals for good study habits.

   Are you going to come to school every day? Are you going to arrive on time? What else are you going to do?

5. Ask members of your team to edit your paragraphs and then rewrite them.

6. Read your paragraphs to your team.

7. As a team, design a goal chart that you can put in your home to remind you of what you want to do.

8. Present your calendar, paragraphs, and goal chart to the class.

PRONUNCIATION

Listen to the vowel sounds in these words. Circle the words that sound like *firm* and underline the words that sound like *farm*. Then listen again and repeat.

(learn)   start   (work)   park   (nurse)   part   heart

card   (clerk)   (shirt)   (hurt)   chart   (journal)   (hurt)

LEARNER LOG

Circle what you learned and write the page number where you learned it.

1. I can talk about ways to study outside of class.
   Yes   Maybe   No   Page *141–142*

2. I can organize a notebook and other study tools.
   Yes   Maybe   No   Page *143–144*

3. I can use time expressions about the future.
   Yes   Maybe   No   Page *149–150*

4. I can use *will* and *going to* for future plans.
   Yes   Maybe   No   Page *146, 148*

5. I can talk about different types of schools.
   Yes   Maybe   No   Page *151*

6. I can make choices about the future.
   Yes   Maybe   No   Page *151–152*

7. I can ask yes/no questions.
   Yes   Maybe   No   Page *153–154*

8. I can evaluate my study skills.
   Yes   Maybe   No   Page *155–156*

Did you answer *No* to any questions? Review the information with a partner.

Rank what you like to do best from 1 to 6. 1 is your favorite activity. Your teacher will help you.

☐ practice listening

☐ practice speaking

☐ practice reading

☐ practice writing

☐ learn new words (vocabulary)

☐ learn grammar

I think I improved most in

(Answers will vary.) _____.

Unit 8 Pronunciation and Learner Log

Pronunciation (*optional*): 10–15 min.

Listen to the vowel sounds in these words. Circle the words which sound like *firm* and underline the words which sound like *farm*. Then listen again and repeat. *(Audio CD Track 48)*

Play the recording and pause after each word.

For additional pronunciation practice: (The following words should be used for pronunciation practice, not for vocabulary instruction.)
Sound like *firm*
first
worst
birth
search
Sound like *farm*
cart
mark
lark
charm

Learner Log

Presentation 1: 10–15 min.

If needed, review the purpose of the Learner Log.

Circle what you learned and write the page number where you learned it. Students research the answers individually. When they've finished, they should share their answers with a partner. These results need not be shared with the class.

Practice 1: 10–15 min.

Rank what you like to do best from 1 to 6. 1 is your favorite activity. Your teacher will help you. Results should be shared with the class in order to demonstrate to students how people learn differently.

Evaluation 1: 10–15 min.

I think I improved most in ——. Students should fill in the blank with assistance from a partner or from you. They may focus on a skill (e.g.,

listening), on a vocabulary area (e.g., numbers), on grammar, and so on. Don't limit them to a single answer. Emphasize that the purpose of completing the sentence is to improve their self-assessment skills. You may want to use this opportunity to ask students to reflect on what they have learned in this book.

Instructor's Notes for Unit 8 Team Project, Pronunciation and Learner Log

_____

_____

_____

_____

_____

_____

_____

_____

_____

_____

_____

_____

_____

_____

_____

_____

_____

_____

Useful Words

Cardinal numbers

1	one
2	two
3	three
4	four
5	five
6	six
7	seven
8	eight
9	nine
10	ten
11	eleven
12	twelve
13	thirteen
14	fourteen
15	fifteen
16	sixteen
17	seventeen
18	eighteen
19	nineteen
20	twenty
21	twenty-one
30	thirty
40	forty
50	fifty
60	sixty
70	seventy
80	eighty
90	ninety
100	one hundred
1000	one thousand
10,000	ten thousand
100,000	one hundred thousand
1,000,000	one million

Ordinal numbers

first	1st
second	2nd
third	3rd
fourth	4th
fifth	5th
sixth	6th
seventh	7th
eighth	8th
ninth	9th
tenth	10th
eleventh	11th
twelfth	12th
thirteenth	13th
fourteenth	14th
fifteenth	15th
sixteenth	16th
seventeenth	17th
eighteenth	18th
nineteenth	19th
twentieth	20th
twenty-first	21st

Days of the week

Sunday
Monday
Tuesday
Wednesday
Thursday
Friday
Saturday

Seasons

winter
spring
summer
fall

Months of the year

January
February
March
April
May
June
July
August
September
October
November
December

Write the date

April 5, 2004 = 4/ 5/ 04

Temperature chart

Degrees Celsius (ºC) and
Degrees Fahrenheit (ºF)

100ºC	—	212ºF
30ºC	—	86ºF
25ºC	—	77ºF
20ºC	—	68ºF
15ºC	—	59ºF
10ºC	—	50ºF
5ºC	—	41ºF
0ºC	—	32ºF
−5ºC	—	23ºF

Weights and measures

Weight:
1 pound (lb.) = 453.6 grams (g)
16 ounces (oz.) = 1 pound (lb.)
1 pound (lb.) = .45 kilogram (kg)

Liquid or Volume:
1 cup (c.) = .24 liter (l)
2 cups (c.) = 1 pint (pt.)
2 pints = 1 quart (qt.)
4 quarts = 1 gallon (gal.)
1 gallon (gal.) = 3.78 liters (l)

Length:
1 inch (in. or ″) = 2.54 centimeters (cm)
1 foot (ft. or ′) = .3048 meters (m)
12 inches (12″) = 1 foot (1′)
1 yard (yd.) = 3 feet (3′) or 0.9144 meters (m)
1 mile (mi.) = 1609.34 meters (m) or 1.609 kilometers (km)

Time:
60 seconds = 1 minute
60 minutes = 1 hour
24 hours = 1 day
28–31 days = 1 month
12 months = 1 year

The Simple Present — *be*

Subject	Verb	Example sentence
I	am ('m)	I am (I'm) Roberto.
you, we, they	are ('re)	You are (You're) a student. We are (We're) happy.
he, she, it	is ('s)	She is (She's) from Mexico.

The Simple Present — *be* (negative)

Subject	Verb	Example sentence
I	am ('m) not	I am not (I'm not) hungry.
you, we, they	are ('re) not	You are not (aren't) from Mexico.
he, she, it	is ('s) not	She is not (isn't) a student.

The Simple Present — *have*

Subject	Verb	Example sentence
I, you, we, they	have	I have three brothers. We have a cat.
he, she, it	has	He has free time. She has black hair.

The Simple Present — *have* (negative)

Subject	do + not	Verb	Example sentence
I, you, we, they	do not (don't)	have	I do not (don't) have children. We do not (don't) have a dog.
he, she, it	does not (doesn't)		He does not (doesn't) have blond hair.

The Simple Present — *Regular verbs*

Subject	Verb	Object
I, you, we, they	bring eat like	sandwiches lunch green salad
he, she, it	brings eats likes	

The Simple Present — *Regular verbs* (negative)

Subject	do + not	Verb	Object
I, you, we, they	do not (don't)	bring eat like	sandwiches lunch green salad
he, she, it	does not (doesn't)		

The Simple Present (yes/no question forms with *do*)

do	Subject	Base	Object	Example question
do	I, you, we, they	like	technology	Do you like technology?
does	he, she, it	have	a diploma	Does he have a diploma?

The Simple Past — *be*

Subject	Past	Example sentence
I, he, she, it	was	He was a mail carrier.
you, we, they	were	They were in the office.

The Simple Past — *Regular verbs*

Subject	Base	Base + *ed*	Example sentence
I, you, he, she, it, we, they	clean	cleaned	I cleaned tables.
	cook	cooked	You cooked hamburgers.
	prepare	prepared	He prepared breakfast.

The Present Continuous

Subject	be	Base + *ing*	Example sentence
I	am	calling	I am calling about the apartment.
you, we, they	are	working	They are looking for a house.
he, she, it	is	looking	She is working right now.

Grammar Reference

Imperative form

(You)	Base	Example sentence
	chop	Chop the potatoes.

Imperative form (negative)

(You)	*do + not (don't)*	Base	Example sentence
	do not (don't)	boil	Do not (don't) boil the water.

Modal Verbs (affirmative and negative forms)

Subject	Modal	Base	Example sentence
I, you, he, she, it, we, they	should	rest	He should rest.
	should not (shouldn't)	go out	You should not (shouldn't) go out.
I, you, he, she, it, we, they	can	drive	I can drive.
	cannot (can't)	type	She cannot (can't) type.
I, you, he, she, it, we, they	must	wear	You must wear eye protection.
	must not	enter	We must not enter this area.
I, you, he, she, it, we, they	will	study	They will study English next year.
	will not (won't)	move	He will not (won't) move to Florida.

The Modal Verb — should (*Wh*- question form)

Question word	Modal	Subject	Base	Example question
What	should	I, you, he, she, it, we, they	do?	What should I do?

Verb + infinitive

Subject	Verb	Infinitive (*to* + base)		Example sentence
I, you, we, they	want	to	exercise	I want to exercise.
he, she, it	wants		walk	She wants to walk.

Future—*going to*

Subject	*be + going to*	Base	Example sentence
I	am going to	be	I am going to be a mechanic.
you, we, they	are going to	work	You are going to work hard.
he, she, it	is going to	save	She is going to save money.

Possessive adjectives

Subject pronoun	Possessive adjective	Example sentence
I	my	*My* shirt is blue. *My* shoes are black.
you	your	*Your* baseball cap is blue. *Your* shorts are brown.
he	his	*His* belt is black. *His* sandals are brown.
she	her	*Her* blouse is pink. *Her* shoes are white.
it	its	*Its* label is red. *Its* doors are green.
we	our	*Our* house is white. *Our* books are blue.
they	their	*Their* school is in Center City. *Their* children are happy.

Demonstrative adjectives

	Near the speaker	Away from the speaker	Example sentence
Singular	this	that	I want *this* umbrella and *that* cap.
Plural	these	those	I want *these* jeans and *those* socks.

Stand Out 1 Vocabulary List

Pre-Unit
Study verbs
listen P6
read P6
speak P6
write P6

Unit 1
Personal information
age 7
divorced 4
height 7
marital status 4
married 4
single 4
weight 7
Hairstyle
bald 8
curly 8
long 8
short 8
straight 8
wavy 8
Family
brother 11
children 11
daughter 11
father 11
husband 11
mother 11
parents 11
sister 11
son 11
wife 11
Hobbies
books 13
computers 13
games 13
movies 13
music 13
parks 13
restaurants 13
sports 13
TV 13

Unit 2
Stores
bookstore 22
clothing store 22
convenience store 22
department store 22
supermarket 22
Money
bill 24
cash 32

check 32
credit card 32
dime 24
nickel 24
penny 24
quarter 24
Clothing
baseball cap 25
belt 27
blouse 25
coat 25
dress 25
hat 25
pants 27
sandal 27
shirt 21
shorts 27
skirt 25
socks 25
suit 25
sweater 25
tennis shoes 25
tie 25
T-shirt 25
Colors
black 27
blue 27
brown 27
gray 8
green 27
orange 27
red 27
white 27
yellow 27
Adjectives
big 30
checked 30
large 30
little 30
medium 30
new 30
small 30
striped 30
used 30

Unit 3
Food and meals
apples 48
avocados 48
bread 48
breakfast 41
burger 45
carrots 48
cereal 54
cheeseburger 45

coffee 54
cola 48
cookies 48
cucumbers 48
dinner 41
french fries 45
ground beef 48
hot dog 45
ice cream 54
lunch 41
milk 48
mustard 48
oranges 48
peanut butter 48
potato chips 48
salad 45
sandwich 45
side order 45
spaghetti 48
tomatoes 48
yogurt 48
Containers/Measurements
bag 49
bottle 49
box 49
can 49
cup 55
gallon 54
jar 49
ounce 54
package 49
pint 54
pound 54
teaspoon 55
Cooking verbs
add 55
boil 55
chop 55
cook 55
drain 55
mix 55
peel 55
whip 55

Unit 4
Housing
apartment 61
balcony 64
bathroom 63
bedroom 63
condominium 61
deck 64
dining room 63
driveway 64
electricity 65

family room 63
first floor 64
front door 63
garage 64
gas 65
hall 63
kitchen 63
living room 63
mobile home 61
porch 64
second floor 64
single-family home 61
stairs 64
swimming pool 64
utilities 65
yard 63
Furniture
bathtub 69
bed 69
chair 69
coffee table 71
end table 71
lamp 71
painting 71
refrigerator 69
sofa 69
trash can 70
Budget
expenses 73
income 73
savings 73

Unit 5
Places in the community
bank 90
bus station 83
city hall 81
DMV (Department of
    Motor Vehicles) 90
fire station 90
high school 83
hospital 90
library 81
mall 83
museum 83
park 81
playground 82
police station 90
post office 81
zoo 83
Body parts
arm 101
back 101
chest 101
ear 101

eyes 101
foot (feet) 101
hand 101
head 101
leg 101
mouth 101
nose 101
stomach 101
throat 101
tooth (teeth) 101

Unit 6
Health
ambulance 111
aspirin 105
cold 103
cough 103
emergency 111
fever 103
flu 103
headache 103

lozenges 105
muscle ache 103
runny nose 103
sore throat 103
syrup 105
temperature 104

Unit 7
Jobs
artist 122
busboy 125
cook 125
homemaker 122
mail carrier 125
mechanic 121
nurse 121
office worker 121
server 121
Employment
application 123
benefits 123

experience 123
full-time 123
insurance 123
interview 128
part-time 123
sick leave 123
vacation 123
Work tools
broom 130
computer 130
copier 130
hammer 130
mop 130
phone 130
saw 130
wrench 130
Work verbs
build 131
deliver 131
drive 131
fix 131

manage 131
sweep 131
type 131

Unit 8
Education
adult program 151
Associate's Degree 151
Bachelor's Degree 151
college 151
counselor 151
degree 157
diploma 148
GED (General Educational
    Development) 148
goal 148
trade school 151
university 151

Stand Out 1 Irregular Verb List

The verbs below are used in *Stand Out 1* and have irregular past tense forms.

Base verb	Simple past	Base verb	Simple past
be	was, were	give	gave
bring	brought	go	went
build	built	have	had
buy	bought	make	made
choose	chose	meet	met
come	came	put	put
do	did	read	read
drive	drove	see	saw
drink	drank	send	sent
draw	drew	sleep	slept
eat	ate	speak	spoke
feel	felt	teach	taught
find	found	write	wrote

Student Book 1 Listening Scripts with Supplemental Listenings from the Activity Bank 1

Pre-Unit
Track 1, Go to student book page P3, Lesson 2, Exercise A.
Track 2, Go to student book page P3, Exercise B.
Track 3, Page P3, Lesson 2, Exercise C.
1. Hi! I'm Susan. S-U-S-A-N
2. Hello! My name's Bill. B-I-L-L
3. How are you? I'm Annette. A-N-N-E-T-T-E
4. Hi! My name's Tony. T-O-N-Y

Track 4, Go to student book page P4, Lesson 3, Exercise C.

Track 5, Page P4, Lesson 3, Exercise C.
a. 5 b. 8 c. 9 d. 3 e. 0 f. 10

Track 6, Page P4, Lesson 3, Exercise E.
My name is Gabriela. My address is 14 Main Street. The zip code is 06119. The phone number is 401-555-7248. There are 16 students in my class.

Track 7, Page P5, Lesson 5, Exercise C.
1. Please stand up.
2. Please sit down.
3. Please read page one in your book.
4. Please take out a piece of paper.
5. Please listen carefully.
6. Please write your name on the paper.

Unit 1
Track 8, Page 2, Lesson 1, Exercise C.
A. Roberto is a new student in Beginning English at President Adult School. Roberto and his family are from Mexico City, Mexico.
B. Eva Malinska is happy to be in the United States. She wants to learn English. In Warsaw, Poland, she learned a bit of English. She wants to help other people in her family learn the language.
C. Gabriela Ramirez is 26. She listens to the radio and reads the newspaper every day in English. She wants to learn quickly. She's from Buenos Aires, Argentina.
D. Duong is a new student. He speaks Vietnamese. Now Duong goes to school to learn English. Duong wants to go to college.

Track 9, Page 4, Lesson 2, Exercise A.
Tatsuya: Excuse me. Is it OK to interview you?
Felipe: Sounds good. Go ahead.
Tatsuya: What's your first name?
Felipe: My first name is Felipe. F-E-L-I-P-E
Tatsuya: Where are you from?
Felipe: I'm from Cuba.
Tatsuya: Are you married or single?
Felipe: I'm single.
Tatsuya: How old are you?
Felipe: Twenty-three years old.
Tatsuya: Thanks, Felipe.
Felipe: No problem.

Track 10, Page 4, Lesson 2, Exercise C.
My name is Tatsuya. This is my new friend, Felipe. Felipe is from Cuba. He is 23 years old. He is single. We are students in this class.

Track 11, Go to student book page 10, Lesson 5, Exercise A.

Track 12, Page 11, Lesson 5, Exercise C.
My name is Roberto Garcia. I am very happily married. My wife's name is Silvia. This is a picture of my family. The older man and woman in the picture are my parents. My mother's name is Rebecca and my father's name is Antonio. I have one sister, Lidia, and one brother, Julio. The girl and boy are my children, Juan and Carla.

Track 13, Page 13, Lesson 6, Exercise A.
Roberto and Silvia are happily married. Roberto likes movies, games, and books. Silvia likes parks, restaurants, and music. They both like sports, computers, and TV.

Track 14, Page 20, Unit 1, Pronunciation.
Practice the /h/ sound at the beginning of words. Listen and repeat.
he his here husband home
hair how who height her

Supplemental Listening Activities for Unit 1
AB Track 2, Page 7, Unit 1, Lesson 3, Supplemental Listening, Activity Bank Worksheet 5.
Listen to the conversations and write the hair and eye color in the chart.

Conversation 1:
Listen to a description of Alan and fill in the chart.
A: Excuse me.
B: Yes?
A: I'm looking for my husband.
B: What does he look like?
A: He is tall and has red hair and green eyes.
B: How old is he?
A: He's in his 60's.
B: I saw him by the information desk.
A: Thanks.

Conversation 2:
Listen to a description of Felipe and fill in the chart.
A: Excuse me. I need to talk to Felipe.
B: I'm sorry. I don't know Felipe.
A: I think he is in this class.
B: What does he look like?
A: He's Cuban, with short brown hair and brown eyes.
B: Oh, yes. I think he's over there.
A: Thanks.

Conversation 3:
Listen to a description of Tren and fill in the chart.
A: I know a wonderful woman.
B: Who is she?
A: She is in my English class.
B: What is she like?
A: She's 33 years old and from Cambodia. She has black hair and brown eyes.

Conversation 4:
Listen to a description of Misha and fill in the chart.
A: Misha is a friend of mine from English class.
B: Oh, I know her.
A: You do?
B: I think so. Does she have blond hair and blue eyes?
A: Yes. She's from Russia.

AB Track 3, Page 16, Unit 1, Lesson 7, Supplemental Listening, Activity Bank Worksheet 12.
Listen to the conversations. When do the people study?
Mark the calendar.

Conversation 1:
Listen to the conversation. Write an *X* under the days Sota studies.
Teacher: Sota, it is very important to study between classes.
Sota: Maybe in the afternoons?
Teacher: Yes, on what days?
Sota: I have time on Monday, Thursday, and Saturday.
Teacher: That's great!

Conversation 2:
Listen to the conversation. Write an *X* under the days Nam studies.
Teacher: Nam, do you study outside class?
Nam: Not really. I work 60 hours a week.
Teacher: Maybe you can study 15 minutes a few days a week.
Nam: Wednesday is my day off. I can study a few minutes on Wednesday and maybe on Thursday too.
Teacher: Good. Wednesday and Thursday.

Conversation 3:
Listen to the conversation. Write an *X* under the days David studies.
David: I'm ready to study every day.
Teacher: You want to study Monday through Saturday?
David: That's right: Monday, Tuesday, Wednesday, Thursday, Friday, and Saturday.
Teacher: Wow. Good luck!

Conversation 4:
Listen to the conversation. Write an *X* under the days Eva studies.
Teacher: Eva, when can you study?
Eva: Well, I'm very busy, but I can study a little bit two days a week.
Teacher: What days?
Eva: Well, maybe I will study on Tuesday and Saturday.
Teacher: That's good.
Eva: Yes. I can study an hour on each of those days.

Unit 2

Track 15, Page 22, Lesson 1, Exercise D.
Van: I need some things for school. Do you want to shop with me?
Nam: No, not today. I have things to do here at home.
Van: OK. Where can I go for all these things?

Nam: What do you need?
Van: I need sneakers, shirts, bread, cheese, and fruit for lunches, a CD player, and a bilingual dictionary.
Nam: Wow, it sounds like a lot.
Van: I know.
Nam: The best place for shoes is Martin's Department Store. You can buy shirts at Martin's also. You can probably also buy a good CD player at Martin's.
Van: All at Martin's?
Nam: Yes, it's a good place for many things, but I think you need to go to Hero's Bookstore for the dictionary. You know Sam's Food Mart around the corner has all you need for your lunches.

Track 16, Page 23, Lesson 2, Exercise C.
Ex. How much is it? It's $22.50.
1. That's $34.15, please.
2. Here's $33.
3. That comes to $15.70.
4. The total cost is $77.95.

Track 17, Page 23, Lesson 2, Exercise D.
Conversation 1:
Customer: Excuse me. How much is this vacuum?
Salesperson: It's $98.99 on sale.
Customer: Thanks, I'll take it.

Conversation 2:
Customer: Excuse me. Can you help me? I'm looking for a washing machine.
Salesperson: This is a good brand.
Customer: Is that right? OK, how much is it?
Salesperson: It's 450 dollars.
Customer: Four hundred and fifty dollars? That much?
Salesperson: I'm afraid so.

Conversation 3:
Customer: I want to buy a ream of white paper.
Salesperson: The paper is over there. It's $6.50.
Customer: Thank you.

Conversation 4:
Customer: I just want this candy bar.
Salesperson: That will be $1.25, please.
Customer: Here you go. One dollar and twenty-five cents.

Conversation 5:
Customer: Every time I buy a phone, I get a bad one. Maybe I should buy an expensive one.
Salesperson: How about this one for $80?

Track 18, Go to student book page 31, Lesson 5, Exercise C.

Track 19, Page 34, Lesson 7, Exercise A.
Part 1
Roberto: Excuse me, I need a cap and an umbrella.
Salesperson: Yes, sir. How about that yellow cap over there?
Roberto: No, I prefer this orange cap.
Salesperson: OK, and how about this umbrella?
Roberto: No, it's too dark. I like that red umbrella.

Part 2
Roberto: I really need some jeans and some socks, too.

Salesperson: We have blue jeans and black jeans. How about those blue jeans?
Roberto: Yes, they look good. And a pair of these socks, please.
Salesperson: Great. I'll ring it all up.
Roberto: Thank you.

Track 20, Page 37, Review, Exercise A.
The tape player is $98.45 with tax; The shirt is $24.50; The TV is 456.78; The vacuum is $168.00; The shoes are $28.98; The dictionary is $18.95; The sweater is $33.99; The shorts are $17.00.

Track 21, Page 40, Unit 2 Pronunciation.
Listen to the /th/ sound in these words. Circle the words which sound like /th/ in thank you. Underline the words which sound like /th/ in this.

(think) these (thirty) those (theater) brother (thing) mother clothing with (bath) (three) father (path)

Supplemental Listening Activities for Unit 2
AB Track 4, Page 26, Unit 2, Lesson 3, Supplemental Listening, Activity Bank Worksheet 3.
Listen to the conversations. Write an *X* under the clothing that the shopper wants to buy.

Conversation 1:
Salesperson: Can I help you?
Shopper: Yes, I need a few things.
Salesperson: OK. Where do you want to start?
Shopper: Well, I need a pair of pants and a shirt for work tomorrow.
Salesperson: Come right this way.

Conversation 2:
Salesperson: What can I do for you?
Shopper: I can't find what I need. I think I'll go somewhere else.
Salesperson: Are you sure? What are you looking for?
Shopper: I'm looking for shoes, very large shoes.
Salesperson: That's no problem. We have large shoes in the back.
Shopper: Oh, great. And do you sell socks?
Salesperson: Of course.

Conversation 3:
Shopper: Excuse me. Where are clothes for children over 12?
Salesperson: They are in the Junior section.
Shopper: Over there?
Salesperson: Yes, over there. What exactly are you looking for?
Shopper: I'm looking for a dress for my daughter and pants and a shirt for my son.
Salesperson: You've come to the right place. Step over here and we will get you started.
Shopper: Thank you.

Conversation 4:
Salesperson: May I help you?
Shopper: Yes, can you direct me to the women's clothing?

Salesperson: The women's clothing is around the corner.
Shopper: Thank you. I need a new outfit for a job interview.
Salesperson: So you want a dress or suit, right?
Shopper: I want a dress and some nice shoes.
Salesperson: I'm sure they can help you over there.
Shopper: Thank you for your help.

AB Track 5, Page 29, Unit 2, Lesson 6, Supplemental Listening, Activity Bank Worksheet 6.
Listen and write the color and clothing.

Conversation 1:
A: I'm looking for Javier.
B: What is he wearing?
A: He is wearing a blue shirt.
B: A blue shirt?
A: Yes.

Conversation 2:
Salesperson: Excuse me. Can I help you?
Shopper: Well, maybe.
Salesperson: What do you need?
Shopper: I need a blouse for work.
Salesperson: What color are you looking for?
Shopper: Something dark. Maybe brown.
Salesperson: Let's see what's on this rack here.

Conversation 3:
Shopper A: Let's go out and buy some nice clothes.
Shopper B: OK. You know I like shopping.
Shopper A: Where should we go?
Shopper B: Let's go to the new store down the street.
Shopper A: OK, is it expensive?
Shopper B: I don't think so. I really want to buy that green dress in the window.
Shopper A: Let's go, then!

Conversation 4:
Salesperson: Can I help you?
Shopper: Yes. I want an extra-large coat.
Salesperson: What color do you want?
Shopper: Do you have green?
Salesperson: I think I can help you. Please step this way.

Conversation 5:
A: Everybody at my work wears the same thing. It's part of the job.
B: What do you wear?
A: Everything is red. I don't like wearing red pants, but this is the rule.
B: Well, at least you can change after work.
A: Yes, I'm glad about that.

Unit 3
Track 22, Page 43, Lesson 2, Exercise A.
Alex: Can I buy you lunch, Natasha?
Natasha: No, but you can help me. How do you work this thing, anyway?
Alex: First you decide what you want. Next, put your money here.
Natasha: I only have two dollars.
Alex: That's OK, the sandwiches are $1.75.

Natasha: OK, I want the tuna sandwich.
Alex: Put your dollar bills in this slot face up, so the president is looking away from you.
Natasha: What is "face up"?
Alex: So the president is looking up.
Natasha: I see.
Alex: Choose the number and take your change.
Natasha: Thank you, Alex. Maybe next time you can buy me lunch.
Alex: I'd love to.

Track 23, Page 45, Lesson 3, Exercise B.
Conversation 1:
Sebastien: I want a cheeseburger, a green salad and an orange juice, please.
Server: No orange juice today. Milk? Cola?
Sebastien: A cola, please.
Server: OK, two minutes. Next.

Conversation 2:
Tranh: What sandwiches do you have?
Server: Ham or cheese.
Tranh: I'll have a ham sandwich.
Server: OK.
Tranh: And a green salad, too.
Server: Of course. What about a drink?
Tranh: No, thanks.
Server: OK, that's a ham sandwich and a green salad, right?
Tranh: That's right, thanks.

Conversation 3:
Miyuki: I want some milk, please, and a hot dog.
Server: Do you want mustard?
Miyuki: No, thanks. Just French fries.
Server: That's fine. Hot dog, no mustard, french fries, and milk coming up.

Track 24, Page 51, Lesson 5, Exercise F.
Duong: We need to go shopping. We are out of everything.
Minh: You're right. Let's make a shopping list.
Duong: Well, I know we need ground beef.
Minh: That's not all. We really need carrots and tomatoes, too.
Duong: OK, I'll write that down, carrots and tomatoes.
Minh: I never buy any spaghetti or milk because you don't like them, but let's buy some cola. OK?
Duong: OK. I'll add it to the list.
Minh: We don't need peanut butter . . .
Duong: Avocados are expensive, but let's buy two?
Minh: That's fine.
Duong: That should be the whole list. I have ground beef, carrots, tomatoes, cola, and avocados on the list.

Track 25, Page 60 Unit 3 Pronunciation.
Can you hear the sounds /j/ and /y/ in these words? Listen and repeat.
jar jelly juice package orange margarine
yes yogurt use mayonnaise menu papaya

Supplemental Listening Activities for Unit 3
AB Track 6, Page 54, Unit 3, Lesson 6, Supplemental

Listening, Activity Bank Worksheet 8.
Listen to the conversations. Write the prices you hear for the different stores. Then circle the cheaper price.

Conversation 1:
A: Look at these prices. Can you believe it?
B: I know it. Prices are higher every day.
A: But look at this. Ground beef at Food Mart is $2.95.
B: Is it cheaper somewhere else?
A: Look. We can go just down the street and buy ground beef at Super A Market for $2.25.
B: That sounds a lot better.

Conversation 2:
A: We need some corn chips for the party tonight.
B: OK, where should I go?
A: Either store is OK. The price is almost the same.
B: You can get a bag at Food Market for $2.50. I don't know about Super A Market . . .
A: Let me look at an old receipt. Yes, it is a little more. Corn chips at Super A Market are $2.75.
B: I'll go to Food Market.

Conversation 3:
A: Oranges are not expensive at this time of year.
B: Especially around here, where they have lots of them.
A: Both Food Market and Super A Market are running specials this week.
B: I see that here in the paper. It looks like Super A Market is a little cheaper though. Oranges there are 79 cents a pound.
A: How much are they at Food Market?
B: 89 cents a pound.

Conversation 4:
A: It's time to go to the store. Is Super A Market OK?
B: Sure, but why? Food Market is much closer.
A: Super A has better prices.
B: Really?
A: Really. For example mayonnaise at Super A is $3.58.
B: And at Food Market?
A: Food Market is $4.99.
B: Wow, that is quite a difference!

AB Track 7, Page 56, Unit 3, Lesson 7, Supplemental Listening, Activity Bank Worksheet 10.

Directions 1:
Listen to the directions for a cake and put the directions in order. Write 1 to 4.
1. Heat oven to 350°.
2. Combine cake mix, water, oil, and eggs in a large bowl.
3. Pour mixture into a pan.
4. Bake for 35 minutes.

Directions 2:
Listen to the directions for tacos and put the directions in order. Write 1 to 5.
1. Fry ground beef.
2. Drain excess grease.
3. Cut tomatoes, onions, cheese, and lettuce.
4. Fry corn tortillas until crisp.

5. Add ground beef, cheese, tomatoes, and lettuce to the fried tortillas.

Directions 3:
Listen to the directions for meatloaf and put the directions in order. Write 1 to 5.
1. Chop half a bell pepper.
2. Add egg, tomato sauce, bell pepper, and rice to ground beef.
3. Form a loaf in a pan.
4. Season with salt and pepper.
5. Cook in the microwave on high for 30 minutes.

Unit 4
Track 26, Page 63, Lesson 2, Exercise A.
Conversation 1:
Saud: I'm looking for a house to rent for my family.
Agent: Would you please sit down?
Saud: Thank you.
Agent: How many bedrooms do you need?
Saud: I need three bedrooms and one bathroom.
Agent: I think we can help you.

Conversation 2:
Silvia: We're interested in a nice apartment in the city.
Agent: I'm sure we can help you. This one has two bathrooms and two bedrooms. Is that OK?
Silvia: Maybe. What's the rent?
Agent: It's only $850 a month.
Silvia: $850 a month? This is going to be more difficult than I thought.

Conversation 3:
Tien: Do you have any properties for a big family?
Agent: Well, let's see.
Tien: I think I need a house with four bedrooms.
Agent: To rent or buy?
Tien: To rent, I think. How much are the rentals here?
Agent: We have one here with two bathrooms for $1300 a month.
Tien: Can we go out and look at it?
Agent: Yes, of course.

Conversation 4:
Felipe: What do you have in a one-bedroom?
Agent: We have this one-bedroom on Sycamore Street.
Felipe: That looks great. How much is the rent?
Agent: It's $750 a month, plus utilities.
Felipe: Is it one bathroom too?
Agent: That's right, one bathroom and one bedroom.

Track 27, Page 66, Lesson 3, Exercise D.
1. This apartment is a large three-bedroom with lots of good features. There is also a pool. All the utilities are paid and it's near a school. Come and visit. You won't be sorry.
2. Apartments come and go, but this is the best. It has three bedrooms and it's only $800 a month. It's on the second floor so you can enjoy a beautiful balcony.
3. This great home is far from the city traffic. Hot summers are no problem. We have air conditioning

and we pay the electricity. Call Margaret at 555-5678.
4. This is a bargain! $700 a month on a lease for this one-bedroom one-bath small apartment. No pets please! Call our manager Fred. He will get you in today! 555-7164.

Track 28, Go to student book page 67, Lesson 4, Exercise A.

Track 29, Page 80, Unit 4 Pronunciation.
Listen to these words. Underline the words which sound like *air*. Circle the words which sound like *ear*. Then listen again and repeat.

where (near) here hair (year) wear chair
(hear) there their (clear) stair pair (tear)

Supplemental Listening Activities for Unit 4
AB Track 8, Page 62, Unit 4, Lesson 1, Supplemental Listening, Activity Bank Worksheet 1.
Listen to the conversations. What kind of housing are they talking about? Write an X in the column for the housing type.

Conversation 1:
A: We really need to move. This place is too small for our big family.
B: How many bedrooms do we need?
A: We need a house with four bedrooms.
B: Can we afford it? Let's look at the prices in the classifieds.

Conversation 2:
A: Where do you live?
B: I live in apartment 203.
A: Is that on the second floor?
B: Yes, it is.

Conversation 3:
A: Can you come to my house to help me with my homework?
B: Sure. Where do you live?
A: I live in a very large house on First Street.
B: Which house is it?
A: It's the large blue one across from the park.
B: OK. I'll be there later.
A: Sounds good.

Conversation 4:
A: Can you help me find Lincoln Avenue?
B: Sure. It's just around the corner where all the mobile homes are.
A: That must be right. I'm looking for my uncle's mobile home.
B: Just go around the corner and you'll see the mobile homes on the left.
A: Thanks.

AB Track 9, Page 64, Unit 4, Lesson 2, Supplemental Listening, Activity Bank Worksheet 4.
Listen to the conversation about housing. Write the number of bedrooms and bathrooms.

Customer: I'm looking for a new place for my family in your community. Can you help me?

Agent: Of course. Our office has all the information you need. What are you looking for?

Customer: Well, I'm not sure. I have a large family and we really want lots of space.

Agent: OK. The condos we have probably are too small. They all have two bedrooms and two baths. Am I right?

Customer: Yes, they sound too small.

Agent: How about a mobile home? There is a very nice doublewide with three bedrooms and two bathrooms at the end of Main Street.

Customer: Three bedrooms, two baths sound good. Is there a yard for the dog?

Agent: No, there isn't. I suppose the apartments on First Street are out, too. They don't have yards although they do have three bedrooms and two baths.

Customer: Yes, I need a yard.

Agent: Well then, you need a house. We have a very large but expensive house on Clayton Way. It has five bedrooms and two bathrooms. How does that sound?

Customer: Maybe we can go and see it.

Unit 5

Track 30, Page 85, Lesson 3, Exercise B.
Conversation 1:

A: Excuse me. I'm looking for the mall. Do you know if it's close by?

B: Yes it is. Turn around and then turn right on Broadway. You can't miss it. There are signs all over.

A: OK, turn around and then turn right on Broadway.

B: That's right. It's only a mile away.

Conversation 2:

A: I'm new here and need to find the post office to mail a package. Can you give me directions?

B: Yes, that's easy. Go straight about a block. It's only a half-mile away on this street.

A: That's great, thank you.

Conversation 3:

A: Let's go to the movies.

B: I can't go right now. I'm waiting for a friend to come over.

A: Why don't you and your friend meet us there?

B: OK, how do you get there?

A: From here you need to turn around and go to Nutwood. Turn right on Fairview. The Movieplex Theaters are on Fairview, not too far down.

B: Great. We'll see you there. What time?

A: I think the movie starts at eight.

Conversation 4:

A: I'm looking for the Museum of Aviation. Do you know where it is?

B: Yes. It's a little far. It's down on Main, downtown.

A: Downtown?

B: Yes, turn right on Center Street, then left on Main. Go about five miles on Main. You'll see it close to the police station.

Conversation 5:

A: Excuse me. Where is Monterey Park? Do you know?

B: I think so. It's not a very big park. I think it's in the residential area on Boulder Lane.

A: Oh, now I understand. I was looking on main streets.

B: Turn left at the next street. Then turn right. Go straight ahead for two blocks and you will see it by a school.

A: Thanks. I hope I find it this time.

B: Good luck.

Track 31, Page 90, Lesson 5, Exercise B.

A. This is a place where people mail letters and packages and buy stamps. It is a government agency.

B. This is a place with trained workers who help the community when there is an emergency like a fire.

C. This is a place where very sick people go for surgery and other problems. Sometimes people go here in an emergency. They sometimes come by ambulance.

D. This is where people go to get a driver's license and identification.

E. This is a place where people put their money. Sometimes they get a checking account and sometimes they get credit cards and loans.

F. This is a place where police officers work. It is the police officers' office.

Track 32, Go to student book page 91, Lesson 5, Exercise D.

Track 33, Page 92, Lesson 6, Exercise C.

Machine: Hello, this is David. I can't come to the phone right now, but your call is very important. Please leave a message after the tone and I will get back to you right away. Beeep.

Gabriela: This is Gabriela. I want to go to the post office tomorrow. Can you go with me? I hope so. I need some help from a friend.

Track 34, Page 98, Review, Exercise C.
Message 1:

Machine: This is Herman. I can't come to the phone right now. Please, leave a message. Beeeep.

Nadia: This is Nadia. I have a question. My number is 555-2344.

Message 2:

Machine: This is Herman. I can't come to the phone right now. Please, leave a message. Beeeep.

Vien: This is Vien. I want to talk. Can you call me? My number is 555-7798.

Message 3:

Machine: This is Herman. I can't come to the phone right now. Please, leave a message. Beeeep.

David: David here. I need information. Please call 555-1234.

Message 4:

Machine: This is Herman. I can't come to the phone right now. Please, leave a message. Beeeep.

Ricardo: My name is Ricardo. I need a phone number. My number is 555-7343.

These words all begin with /s/ together with another consonant. Listen and repeat.

study station straight street sport special
school skirt slow small snow swim

Supplemental Listening Activities for Unit 5
AB Track 10, Page 88, Unit 5, Lesson 4, Supplemental Listening, Activity Bank Worksheet 6.
Listen to the conversations and complete the mall directory.

Conversation 1:
Listen to the directions to Abby's Mexican Grill. Write the name in the directory.
A: Excuse me. I'm looking for a good place to eat.
B: Try Abby's Mexican Grill.
A: Where is it?
B: It's down on the other side of the mall between Rudy's Fine Jewelry and the toy store.
A: Thanks. I will try it out.

Conversation 2:
Listen to the directions to Pet Haven. Write the name in the directory.
A: I want to buy a little dog. Do they have a pet store here?
B: Yes, Pet Haven is just around the corner from The Cookie Cutter.
A: Oh, you mean across from the pizza place?
B: Yes, that's right.

Conversation 3:
Listen to the directions to Ron's Cards and Gifts. Write the name in the directory.
A: I need to find a special card for my mother. She's very sick.
B: Let's try Ron's Cards and Gifts.
A: Where's that?
B: It's next to the furniture store.
A: That's not too far. Let's go.

Conversation 4:
Listen to the directions to Roscoe's Uniform. Write the name in the directory.
A: Did you hear about the new store? It's going to open next week.
B: No, what is it?
A: It's Roscoe's Uniform. It will have clothes for work.
B: Where is it going to be?
A: Across from the Beauty Palace.
B: That will be great.

AB Track 11, Page 93, Unit 5, Lesson 6, Supplemental Listening, Activity Bank Worksheet 10.
Listen to the messages and write down the phone number.

Message 1:
Antonia: Please leave a message after the tone. (Beep)
Alex: Hi, Antonia. I just got in town. This is Alex. Call me and we can do something tonight. My number is 555-9786. I hope all is well. I can't wait to see you. Bye.

Message 2:
Antonia: Please leave a message after the tone. (Beep)
Med. Recep: This is Dr. Pearson's office. We are confirming Antonia's appointment for tomorrow. You have a check-up at 9:00 AM. Please call if you can't make it. Our number is 555-8207.

Message 3:
Antonia: Please leave a message after the tone. (Beep)
Natalie: Hi, Antonia. This is Natalie. Wow, what a great day! Can't wait to talk to you about it. Call me back, OK? You know the number, but just in case, it's 555-1162.

Message 4:
Antonia: Please leave a message after the tone. (Beep)
Antonia's Mother : Antonia, you never call me! I hope you are all right. Your father and I are in town at the Nightlite Hotel. Call us so we can get together. The number here is 555-8947, Room 203.

Unit 6
Track 36, Page 102, Lesson 1, Exercise D.
Conversation 1:
Karen: Doctor, thank you for seeing me on such short notice.
Doctor: What seems to be the trouble?
Karen: Well I'm having trouble with my hand.
Doctor: What do you mean, trouble?
Karen: My hand is very stiff in the morning. I work at a computer and it is getting very difficult to do my work.

Conversation 2:
Doctor: How are you today, Roberto?
Roberto: I'm fine, except my leg hurts all the time.
Doctor: I see. Let's check it out. Where does it hurt?
Roberto: My leg hurts right here near the knee.
Doctor: We probably should take some X-rays.

Conversation 3:
Vien: Doctor, I have a terrible earache.
Doctor: Does it hurt all the time?
Vien: Yes, but especially when I am outside.
Doctor: Hmm. You may have some kind of infection.

Conversation 4:
Doctor: Well, Tino, it seems like you are here every week these days.
Tino: I guess so, doctor. My feet are killing me!
Doctor: I know that you were here last week because of your elbow. Didn't the prescription help?
Tino: Not at all. It seems to be getting worse.

Conversation 5:
Eric: Doctor, I really need your help.
Doctor: What can I do for you?
Eric: My stomach hurts, especially after I eat anything.
Doctor: Well, let's see if we can find something to help you.

Track 37, Go to student book page 104, Lesson 2, Exercise E.

Track 38, Page 108, Lesson 4, Exercise B.
Conversation A:
Doctor: Now, Karen, I know you are in pain. You will need some medicine to help you. I'm writing a prescription for a pain reliever. Please be careful and keep it away from your children.
Karen: OK, doctor, I will keep it out of my children's reach.

Conversation B:
Doctor: You should take two tablets every four hours during the day.
Karen: Yes, OK.
Doctor: It is very important that you don't take too much. Follow the directions carefully and don't take more than two tablets every four hours. OK?
Karen: Yes, doctor, I understand.

Conversation C:
Doctor: It's not good to take this medication if you are expecting a baby.
Karen: It's OK. I'm not pregnant.

Conversation D:
Doctor: This medicine will make you a little tired. Be careful when driving.
Karen: OK, maybe I shouldn't drive at all, to be safe.

Track 39, Page 110, Lesson 5, Exercise C.
Example:
Operator: 911. What is your emergency?
Rodrigo: There is a fire at 9235 W. Brookfield and I think someone is inside.
Operator: What's your name?
Rodrigo: Rodrigo Sandoval. Please hurry.
Operator: We will send the fire department and the paramedics out immediately.

Emergency 1:
Operator: 911. What is your emergency?
Anya: We have a medical emergency here.
Operator: What's happened?
Anya: A woman here at work is having a heart attack.
Operator: Is she conscious?
Anya: Yes, but she is holding her chest in pain.
Operator: What is the address?
Anya: 45 Center Street.
Operator: The ambulance will be there very soon.

Emergency 2:
Operator: 911. What is your emergency?
Felipe: There's a car accident on Murphy and Garden Ave.
Operator: Are there injuries?
Felipe: Maybe.
Operator: What's your name?
Felipe: Felipe Perez.
Operator: Felipe, the police and the paramedics are coming.

Emergency 3:
Operator: 911. What is your emergency?
Brian: My name is Brian Jenkins and there is a man in the house next door.
Operator: You mean there is a robbery?

Brian: Yes, I think so. It's at 2546 Maple Way.
Operator: Thank you, sir. The police will be there right away.

Track 40, Go to student book page 111, Lesson 5, Exercise D.

Track 41, Page 120, Unit 6, Pronunciation.
Listen to the sounds /s/ and /th/. Can you hear the difference? Listen and repeat.

think	sink	thick	sick
thigh	sigh	thumb	sum
mouse	mouth	moss	moth
mass	math	pass	path
a sore throat		a healthy sport	
a thin slice		three spoons	

Supplemental Listening Activities for Unit 6
AB Track 12, Page 113, Unit 6 Lesson 6, Supplemental Listening, Activity Bank Worksheet 10.
Listen to the conversation. Choose the vocabulary word for each number and write it on the chart.

Conversation 1:
A: Excuse me. I need some help. Where can I go to get some information?
B: Go down the hall to the woman at the desk.
A: Thank you so much.

Conversation 2:
A: I need to call my family and tell them that Mary is having a baby. Where can I go?
B: Around the corner are some phones that you can use. They are next to the drinking fountain.
A: Thank you. I will give them a call and be right back.

Conversation 3:
A: I'm looking for my brother. They say he is in room 515, bed 3.
B: You will need to go to the fifth floor. Here are the stairs, and the elevators are around the corner.
A: Thank you.
B: You are welcome.

Conversation 4:
A: My wife is ill and needs to see a doctor right away.
B: I understand that sir, but there are ten patients ahead of you.
A: Well, how long will the wait be?
B: I can't really say because this is an emergency room. Serious emergencies come in and we have to take them first.
A: What do we do until it's our turn?
B: Please have a seat and we will have a nurse talk to your wife shortly.

Unit 7
Track 42, Page 123, Lesson 2, Exercise B.
Conversation 1:
Boss: Roberto, you need to take your vacation right away.
Roberto: Well, I'm not sure that I have time.

Boss: If you don't take vacation now, then you will lose it. You have five days.

Roberto: OK, I'll talk to my wife and see what she says.

Conversation 2:

Anya: I have a problem.

Supervisor: What can I do for you?

Anya: My husband had an accident.

Supervisor: An accident? What happened?

Anya: He had a small car accident and he broke his leg.

Supervisor: What can I do?

Anya: Is he covered by my insurance?

Supervisor: Of course. Your family is all covered by your insurance.

Conversation 3:

Steve: I'm sorry, I have to call in sick.

Manager: I'm sorry to hear that.

Steve: Yes, I have a fever. Maybe I have the flu.

Manager: How long will you be out?

Steve: Do you know how much sick leave I have left?

Manager: I'll check on it for you.

Track 143, Page 129, Lesson 4, Exercise C.

Conversation 1:

Miyuki: Excuse me. I'm interested in a job. Do you have any openings?

Manager: Not right now, but we can keep your name on file.

Miyuki: OK, can I have an application, please?

Conversation 2:

Miyuki: Here is my application. Can I see the manager?

Worker: Not just now, she is busy.

Miyuki: Can I make an appointment, please?

Conversation 3:

Manager: Are you interested in a job as a clerk?

Miyuki: Yes, that's right.

Manager: Do you have any experience?

Miyuki: No, but I'm good at math and I learn quickly.

Conversation 4:

Miyuki: I want to make an appointment to see the manager.

Worker: Just a moment, I'll see if she's free.

Miyuki: Thanks, I'll wait here.

Track 44, Page 132, Lesson 6, Exercise B.

1. This is our manufacturing area. Be sure to always wear a hard hat here because sometimes metal falls from above.
2. Never enter here. This room is for photography development and you could ruin a day's work if you come in at the wrong time.
3. Our factory does not permit smoking anywhere except outside. There are many hazardous chemicals.
4. These machines could hurt your hands, so keep your hands far away from danger.
5. Keep this area clear. We need plenty of room here for cars to pass.
6. Always put this sign up after the restrooms are cleaned because it does get very slippery when wet. We don't want accidents.

Track 45, Page 140 Unit 7 Pronunciation.

Listen to the vowel sound in these words. Underline the words with a long /i/ sound. Circle the words with a short /i/ sound. Then listen again and repeat.

speak   need   quick   teacher   build   little
listen   feel   clean   fix   fill   please

Supplemental Listening Activities for Unit 7
AB Track 13, Page 122, Unit 7, Lesson 1, Supplemental Listening, Activity Bank Worksheet 1.

Conversation 1:

Listen to the conversation. Write Abasi's job title and where he works.

Counselor: It's good to see you again, Abasi. How are you?

Abasi: Just fine, thanks.

Counselor: What do you do now?

Abasi: I work in a factory. I'm an assembly worker.

Counselor: That's a good job.

Conversation 2:

Listen to the conversation. Write Jun's job title and where she works.

Counselor: Jun, you are here from China. Is that right?

Jun: Yes, I arrived last month.

Counselor: You worked as a nurse in a hospital there, right?

Jun: That's right. I worked there for seven years.

Counselor: Very impressive. You have the experience we are looking for.

Conversation 3:

Listen to the conversation. Write Issa's job title and where he works.

Counselor: Issa, your wife told me that you are working in an office now.

Issa: That's right and it's great. I type and file.

Counselor: So you are an administrative assistant?

Issa: Yes. All that practice on the computer really paid off.

Conversation 4:

Listen to the conversation. Write Alonsa's job title and where she works.

Counselor: Alonsa, it is very nice to meet you. What do you do?

Alonsa: I'm a teacher.

Counselor: Great. Where do you teach?

Alonsa: I teach in an elementary school in the city.

Counselor: Wow. Are the kids hard to handle?

Alonsa: A little, but I love them all.

Unit 8
Track 46, Page 146, Lesson 3, Exercise D.

I want to learn English when there is no school, so I'm going to study a lot. I'm making goals so I can remember my plans. I'm going to study every weekday. When I wake up in the morning, I'm going to listen to the radio in English from 6:30 to 6:45. I'm going to listen to the news. Maybe I won't understand, but I can listen and try. From 7:00 a.m. to 7:30 a.m., I'm going to read the newspaper. I'm going to look for words that I understand. After work at night, I'm going to study four pages in the textbook from 8:00 to 8:45. From 9:00 p.m. to 9:15 p.m. I'm going to review my vocabulary notebook and then write in my journal.

Track 47, Page 151, Lesson 5, Exercise A.
Conversation 1:
Ahmed: I want to be a computer technician, but first I need to learn more English.
Counselor: That's very important. Do you have a high school diploma?
Ahmed: No, I don't.
Counselor: Well, that is always a good place to start. Maybe you can get work without it, but it is very important.
Ahmed: Yes, I know. That's one of my plans.
Counselor: You can learn to be a computer technician in a trade school, or you can go to a two-year college.
Ahmed: Which one is better?
Counselor: They are both good, but a trade school will help you find a job when you finish.

Conversation 2:
Counselor: That's great that you want to be a teacher.
Minh: Yes, but I do need to learn English.
Counselor: That's right. You have your high school diploma, so you can start at a two-year college or go right to the university.
Minh: Which is better for me?
Counselor: They are both good. The college is cheaper and you can take English classes while you take other classes.

Conversation 3:
Mario: I just need a little English and I can go to work. I'm already a good mechanic.
Counselor: Do you have a GED or high school diploma?
Mario: No, do I really need one?
Counselor: A GED can really help. A good mechanic has to read instructions and manuals. Please think about it.
Mario: Thanks, I'm going to think about it.

Conversation 4:
Akiko: I want to understand computers in the United States so I can get a good job in web design.
Counselor: First, you have to speak English very well.
Akiko: If I study at home and come to this adult school, I think that will be enough.
Counselor: You should plan to go to college and take technology courses too. It's hard, but you need the experience.

Conversation 5:
Counselor: Alan, you want to be a cook, right?
Alan: That's right.
Counselor: Do you want to be a chef in an expensive restaurant where you can make special food?
Alan: I don't know. I like to cook. Is it hard to be a chef?
Counselor: You need to go to school—maybe a trade school.
Alan: That sounds like a lot of work, but I'll think about it.

Conversation 6:
Counselor: Nursing is a good job. You can take special courses at the state college.
Marie: I already have plans to go to the college here in town. Do I need to be a citizen?
Counselor: No, but you do need to be a state resident or it will cost you a lot of money.
Marie: Good, I am a state resident.

Track 48, Page 160, Unit 8, Pronunciation.
Listen to the vowel sounds in these words. Circle the words which sound like 'firm' and underline the words which sound like 'farm'. Then listen again and repeat.

(learn) start (work) park (nurse) part heart
card (clerk) (shirt) (hurt) chart (journal) (hurt)

Supplemental Listening Activities for Unit 8
AB Track 14, Page 150, Unit 8, Lesson 4, Supplemental Listening, Activity Bank Worksheet 5.
Listen to the conversations and match the names with what they want to do.

Conversation 1:
Counselor: Hello, Rigoberto. What brings you here?
Rigoberto: I need to talk about my future.
Counselor: What do you want to do?
Rigoberto: I'm not sure.
Counselor: What are you good at?
Rigoberto: I'm not sure.
Counselor: Why not get a high school diploma and then maybe you will know what you want to do with your life.
Rigoberto: That sounds like a good idea.

Conversation 2:
Counselor: What are your plans for the future, Anya?
Anya: I want so many things.
Counselor: Like what?
Anya: Well, I guess, first I want to buy a house.
Counselor: Do you have the money?
Anya: Yes, I work very hard and I am saving money.

Conversation 3:
Counselor: Gilberto, you know English now. So what are your plans?
Gilberto: Well, I want to learn a skill to help me everywhere I go.
Counselor: What kind of skill are you interested in?
Gilberto: Computer programming. Is that a good idea?
Counselor: Sounds good to me.

Conversation 4:
Marco: I'm so tired of working here.
Counselor: What's the problem?
Marco: They don't pay enough. I want a new job with better benefits.
Counselor: Marco, did you look in the paper? With your experience, you could go anywhere.

Stand Out 1 Skills Index

TEACHING HINTS

COMPUTERS

Computers can be used in many real-life, task-based ways. We can use this tool to enhance instruction in the context of the lesson. The instructor will find it more workable if he or she presents one computer application along with a related task so students have an opportunity to practice a little at a time. There are various applications that can be used in the classroom:

1. **Word processing** allows students to write paragraphs. They will have a finished product that can include pictures. The spell check feature can be on or off. If it is on, students become more aware of their errors and how they can fix them. Word processing also allows students to make brochures and other interesting products.

2. **Graphs** can be designed in a variety of ways, using spreadsheet programs and chart wizards. Students must understand the information in more detail to be able to develop such graphs—therefore, they receive additional practice in the concepts.

3. **Spreadsheets** allow students to sort and classify information. Spreadsheet templates can be designed by the teacher or the student to display information and calculate formulas.

4. The **Internet** allows students to obtain more information, opening discussion and applying many activities from the lessons to real-life situations.

5. **E-mail** can be used to open up pen pal opportunities, communicate with classmates, get to know other classrooms, and discuss progress and assignments with the teacher.

Suggestions for Using Computers:

- Let students have control of the keyboard. If you need to model the steps by using the student's keyboard, put the computer back where it was before modeling so the student can try the technique or assignment him- or herself.

- Have students work in pairs or small groups. Even when typing a composition, work is enhanced when students work with a partner.

- Allow students the freedom to make mistakes. This is how we learn best.

- Allow students to work at different paces.

- Help students learn to solve their own problems and to assist each other.

COOPERATIVE LEARNING

The purpose of cooperative learning is to create community in the classroom, allow students freedom to speak in smaller settings, provide forums for discussions, accomplish tasks that individuals cannot do alone, provide SCANS and EFF practice, and enhance instruction in a variety of ways.

Cooperative Learning Activities:

- **Corners activities** allow students to learn more about each other by self-classifying into various groups. A corners activity asks students to go to designated places in a room (often corners). Each location represents a certain characteristic or opinion. A discussion among the group members and/or between different groups usually follows.

- **Information gap activities** allow students to practice speaking and listening to each other, clarifying what they don't understand. An information gap activity requires a student to get missing information from another student to complete a task.

- **Jigsaw activities** allow students to become experts in one part of a given topic or task and share their expertise with other members of their group.

Cooperative Learning Suggestions:

1. Groups should be a manageable number, from three to five students.

2. Each member of the group should have a responsibility. Traditional responsibilities include Leader, Secretary, Time Keeper, and Spokesperson. In **Stand Out** team project activities, students choose responsibilities specific to the tasks.

3. Groups should have a task or a product that is recorded and reported.

4. Students should be encouraged to speak English. Some ways to do that are:

- Have a leader whose task it is to make sure everyone speaks English and participates.

- Check with the groups regularly and have them self-assess and report to the class how much English they are speaking.

- Explain the task completely and make sure the students have the experience and knowledge to do it.

- Speak English yourself.

- Encourage; don't reprimand.

- Encourage more fluent students to work with less fluent ones or form groups by student level, so you can support students who need further review and explanation.

DIALOGS

The purpose of dialogs is to help students practice real life conversations. In *Stand Out,* students are given many opportunities to substitute information. To help students prepare for this practice, it is important to present the dialog in a clear manner. It is also important to find different ways for students to practice the dialogs to add variety to their experience.

Dialog Presentation:

1. Present the dialog in context in its entirety by allowing the students to hear the model, either from the recording or read aloud by you.

2. Have the students repeat each line as a class. Work on rhythm and other pronunciation features.

3. Have students take A's role while you take B. Then reverse roles.

4. Ask one student to practice the dialog with you and reverse roles with another student.

5. Ask two students to demonstrate together. Repeat the above steps with word or information substitutions.

Types of Dialog Practice:

- Practice in pairs.

- Have all the students stand and speak to a given number of students.

- Pass out note cards labeled with different substitutions. Ask the students to discover what is on other students' cards by performing the dialog and looking for matches with what is on their personal card.

- Ask students to provide personal information for substitutions.

- Have students perform a task (e.g. mime an action) as they practice the dialog.

- Ask half the class to form a circle facing outward. Ask the other half of the class to form a circle outside of the first, facing inward. Individuals from each circle pair up and perform the dialog. Next have one circle rotate and have the students perform the dialog with a new partner. **Note:** This activity is a good icebreaker in the first weeks of class and can be used for introductions. Limit introductory conversation or small talk to one minute.

DICTATION

The purpose of dictation is to help students improve their listening skills. You can dictate single words, sentences, or an entire paragraph to students. The idea is to get students to understand what you've said before they write it down.

Dictation Suggestions:

- Tell students that the most important part of dictation is to LISTEN FIRST.

- Tell students that you will only be reading the statements or words one time. (You may have to dictate more than once for lower levels.) This will encourage them to listen more carefully.

- Tell students to listen to the whole sentence before they begin writing. Remind them that if they start writing before you've finished speaking, they won't hear the end of what you say.

- Once you've finished dictating, have students check their answers with a partner or group. Encourage them to write down what they missed or fix what they think they got wrong.

- Read the dictation one more time.

- Call on volunteer students to write the dictation on the board.

- Ask the class to check and help correct what's on the board.

FOCUSED LISTENING

The purpose of focused listening is to expose students to real-life listening situations and teach them how to pick out the important information. These activities help students develop strategies they need to be successful listeners outside of the classroom. Focused listening is always accompanied by a specific task.

1. Make it clear to students that they don't need to understand everything spoken to grasp the meaning.

2. Present the context.

3. Make sure the students understand what they are listening for.

4. Help them understand that the recordings are at an authentic pace to help prepare them for real-life experiences.

5. Start with a few examples and allow students to be successful before you expect them to complete the listening in bigger chunks. Evaluate what they are learning before you move to more extensive tasks.

6. After they complete the task, ask for a report.

VOCABULARY

- **PAVE**

The PAVE vocabulary method is a unique way of making vocabulary cards that help students predict the word's meaning, verify their prediction, evaluate, and then create an associative link to help students remember the word.

Prediction	Write the original context in which the word appears. Write the word again, this time predicting its part of speech and definition.
Verification	Check the part of speech and meaning in the dictionary. Write the definition from the dictionary. Also write the sample sentence if there is one.
Evaluation	Look at the sentence written in Verification and write an original or better one if necessary.
Association	Draw an image to help remember the meaning of the word.

PAVE Presentation Suggestions:

- If possible, put up a transparency of a sample vocabulary card using the PAVE method.

- Give the class a new word and have them create a card as a class, using a template on an overhead projector or following one drawn on the board.

- Divide students into small groups and give each group a word to create a card for. Have each group present their word to the class.

- Have students create their own cards with words that are new to them.

- Schedule time each week for vocabulary review or practice.

TEAM PROJECTS

In team projects, students apply all of the objectives they learned in the unit. A project contains task-based activities that generate teamwork through work on one or more products.

Suggestions for Team Projects:

- Set the stage
  -Give an overview.
  -Show examples.
  -Don't be too specific about results.

- Form teams
  -Mix language groups and students of varying ability.

- Assign team positions (all team members are expected to assist with every task)
  Lower levels:
      -Explain leader position.
      -Immediately ask all leaders to stand for recognition.
      -Initially assign roles if class is uncertain how to proceed.
      -Repeat introductions and recognition for all positions.

  Higher levels:
      -Explain all positions.
      -Allow students to discuss and assign positions in their teams.
      -Ask teams to report names and positions.

- Go through the steps
  - Give a few steps at a time.
  - Avoid allowing teams to get too far ahead.
  - Have students keep minutes in an agenda/minutes format.
  - For two-day team projects: Collect work at end of first day with names of team members to be re-distributed on the following day. Ask teams to include names and job positions on their work.

- Work on the project
  - Have assigned students lead efforts.
  - Make sure all students participate in each task.
  - Use computers when possible.
  - Be flexible and adapt when time runs short.

- Facilitate
  - Walk from team to team, listening.
  - Ask questions.
  - Help the leader to make sure everyone is participating.

- Classroom management tips
  - Encourage English use.
  - Have contingency plans for faster teams.
  - Prepare teams for their presentations.
  - Post all or some of the projects in the classroom.

EVALUATION

The purpose of evaluation is twofold: to confirm that your students have mastered the objectives for a given lesson and to evaluate the effectiveness of your own teaching.

Methods of Evaluation:

- Tests or quizzes
  - Original
  - Quizzes created with the *ExamView® Pro Test Bank CD-ROM.*

- Written exercises
  - Peer evaluation:
    Ask students to review each others' written work for ease of comprehension. Do not request that students review each others'

spelling, punctuation, or grammar as this is best left to the teacher.
  - Portfolio:
    Have students maintain a portfolio of their writing assignments. This folder should include copies of the written assignments from team projects as well as individual work.

- Observation
  - Dialog Demonstration:
    See Teaching Hints on Dialog Presentation.

  - Fingers: This approach to evaluation allows students to respond nonverbally as a class to questions when there are a set number of responses. The advantage to this approach is that the instructor can better identify which students understand a concept or idea. For example, an instructor may give the students a series of pictures labeled 1 through 5 and make a series of statements about one picture, without naming its number. Students identify which picture is being talked about by holding up the corresponding number of fingers.

  - Oral Reponses: You can either ask for volunteers to respond, or throw a soft ball or wadded piece of paper randomly to students and have them toss it to each other for questions and answers.

  - Cards: Students are given note cards on which to anonymously write information that will be evaluated later as a class. The teacher may use this activity to ask questions about specific activities students recently attempted or approaches the teacher is using. For example, the teacher can ask students how they feel about a previous activity, choosing from three choices: *I learned a lot from the past activity, I learned a little from the past activity, and I didn't learn anything from the past activity*. Students write their response on the card. Then have one student collect the cards and, as a class, review the responses. Encourage the students to be honest by telling them that you want to be a better instructor and that their responses will help you.

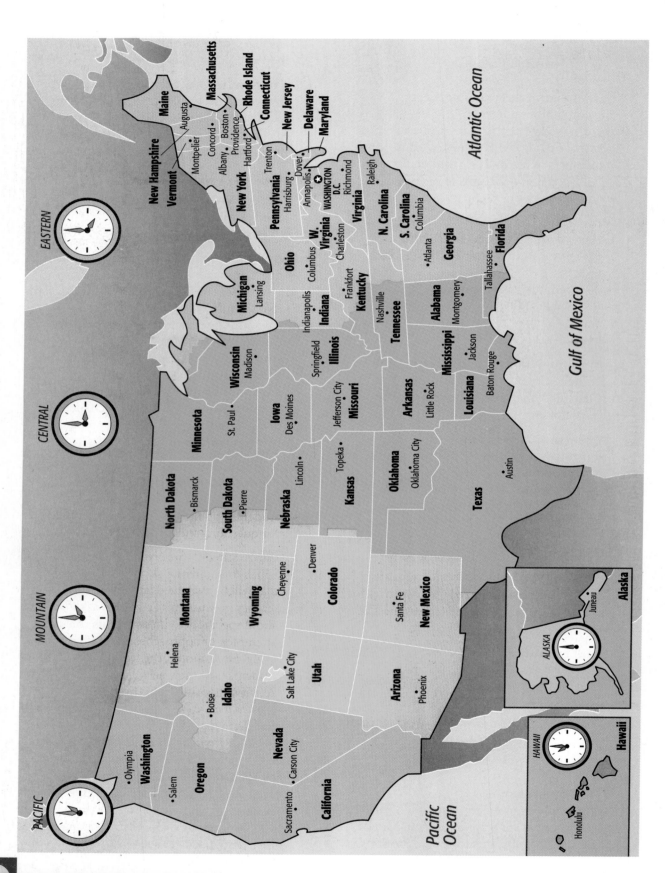

Atlantic Ocean

EASTERN

CENTRAL

MOUNTAIN

PACIFIC

Pacific Ocean

Gulf of Mexico

Maine
Augusta
New Hampshire
Vermont
Montpelier
Concord
Massachusetts
Boston
Albany
Providence
Rhode Island
Hartford
Connecticut
New York
Trenton
New Jersey
Pennsylvania
Harrisburg
Dover
Delaware
Annapolis
Maryland
WASHINGTON
D.C.
Richmond
Virginia
Raleigh
N. Carolina
S. Carolina
Columbia

W.
Virginia
Charleston
Ohio
Columbus
Frankfort
Kentucky
Nashville
Tennessee
Alabama
Montgomery
Georgia
Atlanta
Tallahassee
Florida

Michigan
Lansing
Indianapolis
Indiana
Illinois
Springfield
Missouri
Jefferson City
Arkansas
Little Rock
Mississippi
Jackson
Louisiana
Baton Rouge

Wisconsin
Madison
Iowa
Des Moines
Minnesota
St. Paul

North Dakota
Bismarck
South Dakota
Pierre
Nebraska
Lincoln
Kansas
Topeka
Oklahoma
Oklahoma City
Texas
Austin

Montana
Helena
Wyoming
Cheyenne
Colorado
Denver
New Mexico
Santa Fe

Idaho
Boise
Utah
Salt Lake City
Arizona
Phoenix

Washington
Olympia
Oregon
Salem
Nevada
Carson City
California
Sacramento

ALASKA
Juneau
Alaska

HAWAII
Honolulu
Hawaii

182 **Map of the United States**